THE BIG BOOK OF
Whittling and
Woodcarving

E. J. TANGERMAN

DOVER PUBLICATIONS, INC., NEW YORK

Published in Canada by General Publishing Company, Ltd., 30 Lesmill Road, Don Mills, Toronto, Ontario.
Published in the United Kingdom by Constable and Company, Ltd.

This Dover edition, first published in 1989, is an unabridged and unaltered republication of the work originally published by the McGraw-Hill Book Company, New York, in 1973 with the title *The Modern Book of Whittling and Woodcarving*.

Manufactured in the United States of America
Dover Publications, Inc., 31 East 2nd Street, Mineola, N.Y. 11501

Library of Congress Cataloging-in-Publication Data

Tangerman, E. J. (Elmer John), 1907–
    The big book of whittling and woodcarving.

    Previously published as: The modern book of whittling and woodcarving. 1973.
    1. Wood-carving.   I. Title.
TT199.7.T36 1989   731.4′62   89-25871
ISBN 0-486-26171-9

Contents

✳ By Way of Introduction

This book was actually born more than thirty years ago when I began my collection of simple whittled objects—which was all I could afford at the time. As do most young authors, I had grandiose ideas about a compendium that would encompass whittling and woodcarving (like the legendary circus tent), a tome that would cover everything on the subject.

But my experiences with articles in craft magazines, with readers of my booklets and books, and with my own reading of literature on the subject brought me to the conclusion that there were too many comprehensive tomes already. What was really needed was a roundup of ideas and designs, something that any carver, regardless of his skill, could consult for inspiration and patterns, a treasury of examples rather than a treasure house of erudition. Gibbons, Riemenschneider, Dürer, and the others were undoubtedly great men, but they carved elaborate forms that most of us can't duplicate, and if we could, there would be little demand for them, either in our own homes or in the marketplace.

Through these years, my business made it possible to travel and to meet people around the industrial world, so my collection now numbers some hundreds of examples, not only from Europe, but also from Africa, Asia, the South Pacific, and the Far North as well as from the United States. I have also collected a number of books in several languages and produced a wide variety of carvings myself—a variety which apparently is unusual. None of this would be envied me by the curators of art galleries or museums, but it's the sort of thing that carvers can use.

So . . . As much of all this as I could cram into a wieldy collection is here, together with my own experience and that of hundreds of others who have been kind enough to share their knowledge with me. Not all of it can be valuable or interesting to you, but I hope that much of it will be. I have elected to include here a number of exotic pieces and a great many modern and relatively simple designs not elsewhere available.

Recent years have brought greater emphasis on leisure-time pursuits, creativity and self-expression in an increasingly mass-produced and packaged world, and a paradoxical combination of disdain for tradition and a hankering to return to the soil. Thus my first book, accepted at publication for the library of the Metropolitan Museum of Art and listed by the *Encyclopaedia Britannica* as the source for further information on woodcarving, found itself repeatedly reviewed in *The Whole Earth Catalogs*. In a world in which children must read (if they can find a reference) to learn how to make a wooden whistle or a ball-in-a-cage, in which they can neither use their own jackknives nor borrow those of their fathers ("concealed weapons" is only one reason), in which wood comes from the local lumberyard in nicely squared planks, in which one buys carvings and carving lessons, you'll pardon me for feeling a bit nostalgic.

In any case, I have attempted here to provide a graduated handbook, beginning with simple projects for the knife and moving on into elaborate ones requiring both knowledge and tools, from projects which can be done in an evening to some which can take months. Also, because many readers will already have the needed knowledge and experience, I have elected to discuss tools, woods, and the like at the end of the volume rather than at the beginning. Turn the page, and you're at work. Further, the method of transferring a pattern by drawing proportional squares is well known (see page three)—or easily learned—so I felt it unnecessary to clutter drawings with dimensions and squared grids in most instances, particularly because the publisher has been very understanding in reproducing my drawings at exactly half original size; just measure the drawing and multiply by two (except in a few instances). Thus, a ⅛-in. grid over the illustration and a ¼-in. grid drawn on the wood will give you the original size. Exceptions to this rule are marked or self-evident. Lastly, low-relief panels photographed from dead front are unaccompanied by drawings because they are themselves patterns, either in whole or in part. (I should admit that photographs and drawings are mostly my own, for which I make any necessary apologies.)

From here on, you're on your own, and good luck. You'll find carving an absorbing hobby or occupation, very rewarding when you can say "I made it myself!"

✳ Grooves Can Be Carving Enough

Silhouette Identifies the Figure

ABOVE—Parasitic and long-tailed jaegers were copied directly from pictures in a bird guide and carved in white pine for wall decoration in a cruiser cabin. They can be simply silhouettes with wing pinions and tail feathers suggested by V-grooves made with the knife, low-relief carved, and/or finished by tinting (as in photograph) if color is needed. These two will provide plenty of experience with grain.

LEFT—My front door is teak, designed with panels to be carved. But with the whittled rope molding around the frame and the dogwood flower and leaf corners, elaborate low relief filling the panels would be a bit overpowering. Also, simple local subjects seemed most appropriate. Hence the owl, squirrel, and rabbit. They are outlined with whittled V-grooves, with narrower grooves for details, and slight dishing around the owl's eyes to accent them. There is no modeling. Shown are *two* squirrels; one was a very live visiting friend.

NEXT PAGE, TOP—Marine animals make excellent floating toys for a child's bath. Here again, the silhouette does it. A little chamfering of the edges and V-grooves can be modeling enough, or scales and the like can be carved in also. White pine or soft maple works well. The back can be hollowed out to reduce warpage from alternate soaking and drying, but it's better to carve both sides.

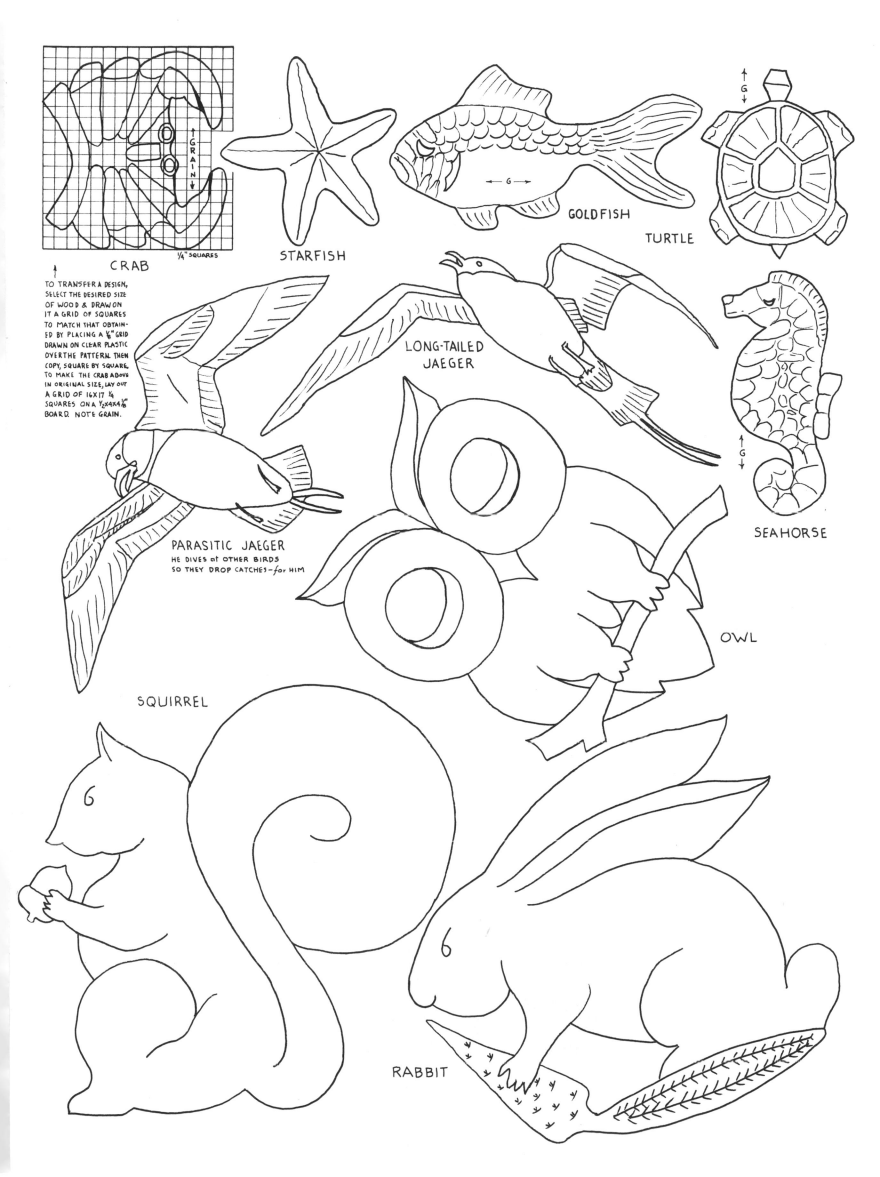

CRAB

1/4" SQUARES

GRAIN

STARFISH

GOLDFISH

G

TURTLE

G

TO TRANSFER A DESIGN, SELECT THE DESIRED SIZE OF WOOD & DRAW ON IT A GRID OF SQUARES TO MATCH THAT OBTAINED BY PLACING A 1/8" GRID DRAWN ON CLEAR PLASTIC OVER THE PATTERN. THEN COPY, SQUARE BY SQUARE. TO MAKE THE CRAB ABOVE IN ORIGINAL SIZE, LAY OUT A GRID OF 16 X 17 1/4 SQUARES ON A 1/2 X 4 X 4 1/8" BOARD. NOTE GRAIN.

LONG-TAILED JAEGER

SEAHORSE

G

PARASITIC JAEGER

HE DIVES at OTHER BIRDS SO THEY DROP CATCHES—for HIM

OWL

SQUIRREL

6

RABBIT

6

✳ Laminated Silhouettes

Simple but Effective

Germany is apparently the source of animals and people made up of wood—and, nowadays, plywood—sections glued or pinned together. Such assemblies may be a derivative of the Noah's Ark, which often had flat animals so they'd pack better inside. Also, animals made of three plies can automatically have separated legs, and it is easy to vary leg positions by varying the pattern of the side pieces. Smaller figures of animals are simply glued up from a body block and two sides, but articulated figures assembled on pins are also readily possible. Quite elaborate and large figures can be made, like the articulated bull, which I duplicated from a German original. He is about 19 in. long, nose to tail, and is good modern art as well. Such figures are side views of the subject; a frontal view can be made, but is usually an appliqué.

Sections are cut with coping, saber, or band saw, and cleaned up and chamfered with the knife. Some modeling and contouring can be done with the knife also, or figures can be modeled and contoured with gouges. For articulated figures, the pins may simply be brads or small screws, but the bull has dowel-rod pins with countersunk caps so the pivots are almost invisible. Finish is commonly with colored paint, but if the wood is good, as it is on the bull, a very effective finish is flat varnish, followed by waxing, or simply waxing alone.

LEFT—Jointed bull in cherry wood. Body is three sections, with head and tail pieces inserted and held by the leg spindles. One-piece head and hooves are recessed to go over adjoining sections. Eye is a dowel, rounded over.

BELOW, FAR LEFT—Duchess from *Alice in Wonderland* is articulated so head, arms, and body can be posed. Joints are held by through wires eyed at ends. Walking doll (see sketch) is similar, once was a common American toy. She had adjustable arms and a double skirt, within which was a rotor carrying six feet, so she appeared to walk when pushed along.

BELOW—Camel, leopard, zebra, and kangaroo with young are all simple assemblies, each of three pieces except for the baby kangaroo, which is a single piece nesting in its mother's pouch.

BELOW, LEFT—Simple animals can be articulated. Here the squirrel pattern from my front door is articulated so when the tail is swung back, the foreleg moves up, carrying a nut to the mouth. This is a one-sided figure, mounted on a cigar-box top of mahogany as a panel. Similar designs can be made with a rabbit, moving the tail, foreleg with carrot, and one ear.

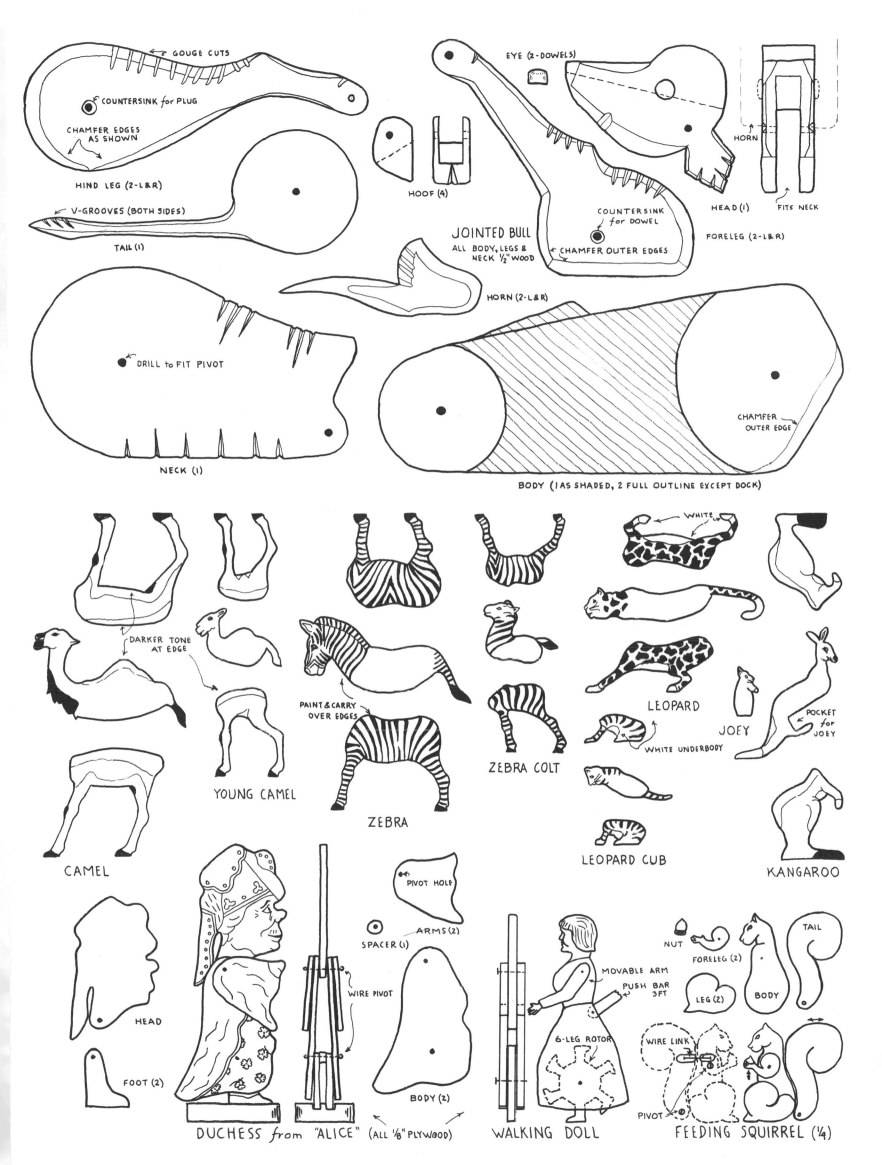

GOUGE CUTS

COUNTERSINK for PLUG

CHAMFER EDGES AS SHOWN

HIND LEG (2-L&R)

V-GROOVES (BOTH SIDES)

TAIL (1)

DRILL to FIT PIVOT

NECK (1)

EYE (2-DOWELS)

HOOF (4)

JOINTED BULL

ALL BODY, LEGS & NECK ½" WOOD

HORN (2-L&R)

COUNTERSINK for DOWEL

CHAMFER OUTER EDGES

HEAD (1)

HORN

FITS NECK

FORELEG (2-L&R)

BODY (1 AS SHADED, 2 FULL OUTLINE EXCEPT DOCK)

CHAMFER OUTER EDGE

DARKER TONE AT EDGE

YOUNG CAMEL

CAMEL

PAINT & CARRY OVER EDGES

ZEBRA

ZEBRA COLT

LEOPARD

LEOPARD CUB

WHITE UNDERBODY

WHITE

JOEY

POCKET for JOEY

KANGAROO

PIVOT HOLE

ARMS (2)

SPACER (1)

WIRE PIVOT

HEAD

FOOT (2)

BODY (2)

DUCHESS from "ALICE" (ALL ⅛" PLYWOOD)

MOVABLE ARM

PUSH BAR 3 FT

6-LEG ROTOR

WALKING DOLL

NUT

FORELEG (2)

LEG (2)

BODY

TAIL

WIRE LINK

PIVOT

FEEDING SQUIRREL (¼)

✳ More Silhouettes

Lapel Pins, Charms, Pendants

"Lapellières"—carved wooden lapel pins for ladies' jackets like some of these—I first described in *Popular Mechanics* in 1942. Many whittlers have made them and others since—not only for pins, but also for brooches, charms, tie clasps, earrings, belt buckles, and pendants. Currently, the rage is pendants on a thong or chain—for both sexes. Whatever fashion may be in the years to come, it is a safe bet that carvings like these will always fit some fashion.

Basically, they are thin wood, sawed to shape and whittled to detail. When necessary, they can be fitted with pins, backings, jump rings, or other "jeweler's findings," available from craft shops, local jewelers, or by mail order. In a pinch, you can do as I have done: Use a safety pin for a backing (if you can find one of those in this zippered world) with a slip of leather to hold it to the wood, or a screw eye and homemade ring to make a pendant. The designs can also be applied to letter openers, purse closings, pipe bowls, neckerchief slides and bolos, napkin rings, wall plaques. I've tried to show some of these examples as well.

The usual whittler selects a particular design, or family of designs (birds or fish for example), depending upon his individual preference, area, or whatever he can sell if he's a professional. These designs lend themselves to quantity production. The blanks for pins or pendants can be sawed in multiple, for example, simply by laying out one piece as a pattern and nailing it to several others with brads through the waste wood. Also, the finishing is faster in multiple, whether it be paint, tint, or varnish and wax.

Hard woods like cherry, walnut, mahogany, and holly are my preference for these

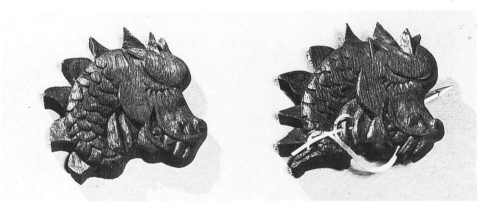

LEFT—"Reluctant Dragon," in mahogany, I carved for the director and producer of a local amateur play so titled. One is highlighted with silver tongue and spear, the latter passing through a fold of skin beneath the neck, as it did in the story. These are, of course, caricatures as well as a mythical figure.

BELOW—A group of lapellières made by the author in cherry thirty years ago are still fashionable. Note the ubiquitous squirrel —for the lady of the house.

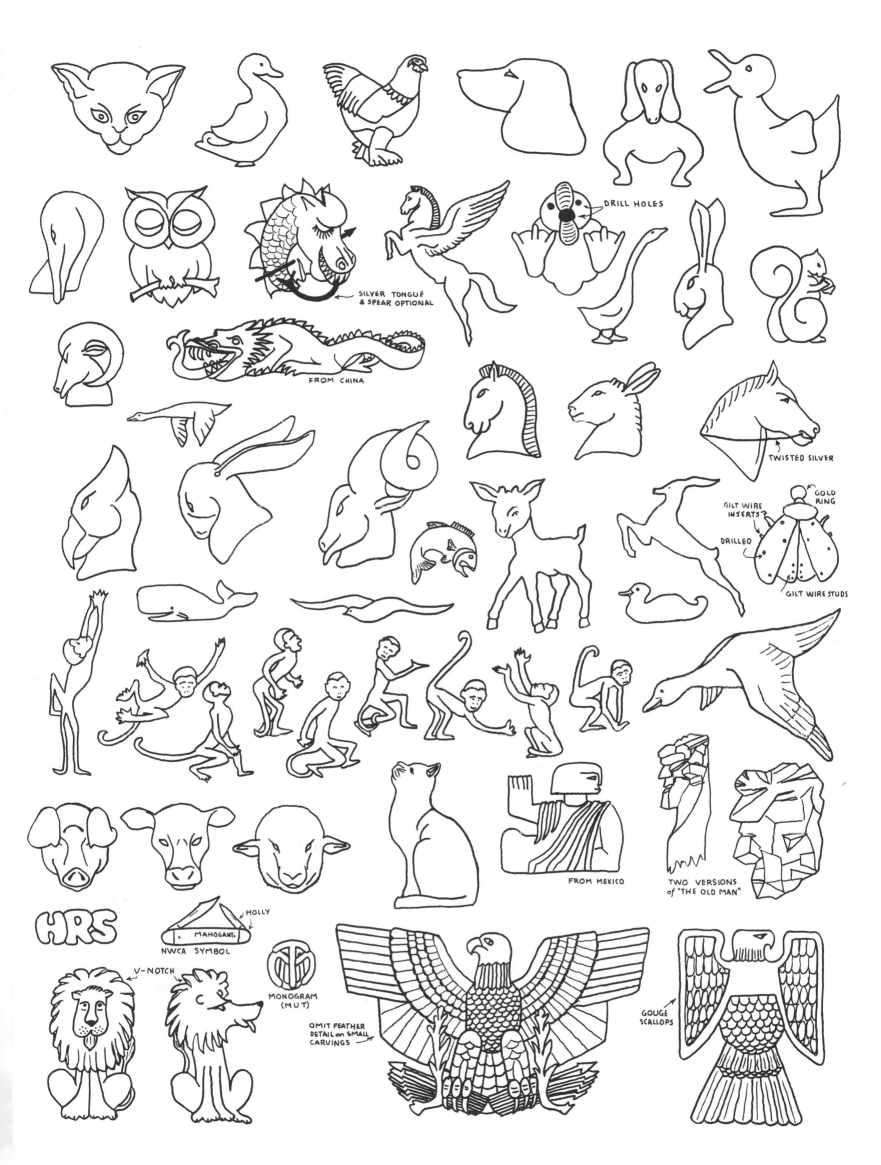

DRILL HOLES

SILVER TONGUE & SPEAR OPTIONAL

FROM CHINA

TWISTED SILVER

GOLD RING

GILT WIRE INSERTS

DRILLED

GILT WIRE STUDS

FROM MEXICO

TWO VERSIONS of "THE OLD MAN"

HRS

HOLLY

MAHOGANY

NWCA SYMBOL

MONOGRAM (MUT)

V-NOTCH

OMIT FEATHER DETAIL on SMALL CARVINGS

GOUGE SCALLOPS

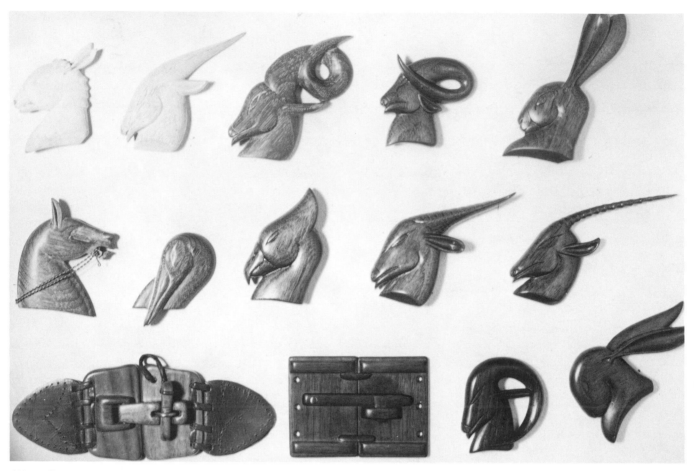

TOP—Pins and buckles by Henry A. Penchoen.

BELOW, LEFT—Screech owl in walnut, for a napkin ring. About 2 in. square, with a 1½-inch belled bore.

BELOW—Ladybug bangle, in cherry.

BOTTOM LEFT—If surfaces of a design are flush and the background cut away, the block may be used as a stamp for fabrics or paper. This block is from India.

BOTTOM RIGHT—Wall plaque, in pine on walnut, has the same design in three stepped sizes.

designs. Most can be sawed out of 3/16- or ¼-in. stock. The exceptions are the monkeys, which, because of their thin sections and elaborate poses, are better in ⅛-in. wood; the "Old Man" as a letter opener, which should be ¾-in. wood to provide strength and grip; and the eagles, which need to be in ½-in. wood if much detail is carved in.

Details can be carved with the knife in most cases; they are simply V-groove lines of various widths and types. A simple V-groove makes a standard line; tilt the V and

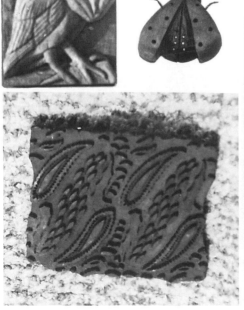

you get a vertical line on one side and a sloping one on the other. The vertical cut gives a sharp shadow, the sloping one a softer one, so the vertical line is good for outlining a figure while the sloping line makes the vertical-outlined subject look as if it were standing above the surface.

Feathered surfaces—on the eagle, for example—are, however, made more easily with the veiner or other small gouge; this gives a rounded surface at the bottom of the depression that is softer in appearance. It is possible, too, to cut away the sides of the veiner groove to make a broader "valley," or to cut away one side and thus achieve an effect similar to that with the tilted V. Feather carving takes a bit of practice and time, but is rewarding in light-and-shadow effect. A veiner can be used to outline the standing edge of the feather; then the opposite edge of the cut can be cut away with a knife or flat gouge so the feathers are a series of steps in cross-section. The veiner can be used to cut the central rib—also to indicate other veining if the feather is large. (This is one of the many cases in which a veiner groove will give the optical effect of a raised rib.)

A good finish for these pieces is flat or eggshell varnish, followed by waxing. Shellac or gloss varnish creates more shine than most people like; what you want is a glow or gloss. Elements to be accented, such as eyes, hooves on a deer, spots on the ladybug shell, and the like, can be touched up with darker stain, paint, or just a soft pencil before varnishing. Or eyes and spots can be drilled so they appear dark. Some of the designs are actually pierced carving—the monogram, grouped initials, the chick in the second row with mouth and eyes that are drilled holes. Also, some of the designs are highlighted with additions of other materials: a silver tongue and spear for the dragon head, a twisted silver-wire rein for the horse head, gold or gilt wire legs for the ladybug—even gilt wire studs in her back for the spots. The wire stud is glued into a drilled hole, then filed smooth. The legs are inset farther.

Figures need not be serious; they can be caricatures, like the two chicks at upper right or the two lions at lower left in the sketches. Also, you can produce your own design from any picture as long as it provides a recognizable silhouette.

RIGHT—"The Old Man of the Mountain," familiar New England rock formation, has been copied countless times. Many are not exact duplicates of the rock formation, but they give the effect because of the silhouette. These two, a pin in mahogany at *LEFT,* and a letter opener in pine at *RIGHT,* illustrate the point. They look like the "Old Man," but differ markedly in detail.

BELOW, LEFT—Sometimes, initials alone are enough. This oak bailing scoop was converted to a serving dish by adding three legs and carving intaglio initials in the handle. They could also be in relief.

BELOW, RIGHT—Napkin rings have single initial in relief. Identification is provided by varying the wood: walnut, holly, mahogany, cherry, rosewood, and teak. The initial is carved in end grain of the pieces. Hole for napkin is 1½ in. in diameter, sawed rather than drilled to prevent splitting, and belled at the ends. Rings are hexagonal, 2 in. high.

✳ Portable, Paintable Farm Barn

Simple Animals Provide 50 Toys in One

This serviceable toy shows how effective even crudely carved animals can be. The barn is also a carrying case for the animals, which are unfinished so they can be painted, chalked, penciled, dyed, stained—or whatever the child's mother will permit.

The barn need not be as large or as elaborate as mine, of course. But individual stalls, operating doors, and other appurtenances help realism and enjoyment and are also educational (as are sex distinctions). The barn opens down the middle on a piano hinge, so it is quite stable and strong. A variety of stall arrangements is provided, including thick plastic "fencing" (easier to see through and install than wire), sliding and liftable bars (made of coffee stirrers). Mangers and roosts are glued in, but can be made removable. The sliding door was a scrap aluminum slab, which also furnished material for the lift latches that lock front lower hinged doors and upper (fake) hay door.

Animals are white pine or basswood (see page 12). To keep them convenient in size and sturdy, most are ¾ in. thick, legs are not separated, and little detail shaping is done; they are essentially silhouettes with heads, horns, and ears outlined with the knife and rough edges chamfered. Colts, piglets, lambs, and kids are of ½-in. stock, as are smaller fowls, except the turkey gobbler, and the cat. (Fowls look more natural with some head and neck shaping.) To make fowl legs look more natural and yet have some

strength, they should be with the grain, or the body can be set above a base on two brads. Or the fowls, particularly the ducks, can simply squat, avoiding the leg problem entirely. Eyes, manes, and foot details can be suggested with a fiber pen. Chicks, ducklings, and goslings can be grouped on whittled bases to avoid loss.

All larger animals can be cut with a jigsaw, coping or saber saw, with close cutting by coping saw. Whittling will take care of ears, horns, mouths, and rough spots. Overall sanding will remove splinters.

The animal population can suit your own fancy, but it may be helpful to the child if they are of particular breeds so the child can locate, or be provided with, a coloring guide. Thus I had a Percheron stallion, Holstein cows, Hampshire sheep and pigs, Dorking chickens, Embden geese—and a collie like "Lassie." I ended up with 54 animals, subdivided as shown in the sketches.

I provided an "owner's medallion" (first name and date) instead of a "hex" sign on the front, and put two "hex" signs on the back, stepped so they don't interfere with opening. The roof eave will also have to be cut away in back so the barn can be opened wide. It's best to make the weather vane removable, in case an adult worries about this metal projection. Spraying the barn interior with white enamel helps the animals stand out, and would not be a very creative child pastime anyway.

Farm barn has two latches . . . opens to reveal two floors of animals in stalls and pens.

 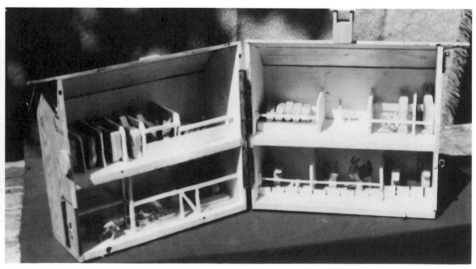

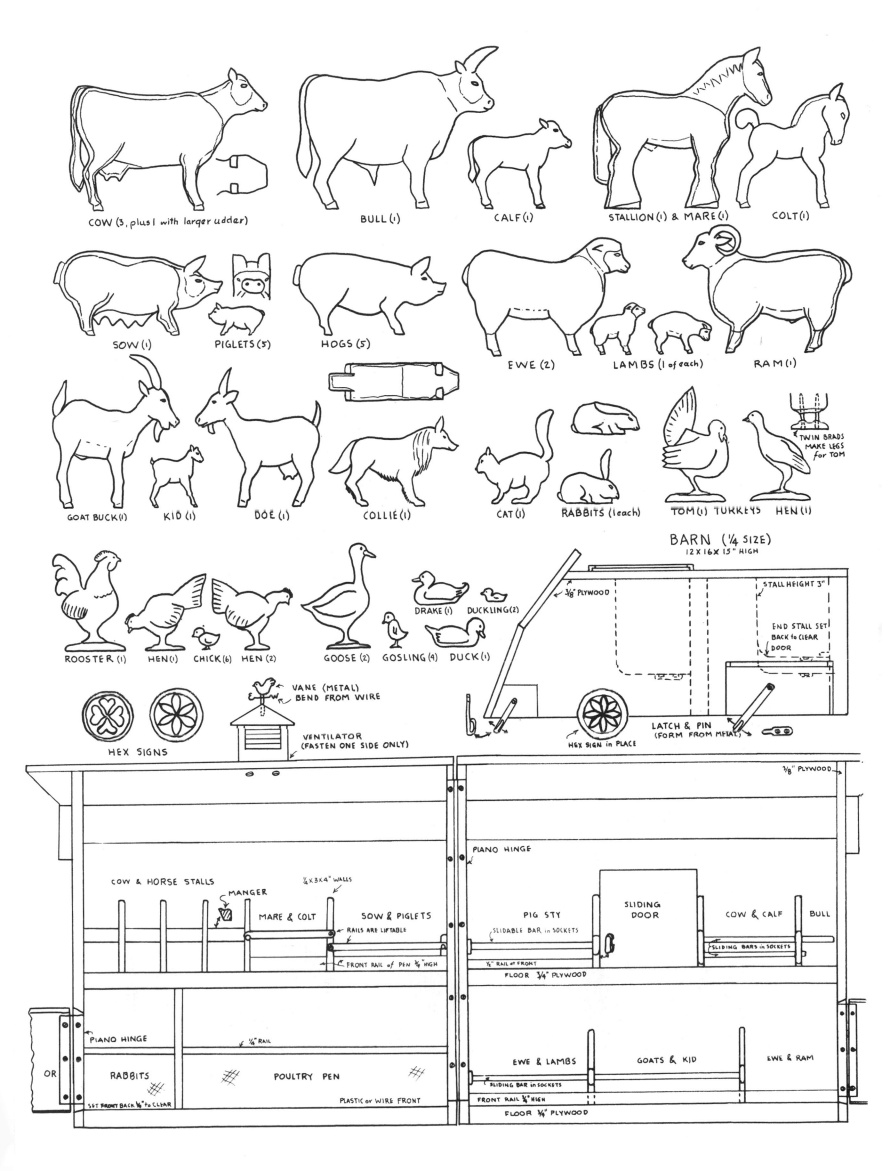

COW (3, plus 1 with larger udder)

BULL (1)

CALF (1)

STALLION (1) & MARE (1)

COLT (1)

SOW (1)

PIGLETS (5)

HOGS (5)

EWE (2)

LAMBS (1 of each)

RAM (1)

GOAT BUCK (1)

KID (1)

DOE (1)

COLLIE (1)

CAT (1)

RABBITS (1 each)

TOM (1) TURKEYS HEN (1)

TWIN BRADS MAKE LEGS for TOM

ROOSTER (1)

HEN (1)

CHICK (6)

HEN (2)

GOOSE (2)

GOSLING (4)

DUCK (1)

DRAKE (1)

DUCKLING (2)

BARN (1/4 SIZE)
12 X 16 X 15" HIGH

3/8" PLYWOOD

STALL HEIGHT 3"

END STALL SET BACK to CLEAR DOOR

LATCH & PIN (FORM FROM METAL)

HEX SIGN in PLACE

HEX SIGNS

VANE (METAL) BEND FROM WIRE

VENTILATOR (FASTEN ONE SIDE ONLY)

1/8" PLYWOOD

COW & HORSE STALLS

MANGER

1/4 X 3 X 4" WALLS

MARE & COLT

SOW & PIGLETS

RAILS ARE LIFTABLE

FRONT RAIL of PEN 3/4" HIGH

PIANO HINGE

PIG STY

SLIDABLE BAR in SOCKETS

1/2" RAIL at FRONT

SLIDING DOOR

COW & CALF

BULL

SLIDING BARS in SOCKETS

FLOOR 3/4" PLYWOOD

PIANO HINGE

1/4" RAIL

OR

RABBITS

SET FRONT BACK 1/8" to CLEAR

POULTRY PEN

PLASTIC or WIRE FRONT

EWE & LAMBS

SLIDING BAR in SOCKETS

FRONT RAIL 3/4" HIGH

GOATS & KID

EWE & RAM

FLOOR 3/4" PLYWOOD

Farm Barn—continued

The farm population, grouped *BELOW*, is mostly of ¾-in. white pine or basswood except for young, which are ½ in. Legs are not separated, and features are drawn in with a fiber pen, so the child can color animals as and when he wishes.

✳ Low Relief for 3-D Effects

Men, Animals, Spoons, Batons, a Mobile

Man has always decorated his tools, staffs and personal effects, sometimes with traditional figures, sometimes with abstract designs. Often, only surface carving is done — the object itself supplies the third dimension. Thus the 4-way head (page 15) appears three-dimensional although it is carved in low relief, as do the Indians below. Primitive designs may be simple and geometric, as on the Taiwanese spear, complex and fluid, as on the Alaskan and Viking spoons, or may be stylized elements (sketches on next page).

BELOW—Indian caricatures in basswood were vacation whittling in scraps. Simple grooves create the character.

BOTTOM—Spoons of horn carved by Alaskan Indians (sketch on next page) use motifs like those on totem poles, slant-eyed gods and animals. Low-relief carving produces in-the-round figures because of the shape of the horn. Some lines and background are cut through to the hollow core—pierced carving.

BOTTOM RIGHT—Vikings are said to have carved spoons like these for their brides, all of one piece of birch. Bowls have scratch designs, handles are pierce-carved and joined by an elaborate block-and-link chain.

RIGHT—This stylized Swedish horse is a very different silhouette, with saddle and harness suggested by V-grooves. Thin wood slabs glued in slots represent mane and tail, and sharp edges are chamfered. The result is a strong, dynamic figure.

BELOW—Russian wall hanger, in pine, has a hook which lifts the owl's wings when a load is applied. Other similar designs: man, bear, eagle.

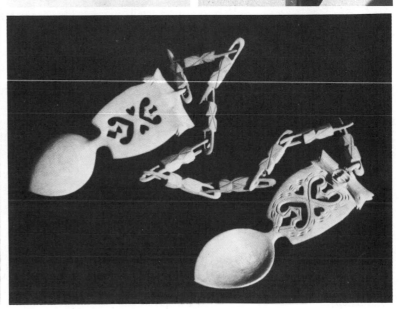

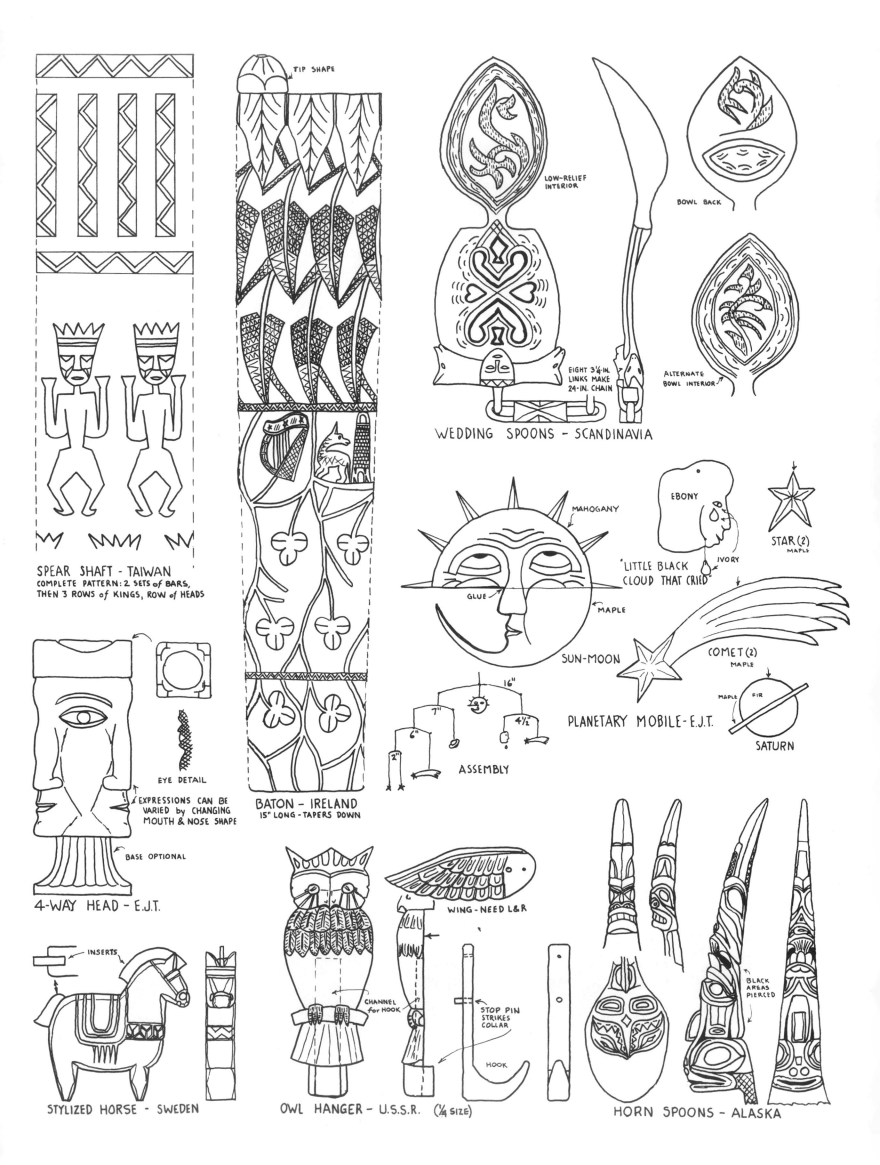

SPEAR SHAFT - TAIWAN
COMPLETE PATTERN: 2 SETS of BARS,
THEN 3 ROWS of KINGS, ROW of HEADS

EYE DETAIL

EXPRESSIONS CAN BE
VARIED by CHANGING
MOUTH & NOSE SHAPE

BASE OPTIONAL

4-WAY HEAD - E.J.T.

TIP SHAPE

BATON - IRELAND
15" LONG - TAPERS DOWN

LOW-RELIEF INTERIOR

EIGHT 3¼-IN.
LINKS MAKE
24-IN. CHAIN

WEDDING SPOONS - SCANDINAVIA

BOWL BACK

ALTERNATE
BOWL INTERIOR

MAHOGANY

GLUE

MAPLE

SUN-MOON

16"
7"
6"
2"
4½

ASSEMBLY

EBONY

"LITTLE BLACK
CLOUD THAT CRIED"

IVORY

STAR (2)
MAPLE

COMET (2)
MAPLE

PLANETARY MOBILE - E.J.T.

MAPLE   FIR

SATURN

INSERTS

STYLIZED HORSE - SWEDEN

OWL HANGER - U.S.S.R.   (¼ SIZE)

CHANNEL
for HOOK

WING - NEED L&R

STOP PIN
STRIKES
COLLAR

HOOK

BLACK
AREAS
PIERCED

HORN SPOONS - ALASKA

COFFEE   COCOA   FRUITS   PEARLS

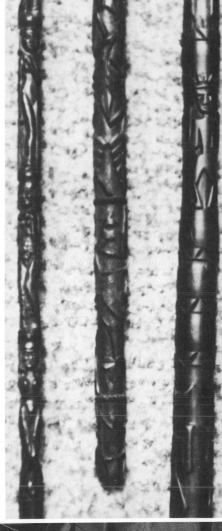

ABOVE—Four of a series of five 6-ft. figures in mahogany by F. Narváez of Venezuela, shown at N.Y. World's Fair, 1939. Left to right: Coffee, Cocoa, Fruits, Pearls. Each is a block, primarily, but surface carving converts the block to a bulky figure or figures. Similar design can be used to produce sturdy totem poles.

FAR RIGHT—Baton at *LEFT* is Macassar ebony, with piano-key ivory inserts. It shows the four seasons as female figures; I adapted it from low-relief panels on the prewar *Queen Mary*. Length 20 in. The *CENTER* baton is Irish, with harp, castle, and shamrock elements in ebony. Farthest *RIGHT* is a section of a 5-ft. spear from Taiwan (see sketches).

RIGHT—4-way head, in walnut, was suggested by a low-relief Celtic head in Paris and Maya cornice corners at Tulum, Mexico. Height should be 2 to 2½ times width.

BOTTOM RIGHT—Solar mobile is based on setting sun combined with moon crescent sharing nose bridge and one eye.

BELOW—Mexican one-piece whirlers for chocolate are spun between the palms. Head is notched, hollowed, has various designs. Rings on spindle float free. Combs are notched plates of hard wood with backbone design.

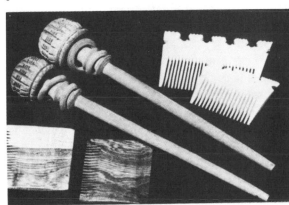

✳ More 3-D Effects with Low-Relief Carving

Calabashes and the Magi Candlesticks

Low-relief carving may range from surface scratching to a decided depth, but it does suggest a flat surface, or, more properly, carving a design on a plane. But there are times when the surface isn't flat, or when the effect of the low-relief carving is to produce a three-dimensional object. Some examples of the latter have been given, in the preceding article, as well as in the multi-ply assemblies (page 4) and the 4-way head (page 136). Or low relief may be combined with in-the-round, as on the "bug tree" (page 139), or the "totem pole" (page 136). The latter is part in-the-round (upper end) and part low relief, but the two blend without trouble.

Low relief applied to a cylinder or other regular surface poses no more problems than applying it to a plane, except that it must be properly spaced to join itself in a continuous pattern or picture. The breadboard is a good example (page 123), because words can be spaced differently or the width of the intervening element (dots or a wheat sheaf) changed to take up or lose space. But if the pattern must go on a compound curve, the problems begin to mount, because a two-dimensional pattern, like a Mercator projection, exaggerates distances near poles.

BELOW—Pipe from Arnhem Land, northern Australia, is made from milkwood by an aborigine, depicts lizards in simple outline and set out by a grooved background. The surface is dyed or painted before carving is begun.

BOTTOM—Calabashes carved in Peru (two in FRONT) and Mexico are done with the knife, then tinted. That at RIGHT has black background, while the LEFT one is in three tones with a light background—more modern.

The calabashes shown here are a good example of the problem. I have drawn the major band patterns in two dimensions, but simply to copy them on a ball or calabash of similar dimensions would be a difficult job, because there'd be too much pattern along the edges. It is necessary to compress the pattern there as it is applied, putting animal feet closer together, or heads closer together, as the design progresses to make the band come out even. It may also be necessary to alter the design slightly to compensate for irregularities or nonregular contours.

Actually, the easiest way to apply such a design is to follow the method used by the Indians who carved these three calabashes and who know nothing about such educated niceties as compound curves and Mercator projections. They just draw the design as they go, putting elements in their positions to suit, and adding or subtracting minor design elements like bushes to come out even. More probably, they do not draw the design at all, but simply carve it, making necessary adjustments as they become necessary. Thus, on one calabash, a top star has 11 points (not a "proper" 8 or 12), while the next band has 10, and the picture band has a cactus or two that are there to make the design uniform around the object. The carver probably doesn't know that the perimeter of a calabash is 3.14159 times the diameter, and if he does know about pi, he probably hasn't a pencil—or, more likely, is teaching school rather than carving.

The flat calabash is the simplest of the three in that the band design of llamas and peasants is repeated, and one pair of peasants is suspiciously fatter than the other. Made in Peru by a woman, this piece has a removable top cut along the central lines of the second star ring and with one star point with a flat end so the top can be indexed easily. The pear-shaped calabash is also Peruvian in origin, but is much finer and more-detailed work with a continuous band interrupted only by the tree which I have shown at the ends and which is obviously a filler. The regular designs in the top bands are not interrelated: the top flower has 16 petals, the band below it has 23 points, and the third band,

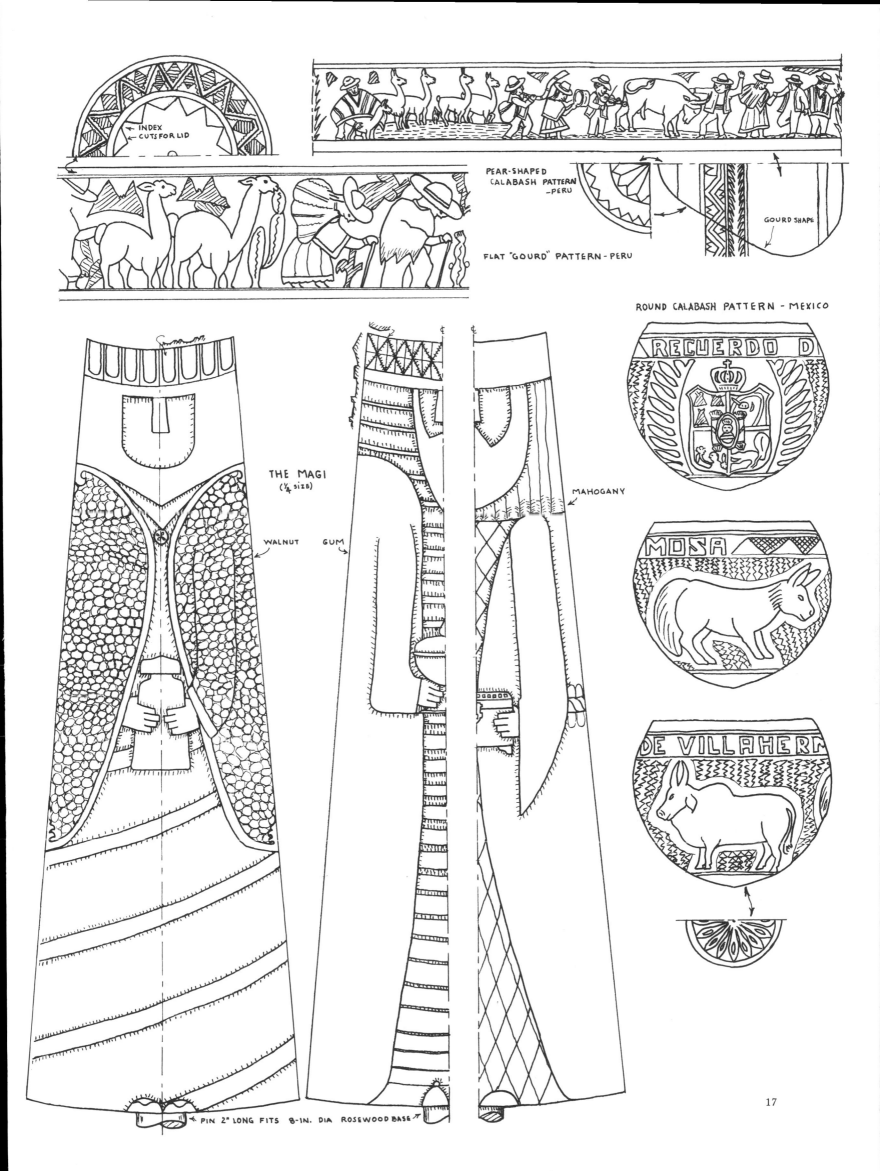

INDEX
CUTS FOR LID

PEAR-SHAPED
CALABASH PATTERN
—PERU

GOURD SHAPE

FLAT "GOURD" PATTERN—PERU

ROUND CALABASH PATTERN — MEXICO

RECUERDO D

MOSA

DE VILLAHERM

THE MAGI
(⅛ SIZE)

WALNUT

GUM

MAHOGANY

PIN 2" LONG FITS 8-IN. DIA ROSEWOOD BASE

17

The Magi are mahogany (*LEFT*), walnut, and gum. Each is 36 in. high, including candle, 4 in. diameter at the base, 2 in. at the top, with an 8-in.-diameter rosewood base. Finish is flat varnish and wax, to create a soft "glow," and carving is quite shallow.

with the triangular wave design, has a spacer in it as I have sketched at the top.

The third calabash, an open cup, is from Villahermosa, Mexico, and is much more formal. It bears the coat of arms of the city and two animals, one obviously a Brahma cow, the other anything from a wolf to a burro. The flower on the bottom of this one is also quite regular—16 petals, and the lettering is well spaced and executed, although the beginning and end are separated by a series of triangles to take up the space.

Calabashes are carved with the knife alone, usually while still green. It is a painstaking, slow job. They are then allowed to dry and are tinted in tones ranging from the shiny light yellow of the skin itself to a dark chocolate brown. The carved surfaces are rough and almost white, so provide a good background. In recent years, because more colors have become available through traders and agents, calabashes may have tones of red, or even blue and green.

Somewhat similar in technique is the pipe from Northern Australia. Made in a soft wood like balsa, it is painted dark outside,

then the design is produced by cutting parallel gouge lines in the background around an outline of the figure—in this case a lizard. This idea has been adapted, incidentally, in "personalizing" native carvings in the South Pacific. There wooden pieces like long trays will be carved to shape, then painted. The carver puts on a geometric design with a small gouge, which exposes the light wood under the paint. The peddler in the market, who poses as a carver, also has a small gouge, with which he carves in the buyer's name and "Souvenir of Fiji."

The Mexican calabash in the group has an interesting background pattern, which looks like stacked triangles. It is actually a series of parallel light-colored wavy lines made by cutting away the dark skin by rocking a small flat gouge sideways as it is pushed forward. This produces a tight series of S-curves and an irregular pattern.

In rather sharp contrast to these is The Magi—three candlesticks 32 in. high (plus 2 in. for base and 2 in. for candle) and each of a different wood. I first planned tinted candlesticks and tried models at one-fourth scale. They proved so disappointing that I shifted to the idea of three natural tones of the same color from a middle yellow or tan to a dark brown, assuming they would be displayed against a light background. Wood available 4 × 4 × 36 in. (2 in. needed for the base pin) included poplar or gum, mahogany, and black walnut. Maple was too white, teak had a somewhat different color, pine was again too light, oak had too much pattern. Besides, among the tales about the Three Wise Men is one that says one was Chinese, one Persian, one black.

The blocks had to be selected to avoid checks and end cracks, then turned on a wood lathe. Each was also provided with an 8-in.-diameter rosewood base 2 in. deep. Layout is difficult because the piece is so long, but can be done once a vertical centerline is established. It is easier on the work than on a pattern. Two of the three are symmetrical, and the third could be with elimination of the arm lines. Carving is quite shallow—less than $\frac{1}{8}$ in. deep—and the faces are not defined beyond the nose and beard. The graduated-width bands making up the inner gown of the poplar king were a difficult job, both to lay out and carve, and the figure might look almost as well with uniform bands or even a pattern of some sort.

✳Curls and Fans

Tricks with Wet Wood

The one-piece fan is a standard whittler's trick which I elaborated into winged birds, finned fish, flowers, and finally an Indian head with shaped Sioux headdress, and thought I was being quite original. But the Japanese, German, and Swedish applications of the fan principle make my best efforts look pale.

The Japanese are partial to roosters carved at the top of a 1×1×6-in. stick, with the side of the stick curl-carved to form a long tail down the block. The Germans make trees by cutting curls on all four sides of a ¼-in. stick, progressively shorter and narrower, of course, near the top (see *CENTER, BELOW*). But the Swedes make a wide variety of curl and fan carvings, ranging from simple birds with fan wings and tail to complete boxes. The trick, of course, is to use straight-grained knot-free white pine and to soak it well before making the curls. A sharp knife also helps.

At *TOP RIGHT* is my best effort to date, a low-relief Santa Claus about 6 in. square, with beard, moustache, eyebrows, hair, and cap pompom all curls made with a flat gouge. It is tinted and provided a Christmas-card illustration one year.

UNDER it is a 4-in. hollow cube from Sweden, made of six crosses. Each cross is intersecting half-jointed pieces about 9/32×1 in., with curls carved on each side so they fill the opening and complete the square. Note that the longer curls have smaller curls cut along their edges as well, as do the tree and larger rooster below. That rooster, incidentally, is an assembly, with separate wings, tail, comb, wattles, and legs—with curl spurs—glued in. The bird at *LOWER RIGHT* is about 8 in. long, made of two half-jointed blocks, with the body silhouette well shaped from the side, less so from above (as shown). The German piece, intended to hold a place card, has a 1-in. dwarf restraining an armadillo from chasing a ½-in. rabbit, all well-carved and tinted.

Wetting soft woods to inhibit splitting during carving is a common trick among professionals. In Oberammergau, Germany, large figure panels and figure blanks hogged out on a profiling machine are finish-carved by hand while wet. Southern Highlands carvers boil walnut, pecan, and other fruit and nut wood blanks before carving. Many primitive carvers prefer to carve green wood—but their carvings develop checks when subjected to our steam-heated winter atmosphere. Generally speaking, small pieces can be carved more easily while wet, but the danger of checking counterbalances these advantages in larger pieces, at least in my experience.

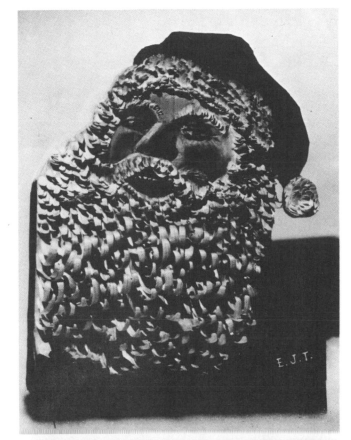

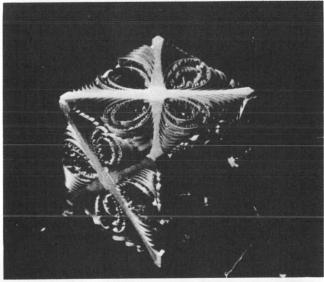

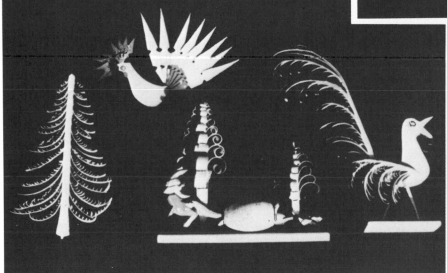

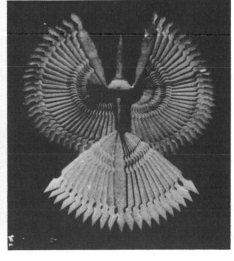

✳ Whittled Footwear

Sandals, Sabots, Clogs, Klompen, Geta, Zori

Wooden shoes were first made for wear outdoors in mud and cold, not for dress. They are clumsy by comparison with leather sandals or shoes, but that doesn't deter the ladies, who are currently wearing thick-soled "Swedish clogs." Such shoes, French sabots, bathing or garden sandals, and even the all-wood Dutch shoes (Klompen) can be homemade, and decorated as well. I have made several pairs of various types, and carved surface designs on a pair of willow shoes big enough to wear—and now dare not wear them outside for fear of battering the carving. (To tell the truth, they're no loss; they hurt my feet.)

Simple sandals are very easy. I told about them in *Popular Science Monthly*, September 1936! Start with ¾-in. wood—pine or basswood wears reasonably well, but maple is better—and outline your foot as at *A*, Fig. 1. Indicate the line of the ball of your foot and the center of your heel, or step on the outline with wet foot, which locates the two major support points. Draw lines across grain at these points (*B*) and outline the pad (*C*). Saw out the outline (this can be quite rounded, even slightly larger than the foot) and hollow out to the pad marks, testing to see that they fit (*C*). This is done by making stop cuts along the cross lines and hollowing toward them from each side. These pad sockets can be sunk about ¼ in. and sanded smooth (*D* and *E*). Copy the heel location on the underside from a pair of your regular shoes, and make a notch about ¼ in. deep, fairing it forward into the sole (*F*). This is not necessary, but it does make the shoe lighter and provides something to catch the shoe on if you slip. Also slope the sole up at the toe as shown (*F*), to make walking easier.

A single strap of leather across will make a beach sandal, but will not hold the shoe in line as well as crossed straps, Fig. 2. Or you can put in the Far East toe peg, which is a whittled knob on a neck streamlined to fit between your big and second toes. The peg looks roughly like a toadstool with a shank long enough to fit the toes snugly and go down into a drilled hole. Drill a hole crosswise in the peg tight under the head and lengthen it into a slot for the thong, which is then fastened at the sides along the instep.

The simple sole is also the base for the French sabot, Fig. 4. This is quite comfortable and easy to wear, and can be made with or without the heel leather. The leather size will vary with your foot size, of course, but a toepiece takes a square roughly the length of the sole (to allow for tucking at the toe), and the heelpiece takes a piece as long as the sole but only half as wide. For me, these pieces are about 1×1 ft. and ½×1 ft. Use a thin and flexible leather like sheepskin but not one that will stretch too much—or use plastic. Cut it to the rough shapes of the patterns, then try it over your foot. The leather is simply tacked around the shoe edge. (The flatter curve of the heel leather is the one tacked.) Tack the toe leather at the sides first, making sure it fits your instep, and stretch it forward as you tack. Then make two tucks or folds at the front as shown

General-utility sandals—wood with monogrammed leather straps—and French sabots made for a child are pictured here. Both have simplified foot outlines for soles. Hollows are carved for the heel and ball of the foot, and the sole is notched for a heel on the bottom. This reduces weight and the chance of slipping on inclines. The Swedish clog, current vogue, is like these, but of wood 1½ to 2 in. thick, and sometimes sloped on top like the Fiji sandals shown.

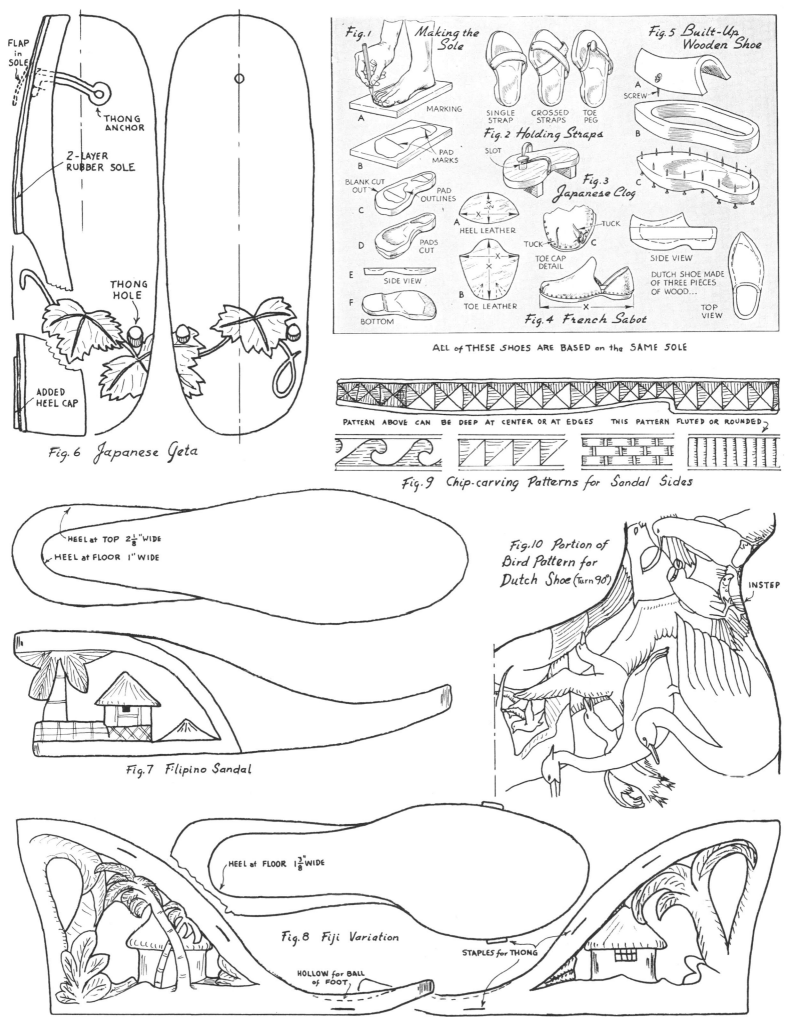

FLAP in SOLE

THONG ANCHOR

2-LAYER RUBBER SOLE

THONG HOLE

ADDED HEEL CAP

Fig. 6 Japanese Geta

Fig. 1 Making the Sole

MARKING

A

B
PAD MARKS

BLANK CUT OUT
C
PAD OUTLINES

D
PADS CUT

E
SIDE VIEW

F
BOTTOM

SINGLE STRAP   CROSSED STRAPS   TOE PEG

Fig. 2 Holding Straps

SLOT

Fig. 3 Japanese Clog

HEEL LEATHER

TOE LEATHER

TUCK   TUCK

TOE CAP DETAIL

C

Fig. 4 French Sabot

Fig. 5 Built-Up Wooden Shoe

A SCREW

B

C

SIDE VIEW

DUTCH SHOE MADE OF THREE PIECES OF WOOD...

TOP VIEW

ALL of THESE SHOES ARE BASED on the SAME SOLE

PATTERN ABOVE CAN BE DEEP AT CENTER OR AT EDGES   THIS PATTERN FLUTED OR ROUNDED

Fig. 9 Chip-carving Patterns for Sandal Sides

HEEL at TOP 2⅛" WIDE

HEEL at FLOOR 1" WIDE

Fig. 7 Filipino Sandal

Fig. 10 Portion of Bird Pattern for Dutch Shoe (Turn 90°)

INSTEP

HEEL at FLOOR 1⅜" WIDE

Fig. 8 Fiji Variation

STAPLES for THONG

HOLLOW for BALL of FOOT

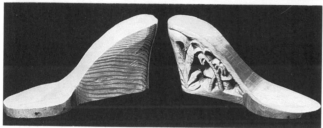

High-heeled dress sandals have a different Fijian scene on each side, and the heel is pierced. Tinted and varnished.

before you tack; this forms the toe cap. To produce the vogue—the Swedish shaped-front clog, or the "Dr. Scholl" with its single cross strap, start with a thicker board.

To make a Dutch shoe of one piece practically demands special tools like shaped drawknives and long-handled bent spoon gouges; my grandfather had them in Hannover when he made *Holzschuhe*. But you can build up a Dutch shoe in three pieces (Fig. 5), by leaving a longer point at the toe of the sole section and adding about ½ in. around the rest, then sawing out a 1½ in. for men—about 1 in. for children—collar and a cap the same thickness to be glued and screwed on top. The assembly is then shaped.

The Japaneze *zori*, or clog shoe, Fig. 3, is simply a sandal with toe peg and two 1-in.-high crosspieces nailed or screwed to the bottom. It's good for mud and falling flat on your nose a time or two until you get used to the elevation. A modern style of Japanese *geta* (sandal with toe peg) is sketched in Fig. 6. Note that the soles are not shaped to the foot at all, but are simply rounded at the ends. Also, the toe peg is replaced by a leather loop tacked into a slot in the bottom and covered by the outer rubber sole. These soles are specially made and are only about ⅛

in. thick, a soft rubber "shock absorber" with a harder rubber outer sole. A small tab is cut in the outer sole and a hole in the inner one to allow the toe loop to be tacked in place on the wood, then the tab is stapled back.

Note that the toe loop is exactly in the middle of the shoe, so the shoe fits either foot. Also, the thongs pass through the loop and through holes at the instep just forward of the heel, where they can be tied or tacked underneath. The shoes do have a right and left, however, because of the low-relief design carved along the heel line. This is in *very* low relief to avoid hurting the foot, and there are no sharp edges. But the design is carried right across the two shoes, so they should be worn with the vine ends to the outside. *Geta* are carefully lacquered and the design touched up in gold or colors. Also, the thong is decorative. Remember that the Japanese leave their shoes outside the house.

Before World War II, a traveling friend brought back from the Philippines a pair of sandals like those in Fig. 7, each a pierced carving in hard wood and painted in colors. The design is repeated in reverse on the opposite side of the heel. Note that this shoe also will go on either foot. It is held on by thongs from staples at the sides.

I made my own variation, a higher shoe with a Fijian round grass shack rather than the square woven-mat hut on sticks of the Philippines. They can be in white pine, basswood, willow, or a harder wood. I also varied the design somewhat between the sides, making one look like the opposite side of the house and with different foliage. It is also possible to vary designs from one shoe to the other, thus having four scenes.

Height and heel shape can be taken from a shoe of the intended wearer. The blank is sawed out, the pierced areas drilled through and sawed to shape, and the blank thinned down if desired, so the heel at the floor is narrower than the heel at the sole. It is helpful to the wearer if sockets are made for the ball and heel of the foot, as in Fig. 1, particularly because of heel height. Then the design is carved. It is unnecessary to pierce the carving, but it makes the shoe look as well as feel lighter. Sturdy staples driven in where indicated at the sides, or though holes, provide an anchorage for the thongs—ribbon or leather. Designs like those in Fig. 9 can also be expanded to decorate the sides.

✳Dynamic Wooden Toys, Mostly Slavic

Articulated Pine Assemblies

RIGHT—This Russian bear, about 10 in. tall, hangs on the wall. A pull on the cord lifts his arms and his jointed legs (see sketch, next page). Rough fur texture is gouge cuts; head and mouth are carefully carved. Joints must move easily, and strings for opposite limbs are yoked separately to central cord. Pivots can be wood screws set in drilled and countersunk holes. String is better than wire for the operating cords.

Sketches—next page.

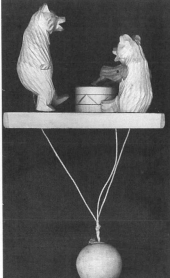
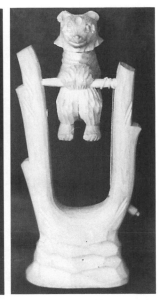

BELOW—Polish smiths are a bear and a man, both crude, pivoted so opposed endwise slat movement causes them to alternate in hitting anvil. Figures are pivoted to both slides, anvil to upper slide only, so it stays vertical. Bear is furred with gouge cuts.

BOTTOM—Russian fisherman has right arm lifted by a cord when his body swings back, rocked by plunger in base (see sketch). This lifts nose of a fish pivoted in base slot.

ABOVE—Russian dancing bears are like chicken-pecking toys from Japan and Sweden. Strings which pull arms of drummer and loose leg of dancer go through hole in base to ball. When ball is swung in a circle, limbs move alternately.

BELOW—Russian scissor toy is basically a pantograph with a whittled figure at each joint, and a man at the outer end in this case. When the scissor is closed (*BELOW*), herd is compact; when opened (*BOTTOM*) animals move into a line.

ABOVE—Bear acrobat must be balanced on his bar. Support is a fork, so ends of bar can be sprung into sockets. Operating string, wound on bar, passes through hole in yoke base. Russian.

BELOW (CENTER)—Whammydiddle is simply a notched stick with plug propeller. When notches are stroked with wand, propeller rotates. Rotational direction can be changed by touching stick at side of notches during stroking. Notches must be regular in spacing and size, propeller balanced and freely rotating.

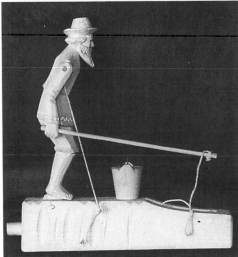

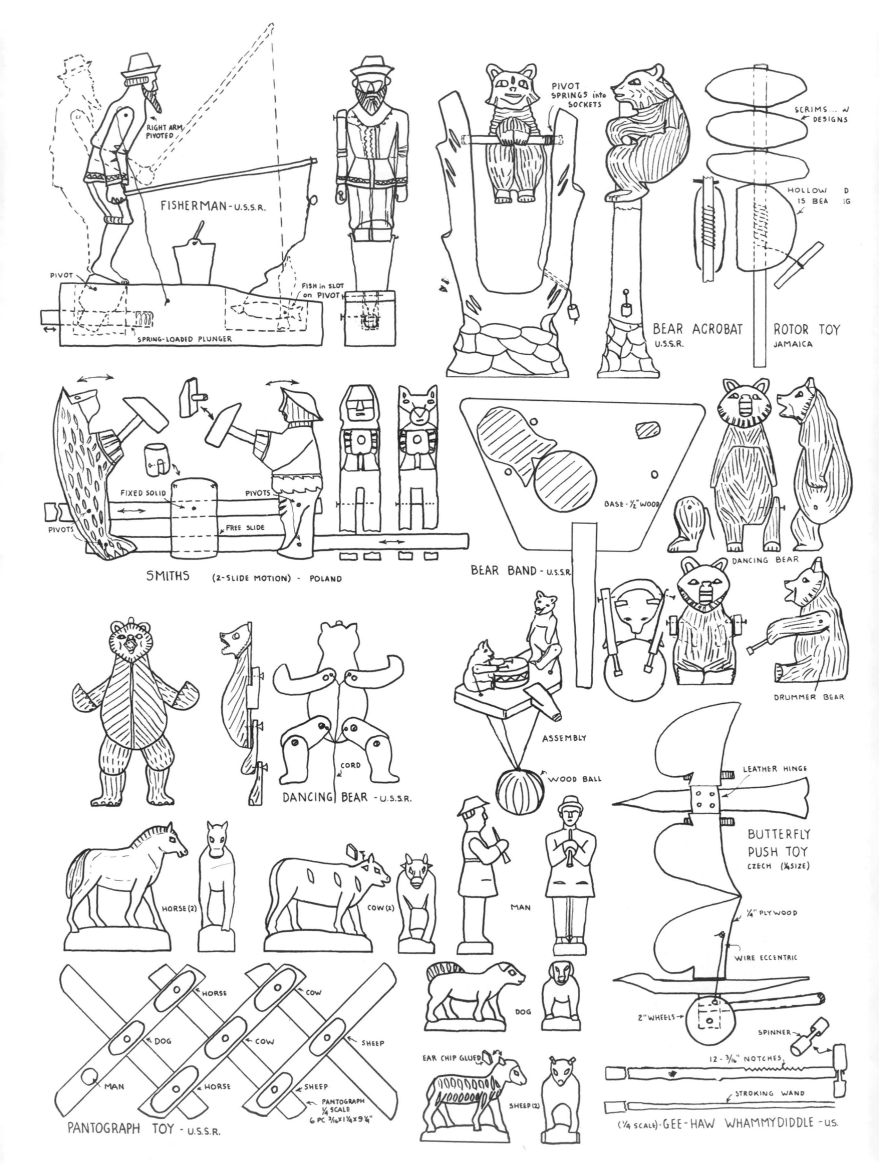

FISHERMAN - U.S.S.R.

RIGHT ARM PIVOTED

PIVOT

FISH in SLOT on PIVOT

SPRING-LOADED PLUNGER

PIVOT SPRINGS into SOCKETS

BEAR ACROBAT U.S.S.R.

ROTOR TOY JAMAICA

SCRIMS... DESIGNS

HOLLOW IS BEA

SMITHS (2-SLIDE MOTION) - POLAND

FIXED SOLID

PIVOTS

FREE SLIDE

PIVOTS

BEAR BAND - U.S.S.R.

BASE - ½" WOOD

DANCING BEAR

DRUMMER BEAR

DANCING BEAR - U.S.S.R.

CORD

ASSEMBLY

WOOD BALL

BUTTERFLY PUSH TOY CZECH (½ SIZE)

LEATHER HINGE

¼" PLYWOOD

WIRE ECCENTRIC

HORSE (2)

COW (2)

MAN

DOG

2" WHEELS

PANTOGRAPH TOY - U.S.S.R.

HORSE   COW

DOG   COW   SHEEP

MAN   HORSE   SHEEP

PANTOGRAPH ¼ SCALE 6 PC 3/16"x1¼"x9¼"

EAR CHIP GLUED

SHEEP (2)

SPINNER

12 - 3/16" NOTCHES

STROKING WAND

(¼ SCALE) - GEE-HAW WHAMMYDIDDLE - US.

✳ More Carved Wooden Toys

Seven Classics from Bogorodsk

Bogorodsk, near Moscow, has long been the center for Russian carved wooden toys. It has been a cottage industry, whole families carving local birch and aspen often with only a hatchet, chisel, a small gouge or two and knives. Even the lathe-turned objects like nested dolls were made on foot-power lathes. The government has now developed the industry, encouraged standardization, and collected typical examples in museums. Those shown here are in the Toy Museum, Academy of Arts, Moscow.

The goats at *LEFT BOTTOM* are on tilting platforms weighted forward. Twisting the center key lifts their inner ends by winding up cords, then, when reversed, allows them to fall back and bump heads. The three singing bears at *BOTTOM RIGHT* are not animated, but all the others are. The bear at *TOP RIGHT* has a plunger which pulls a string so the bear lifts his arm and threatens the leaping dog. (This double movement is based on the fisherman mechanism at left.) The bear (*BELOW, LEFT*) lifts his arm to drink, meanwhile tilting back while the dog tilts forward. The heads of the fox and crane tip (*BELOW, RIGHT*) alternately toward the center vase, pulled by strings on a swinging ball, re-creating a part of the old Aesop fable. The wood sawyers (*RIGHT*) are animated like the Polish smiths on the previous page, and the two bulls *BELOW* them are on platforms pivoted at the front, so they clash when a bottom string is pulled. All these are easy variations of figures previously sketched, except for the bucking goats.

✳ Basics in Carving Animals

Elephants and Deer Provide Practice

Animals, wild or domesticated, have fascinated the carver since the beginning of time. We have likenesses in low relief scratched in caves and animals in the round dating back to the Stone Age, whittled and carved by all peoples, from the Eskimo to the Australian aborigine. Many primitive and backwoods people are carving them today, not to mention some respected artists.

Animals tend to be recognizable by the silhouette (side view) alone, so it is relatively easy to carve one. Usable side views can be found in a good dictionary, encyclopedia, or child's book on animals; all that's necessary is to copy them to size, cut them out, and round them up a bit.

It is possible, however, to make very real likenesses of particular breeds, even of particular animals. Some years ago, I had two commissions in quick succession, one to make the head of an Arab stallion, the other the head of an English bulldog. In both instances, the owners were as insistent about certain details as are parents when you carve the head of a child.

One problem with carving animals is the grain. If it goes the length of the body, the legs, and often the tail and ears, are crossgrain. If grain goes with the legs, horns, tail, and tusk can cause trouble. Also, the skins of animals are usually not smooth; they have a characteristic texture, which is sometimes hard to imitate in a carving. Thirdly, their limbs are not jointed like ours, so you may end up with an animal that has a joint or two reversed, or a muscle bulge in the wrong place, particularly if you vary the pose from standard. The best thing to do is, of course, to study the animal itself in the

desired pose; but, failing that, you must find good references. I use *Animal Drawing and Painting*, by Walter Wilwerding (Dover) and *500 Animals from A to Z*, by Gergely and Davis (American Heritage). For real detail, best is *An Atlas of Animal Anatomy for Artists*, by Ellenberger, Baum, and Dittrich (Dover).

A good "break-in" animal to carve is the elephant, because he's bulky and his legs are thick. Years ago, I produced two sets of designs, one quite simple and the other more detailed, both called "Jumbo" by the editors. Jumbo I is in several poses (see sketches), three vertical to minimize grain problems. This Jumbo can be anything from ¾ to 1¼ in. thick in white pine or basswood.

Carving is largely chamfering the edges, except for ears and face details. Leave the body quite blocky and with your knife cuts showing; this helps the massive look of the beast. Cut a V-notch between legs and body and thin down behind the ears so they can be carved. The tail and nose are very thin, rounded—and don't forget the little finger at the outer top end of the snout. The junction of the tusks and mouth is important; study the step-by-step drawings carefully to get this right. The eyes are little pyramidal notches. Cut a series of V-notches around each foot to simulate toes, and put in wrinkles at the knees and "shoulders."

To color Jumbo I, I prefer a dark gray flat paint, painted on, then wiped off somewhat with a cloth. This accents notches and gives him a patchy appearance, somewhat like a real elephant. The inside of his mouth, inside tip of his trunk, toes, and eyes can be touched up with pink. The tusks are white,

Three poses of Jumbo I (*LEFT*) and Jumbo II, showing rough, carved and finish steps.

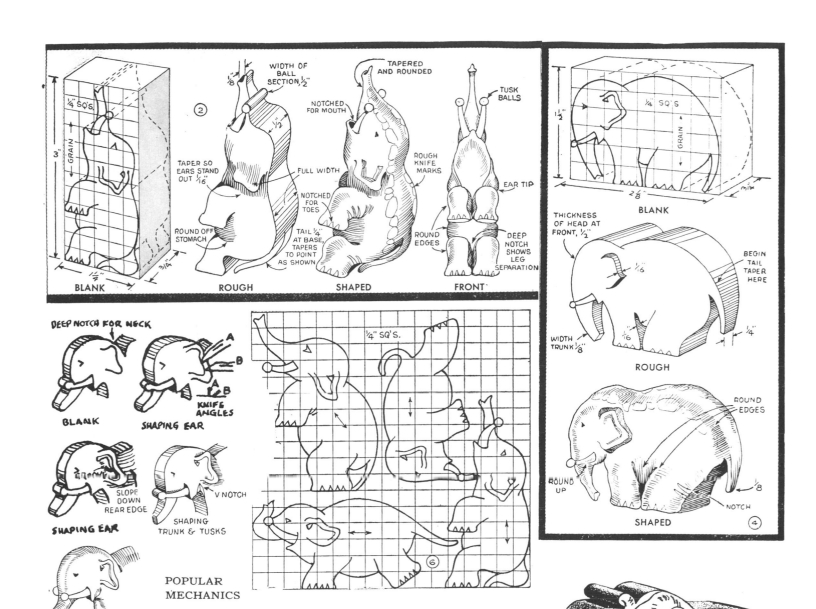

Figure 2 (Rough): WIDTH OF BALL SECTION, ½" · TAPERED AND ROUNDED · NOTCHED FOR MOUTH · ⅛ · ½ · TAPER SO EARS STAND OUT ¹⁄₁₆" · FULL WIDTH · NOTCHED FOR TOES · ROUND OFF STOMACH · TAIL ¼" AT BASE, TAPERS TO POINT AS SHOWN · BLANK · ¼ SQ'S · GRAIN · 3" · 1½" · ¾" · ROUGH · SHAPED · ROUGH KNIFE MARKS · ROUND EDGES · FRONT · TUSK BALLS · EAR TIP · DEEP NOTCH SHOWS LEG SEPARATION

DEEP NOTCH FOR NECK · BLANK · SHAPING EAR · A · B · KNIFE ANGLES · SLOPE DOWN REAR EDGE · SHAPING EAR · V NOTCH · SHAPING TRUNK & TUSKS · FINISHING

¼" SQ'S. · 6

POPULAR MECHANICS

AUGUST, 1941

BLANK · ¼ SQ'S · GRAIN · 1½" · 2⅜" · ROUGH · THICKNESS OF HEAD AT FRONT, ½" · WIDTH TRUNK ⅛" · ¹⁄₁₆ · ¹⁄₁₆ · ¼ · BEGIN TAIL TAPER HERE · SHAPED · ROUND EDGES · ROUND UP · NOTCH · ⅛ · 4

"JUMBO" I & II →

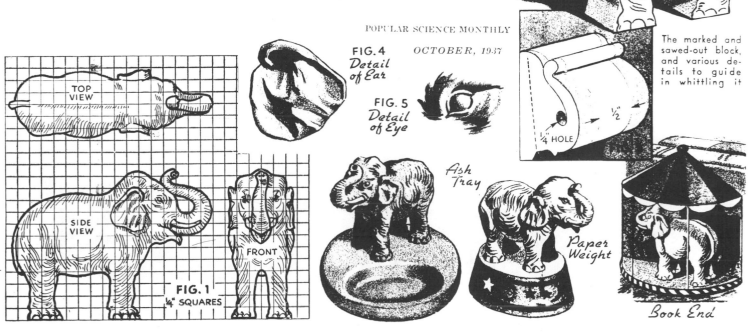

POPULAR SCIENCE MONTHLY

OCTOBER, 1937

FIG. 2

FIG. 4 — Detail of Ear

FIG. 5 — Detail of Eye

The marked and sawed-out block, and various details to guide in whittling it

½" · ¼" HOLE

TOP VIEW · SIDE VIEW · FRONT · FIG. 1 — ¼" SQUARES

Ash Tray · Paper Weight · Book End

with gilt balls. (The fabled "white elephant" —if you want one—is actually a light gray or dirty white.) You can also carve this elephant in a better wood, like mahogany or teak, and finish him with varnish. For the horizontal pose, you can add a palanquin— the little open "house" on his back—and an Indian mahout sitting on his head. In that case, carve V-grooves to show a headcloth and a body cloth and paint them in gay colors, touching up with gilt.

Jumbo II is more elaborately carved, made from a block $1\frac{3}{8} \times 3\frac{1}{8} \times 4\frac{1}{8}$ in. After the silhouette is sawed out, drill a ¼-in. hole through the trunk, as in Fig. 3, and thin down the trunk *only to the mouth and tusk edges* to ½ in. at the outer edge, Fig. 3. Outline the ears with the knife point, then cut the wood away all around about ⅛ in. Also score along the tusks and shape the trunk and mouth. Round up the rest of the body, allowing wood for the tail, and remembering

that the feet flare out from the legs. The legs are, of course, separated by a deep V-notch, or you can saw between them carefully from feet to belly and shape the legs completely.

Do not quite cut through between the outer end of the trunk and the head, but make it look as if you had. In the center of the hump that marks Jumbo's eye, lay out a slanting oval, as in Fig. 5, and cut a V-notch all around it, shaping the center into an eyeball. Curve the wood outside it to form the heavy, pouchy eyelids. Finish the ears, Fig. 4. Wrinkles are easiest to put in with a veiner or small V-tool, but can be done with the knife in a little more time.

Jumbo II can be painted white, gray, or black. An interesting variation is to paint him a light greenish-gray. Then when he's dry, brush dark brown over him and rub it off the high spots. He'll have a sort of jungle antique look. A touch of black on Jumbo's

LEFT—"Cottontail," 7 in. long, is mahogany with a maple tail tuft. The hare and tortoise, one piece of mahogany, 12 in. long, is adapted from a soap carving. I made both from discarded World War II aircraft patterns.

LEFT—These six deer, as described here, provide good training in cross-grain cutting. They are largely chamfered silhouettes, with long, thin legs. Sketches, page 34.

BOTTOM—Three carvings made by students at the Swiss Federal Woodcarving School at Brienz. At *FAR LEFT* is an insect model about 2 ft. long, planned for high-school biology classes. The buffalo at *CENTER* is a dynamic pose, with an interesting surface texture of small flat-gouge scallops. Woodchuck pair *BELOW* are stocky and stolid like the animals, done in dark wood with smooth finish.

eye, a little red about the mouth and trunk tip, and white or ivory on the tusks, and he is complete. Several possible mountings are shown, but I prefer him unmounted.

For contrast, and training in handling cross-grain cutting, try the five poses of the deer (patterns on page 34) which I first described in *Popular Mechanics* for January 1945. The blanks can be cut with scroll saw or jigsaw, but be careful to have the grain run as indicated. White pine or basswood ¾ in. thick is used. Thin the neck to a bit over ⅜ in. and narrow the back between the legs to ½ in. This will make the legs and shoulders stand out. Saw up to the belly between the legs and thin them down so they taper from about ⁵⁄₁₆ in. at the top to ³⁄₁₆ in. or

slightly less at the hoof. Thin the tail to ¼ in. thick and taper it in slightly on all sides from tip to base. Now take shaving cuts along the top of the "shoulders" and "hips," so the upper part of the body is thinned. Chamfer all edges and notch a bit where the legs join the body.

Now do the head. Note that the nose is really a 4-sided pyramid sloping from just in front of the ears, and chamfered to make it 8-sided. Two of the chamfers on the top are hollowed out to make eye notches, back to the forehead. The ears should be separated by sawing, then shaping, and the back carved in an arc to give them a forward tilt. The fronts are hollowed out with a deep V-groove, enlarging from tip to base.

BELOW—The goose, from Denmark, in teak, is an interesting design, suggesting rather than defining the shape. The dachshund with her is from Switzerland, and very precise in detail. Each is about 4 in. long.

BOTTOM—Two sleeping kittens by the author, in walnut. The upper is 7 in. long, the lower 6½ in. Grain lines add a curved look to back and neck of the curled-up kitten, and color variation from growth wood also adds interest, Finish, flat varnish and wax.

CENTER—Hare from Kenya, Africa, and fish from Ponape, South Pacific, both in heavy dark woods, were purchased in a museum in Hawaii. Both have the simple power of primitive work.

BELOW—Elizabethan fox in holly features a stylized oversize tail and neck ruff. I also provided horsehair whiskers.

BOTTOM—Deer and moose from northeastern United States contrast sharply with the simple designs of the facing page. Horns are carved separately.

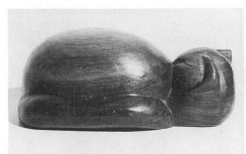

✳ Surface Texture

What It Can Do to Help

Sculptors have long used textural devices to add aesthetic value or interest to a work; the sculptor in clay leaves a surface looking daubed and with finger marks; a sculptor in metal leaves areas showing mold marks; a sculptor in wood leaves tool marks, even carefully adds them after the piece is completed. Many artists in oils try to make their canvases three-dimensional by slabbing on the pigment with a palette knife or building gesso contours. Thus it is no surprise when a bird carver adds color to identify the particular species, or an animal carver attempts to suggest the texture of an animal's pelt. The temptation to do the latter is strengthened by the fact that animals don't have the color range of birds, and the distinction between species is sometimes largely one of color. Thus a zebra may be distinguished from a donkey by parallel shallow gouge cuts or a spotted dog from a plain-color one by stain-ing or bleaching areas, or by gouge-cut pits. Coarse hair is suggested by a rasped or roughened surface, long hair by long V-tool or veiner cuts in appropriate areas.

Some surface textures have been used for so long by particular carvers that they become a form of identification. Thus the Swiss finish their bears with an all-over pattern of shallow gouge pits; several of the émigré French-Canadian carvers in New Hampshire experimented extensively with pyrography—burning marks to simulate change of color in a raccoon's stripes, for example; the Japanese make a variety of stylized figures in a kind of cedar that shows alternate stripes of light yellow and dark brown (summer and winter growth wood), designing the figure and placing the grain to make most effective use of the color change. In the latter case, they sometimes sand-blast the figure to make definite ridges by

LEFT—Japanese badger is always cut from two-tone cedar so growth lines accentuate his fatness and toe tips. Other animals *(LEFT, BELOW)* are similarly designed. Turtle, goldfish, and toad (next page) are ideal subjects for such treatment.

BELOW—Bears have a rough coat which suggests gouge channeling. The upper group, from Switzerland, includes a variety of treatments, from a rasped surface *(RIGHT)* through channeling and slabbing *(LEFT)* to smooth *(CENTER)*. The Indian bears, however, are gouged and polished, and have ivory claws, teeth, and eyes.

TIGER – JAPAN

WILD BOAR – JAPAN

BADGER – JAPAN

HAT SEPARATE
GLASS EYES

GLASS TIPS

TAIL HOLLOWED   GOLDFISH – JAPAN

GLASS EYES

ALL OF THESE JAPANESE FIGURES
ARE DESIGNED & ERODED to EMPHASIZE GRAIN
AS DETAILED ON THE FIVE
at LEFT & BELOW

DRAGON – JAPAN

TURTLE – JAPAN

REAR VIEW

GLASS EYES →

TOAD – JAPAN

BEAVER – U.S.

RACCOON – U.S.

SMALL
GOUGE LINES

KIWI – AUSTRALIA

SNAKE – JAPAN

ALL FOUR OF THESE U.S.
FIGURES FINISHED WITH
PYROTECHNIC PENCIL

GROUNDHOG – U.S.

RABBIT – U.S.

COW CARICATURE – U.S.

BABY BURRO
MEXICO

VEINER SPOTS

FLAT-GOUGE
SCALLOPS

VEINER GROOVING

SPANIEL – U.S.

SPANIEL CARICATURE – U.S.

GOAT – U.S.

FLAT-GOUGE SCALLOPS

CHIPMUNK – U.S.

TINTED STRIPES
PYROTECHNIC PENCIL

THREE
MONKEYS
– JAPAN

SIDE VIEW
TOP VIEW

V-TOOL GROOVING

eroding the softer summer wood. One German sculptress some years back finished all her portrait heads with an all-over pattern of tiny planes purely for the effect. And carvers all over the world have used parallel notches to simulate the "lie" of long hair on a horse's mane or a dog's coat.

Some examples of these techniques are shown here. You'll find others in other pages of this book—like rasping or blasting a surface to indicate a rough pelt, slabbing the hide of a rhinoceros to simulate the plating, and so on. It's a matter of trial and error, but if you can simulate a texture with the tools alone, that's usually better than attempting it by adding or subtracting color.

LEFT—Swiss bitch and pups, all one piece and about 3 ft. long, show extreme detail in hide texture, produced with carving tools, as contrasted with the kiwi from Australia, which has crude knife V's to simulate its coarse feathering.

LEFT, BELOW—Three caricatured animals are carefully slabbed with the knife, as constrasted with the spaniel, in which knife V's simulate his shaggy coat. The three monkeys *(UPPER RIGHT)* are V-grooved over body and legs to represent their long hair.

BELOW—Burning and notching were both used in finishing these New Hampshire animals. (Photo *BELOW* retouched to show line locations.) Woodchuck at *FAR LEFT* has only occasional notches, while that at right has fine vertical V's and that at *FAR RIGHT* in retouched group has flat-gouge scallops.

BOTTOM—Teakwood silhouettes from India have patterns of brass strip driven into the wood and polished smooth. Animals are about 3 in. long, so very fine strip is required. Features, harness and trappings, and just plain decorative spots are all applied in this painstaking way. Only woods like teak can be used because of danger of splitting.

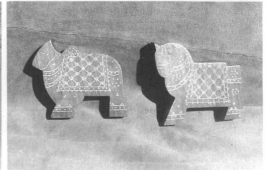

✳ More Animals to Carve

Five Pages of Ideas and Patterns

Because animals are so favored as subjects, carvings may be caricatured, stylized, adapted and distorted as well as realistic, and a wide range of finishes and surfaces may be applied. In these five pages, I have tried to provide a variety that suggests many of the possibilities. Sketches and photos will explain many details. The giraffes *(BELOW)*, for example, are blocky American caricatures, while the curled fawn *(BOTTOM CENTER)* is realistic but a very complex pose. The Mexican cat *(CENTER)* is a bit more blocky, must be posed on a ledge to clear its tail (which is very vulnerable), and has actual horse-hair whiskers. Both the fawn and the cat are delicately tinted, the fawn tan with lighter underbody and dark big eyes and ears, while the cat is in tones of gray. The cat is left with some knife and gouge marks, while the fawn is carefully sanded into smooth, flowing lines. My sheep, in basswood *(BOTTOM LEFT)* retains the knife marks as well, to represent his coat.

Stylized mythological animals were once quite familiar for cane and umbrella heads, but I have never seen a shepherd's crook as elaborately done as the Greek one *(RIGHT)*. It is apparently a dragon or fish head, as is the umbrella with it, and both are in hard woods, the handle a dark red and the crook a dark yellow, both finished only by rubbing with wax. The Mexican circus horse *(RIGHT)* is in a very soft wood, about 8 in. high, and is made easily in parts, with the legs glued and nailed on. He is painted in fairly gaudy colors and antiqued, in contrast to the burro, which is plain-varnished, with only tinting of eyes, mouth, mane, and hooves. The spotting of some baby burros is simulated by depressions cut with a small gouge. The precision and strength of Swiss carving is typified by the chamois and kids *(BOTTOM RIGHT)*, each carved from one piece of wood complete with base. No tinting is done, muscle lines and other features being suggested by gouge grooves and lines. Finish is also a restrained glow.

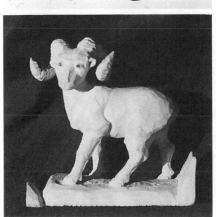

CHAMOIS - SWITZERLAND

GAMBOLING KID - SWISS

BIG-HORN SHEEP - EJT

FAWN (Complex Pose) - SWISS

GAMBOLING KID

FAWN

PIGLET RUNNING - USA - FAWN or DOE

STYLIZED DEER in FIVE POSES & STYLIZED FAWNS - USA

GIRAFFES
in caricature

ARMADILLO (Stylized) - MEXICO

MOOSE (Stylized) - FINLAND

34

BOVINES, like horses, are common subjects—the cow in the Western world, the carabao in the Eastern. They range from the 4-in. crude cedar one with thorn horns *(CENTER)* made by a Tarahumara Indian in Mexico who burned holes for horns, ears, and tail (but added only the horns), to the very well-done span of oxen (4 in.) and sledge *(BELOW RIGHT)* from New Hampshire. The latter includes a whittled and assembled yoke, an ax and a pipe that obscures the driver's face—all whittled. The 6-in. resting cow *(BOTTOM RIGHT)* in pine, was made by a Mexican guard at a ruin and is an excellent example of primitive carving. (The armadillo with him, on the other hand, is a crude assembly of whittled pieces.) The carabaos *(BOTTOM LEFT)* from the Philippines, about 4 in. long, are in a hard mahogany, stained still darker, and show the blocky lines of primitive work. They contrast sharply with the skilled carving of a man on a carabao *(LOWER LEFT),* which even has such details as the guiding rope and designs on the man's loincloth and separate hat. This figure, about 10 in. high, is one piece, including the base, except for the hat.

DACHSHUNDE are fun to carve, partly because their overlong bodies and hound heads permit easy caricature. *BELOW,* however, is a Swiss seated pose that is very precise and realistic, even to an integral-carved collar with a hole for a lead. Grain is vertical in this design, so the ears are not too delicate. While the piece is rounded, some tool marks—very shallow, made with a flat gouge—give it character and texture. Nostrils, eyes, and collar are tinted, and the back is shaded. Finish is a flat varnish, with waxing. *LEFT CENTER* is a simple donkey or burro pose, with head slightly larger than life. It is pine, but finished with a dark stain and flat varnish.

BELOW are American small carvings, the boxer and puppy from New Hampshire, the piglet and rabbit from the Southern Highlands. Only the boxer shows tool marks, and he and the puppy are tinted. The piglet, probably pecan, is simply waxed. The rabbit looks ghostly because he is maple. *CENTER RIGHT* are two carvings by E. Jerome Frye, a bull in poplar (obviously inspired by Ferdinand) and a calf in white pine, each integral with its support. Both were originally modeled in clay, then copied in detail, the bull's horns being separately carved from maple and inserted in drilled holes. Both are tinted with walnut stain, then waxed. Clay models teach students how to design animal heads or portraits because they telegraph trouble that surprises the direct carver. These animals were Mr. Frye's first, so he went through this additional step, then transferred dimensions by caliper and scale. The model would be a help in getting Ferdinand's face right.

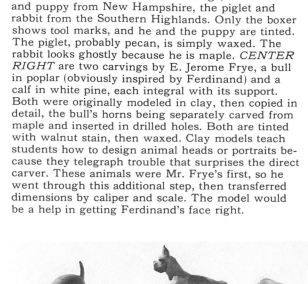

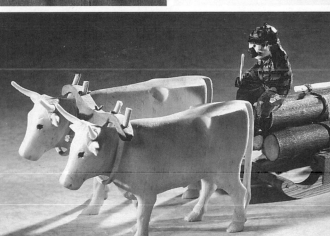

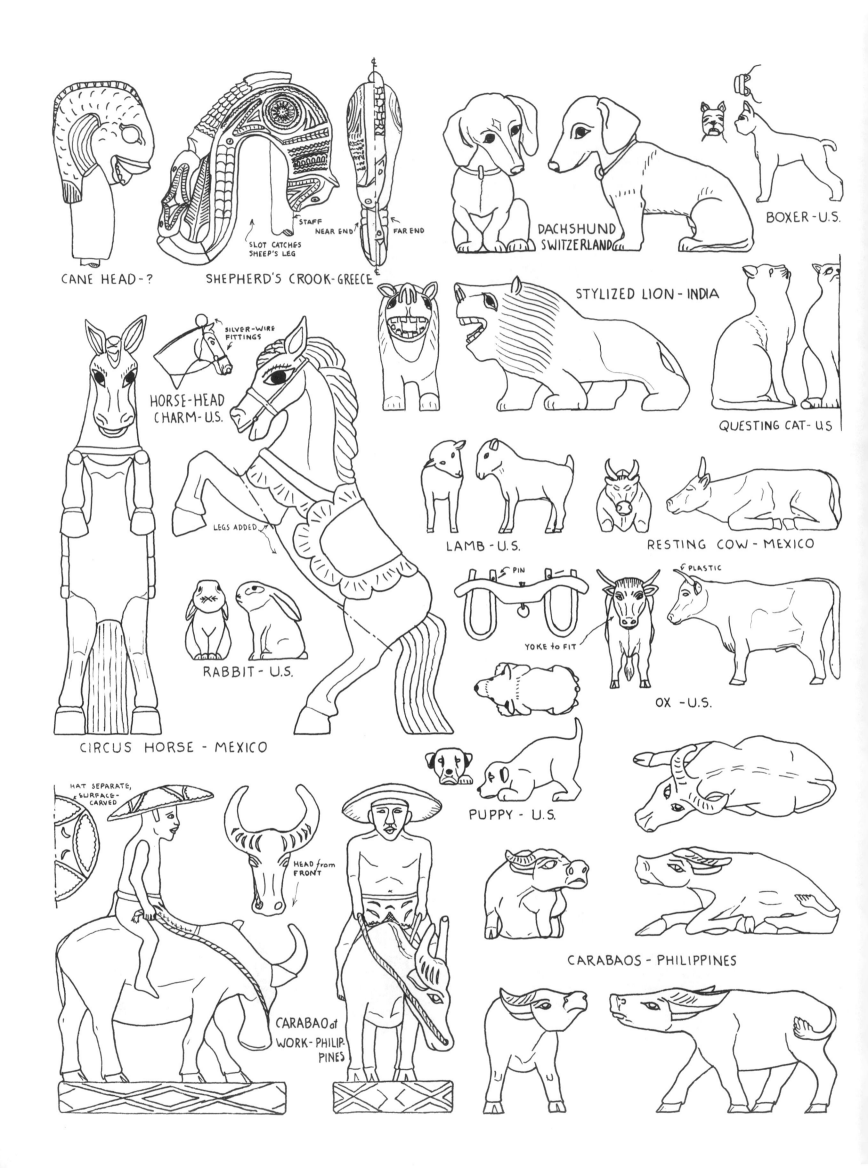

CANE HEAD - ?

SHEPHERD'S CROOK - GREECE

STAFF

NEAR END   FAR END

SLOT CATCHES SHEEP'S LEG

DACHSHUND SWITZERLAND

BOXER - U.S.

STYLIZED LION - INDIA

QUESTING CAT - U.S.

HORSE-HEAD CHARM - U.S.

SILVER-WIRE FITTINGS

LEGS ADDED

RABBIT - U.S.

CIRCUS HORSE - MEXICO

LAMB - U.S.

RESTING COW - MEXICO

YOKE to FIT

PIN

PLASTIC

OX - U.S.

PUPPY - U.S.

HAT SEPARATE, SURFACE-CARVED

HEAD from FRONT

CARABAO at WORK - PHILIPPINES

CARABAOS - PHILIPPINES

CATS, big or little, "flow" as they walk and are usually sleek, so carvings should have polish. The pair of domestic cats *(ABOVE)* from our Southern Highlands are sanded and polished. The lion from India *(TOP)* has oversize head and mane, while the ironwood jaguar *(ABOVE)* from Peru is lengthened to stress physical traits.

DEER and fawns are favored carving subjects in many countries. The group *(TOP)* includes three blocky miniatures and a well-rounded one (see sketches), all tinted brown with white spots. Compare them with the long-eared, big-eyed fawn *(RIGHT)* and his lined coat. The lamb with him is smooth. The deer from Bali *(UPPER RIGHT)* is stylized, has widened hindquarters to make the base triangular. Note how the ears reinforce the horns. South Germans use the deer for designs carved in deer-horn, often pierced, in buttons, martingales, slides, etc., even on their underslung pipes *(TOP RIGHT)*. Indians also make the deer, principally in ivory, but they favor the lion. A standard design *(RIGHT)* has ivory eyes and teeth, just as the Peruvian jaguar above has turquoise eyes, to emphasize them. This particular lion is a miniature copy in rosewood presented to me by Willard Bondhus. With it is a Hindu god in sandalwood, a fragrant hard wood now growing very scarce because everybody has carved it—even Solomon for his temple. Each of these figures is about 2 in. high. The bear *(RIGHT)* is poplar, stained walnut, then thin-shellacked and waxed. Some carving planes are left to suggest his rough coat. With him is a mountain lion or puma, also of poplar, but in this case only the base is stained walnut. The figure is polished with clear wax only, which combines with the yellow tinge of the wood to give a natural tawny color. Each figure is carved integral, is about 8 in. high, and was made by E. Jerome Frye some years ago.

NOTE—Many of the figures on these pages are also sketched, but in some cases I felt it unnecessary because the pose was simple and the view in the photograph is essentially a pattern silhouette. Designs can be transferred with the grid from a photo just as readily as from a sketch.

✳ My Kingdom for a Horse

How to Carve Equines

The horse, which modern research tells us seems to have originated in north-central Asia, actually preceded man on earth, and primitive man used him as food before he was domesticated. There have always been horses in most of the areas occupied by man —in Europe, China, and down through Persia, India, Arabia and even Egypt. Surprisingly, it was vast numbers of horses that enabled the Huns to beat the Romans. The Crusaders brought the powerful Arab horses to Europe when they returned. In Spain, the pick of Arab and Barb strains brought by the Moors soon became the source of Europe's best horses, because the horse strains of the Arab areas far surpassed those of Asia and Europe.

Even before the siege of Troy and the wooden horse, equines had helped man work his way up from savagery—the early Asian and European civilizations were all horse breeders and horse users. The "man on horseback" was the symbol of power, and the image of the horse was on coins, temples, even worshipped as divine. Thus it is no surprise that the horse has been a favored subject of carvers and sculptors from China and India through Europe to the United States. While a recognizable one can be made with a block and four sticks, as shown below, the animal can also tax a sculptor.

Among the oldest of existing horse images are those carved in China, the so-called "Peking horses," originally a series of statues along the road to the royal mausoleum, as I understand the story. The series includes eight poses ranging from the awesome to the almost-ridiculous, because one of the originals is a horse rolling on his back. Be that as it may, one of the most familiar Chinese carving subjects is this same series of horses, in various woods, ivory, semi-precious and precious stones. I have one set, of ivory, about 4 in. long, on rosewood bases that cost about $50 in Hong Kong, another of solid rosewood that cost around $20. (That's

BELOW—Crude horses whittled by a New Hampshire farmer draw a buggy with sections of spools for wheels. 12 in. long overall, white pine. Legs are slats in drilled holes. Contrast this with *BOTTOM*—Russian carving, also in pine, of the boy who helped his father cut wood (Pushkin), has horse, sledge, and harness meticulously detailed. 15 in. long overall. *BOTTOM RIGHT*—Russian troika model of a military group, complete with small cannon, with three horses carved from a single piece of wood. Photo taken through glass in a Moscow museum.

BELOW LEFT—12-in. horse in cherry by W. J. Hayman, captain of the guards at the Cooper-Bessemer plant, Grove City, Pennsylvania. Carved with knives and files. *BELOW RIGHT*—Percheron in basswood, by John T. Tangerman at age 14. About 4 in. long, it was whittled.

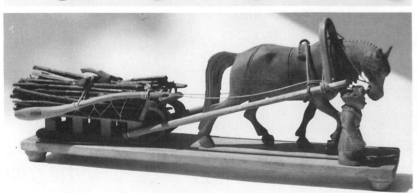

scarcely an incentive for an American to go into the business, although a number of Americans now specialize in carvings of horses that sell at sculpture prices.)

Oriental tools for such work tend to be small and are chisels rather than knives. Each carver owns his own and will not sell them because they're his livelihood. The woodcarver has perhaps a half-dozen tools— small firmers and gouges and a club or small hammer to drive them. The ivory carver has tools with chisel tips and rasp sides, so each serves a double purpose. In each case, the carver is a specialist—he makes only horses —and he has only the tools he requires. (Incidentally, a set of eight horses about 5 in. long, each in a different semiprecious stone, can cost $2,000 or even more.)

For a tryout, I'd suggest the series of Italian caricatured horses sketched and pictured on the next two pages. They're fun to make and to have; mine are only about 2½ in. tall, but you'll probably want them larger, at least for a first try. Use ¾-in. basswood, white or sugar pine, and have the grain run with the legs. Lay out the blank on two faces, cut to the outlines with a coping saw, and follow the step-by-step sketches. The head is the difficult part; it can be either simple or elaborate, so again I have provided step-by-step sketches for both types. Finish can be natural, or flat varnish and wax. In either case, you'll probably want to darken the nostrils, inside the mouth, the eyes, inside the ear notches, and the mane and tail; it adds a little distinction.

Eric Zimmerman of Greensburg, Pennsylvania, has whittled horses for years and has upwards of 80 poses, carved since 1949. He leaves the finish natural, gets color by choice of wood. In some instances he adds riders, a wagon, or other element, but usually he makes the horse alone—he likes horses. But other people miss the accessories, so he provides them on occasion, even though he doesn't sell his carvings.

BELOW—Three of the Peking horses in rosewood, 3 in. long and without bases, a more modern adaptation of the traditional ones at right. *BOTTOM*—Brewery teams have always been typical of heavy work horses. This pair, 2 ft. high, are pulling a model wine wagon, however; they were shown at a Chicago Trade Fair in 1950.

BELOW—Peking horses in ivory, with rosewood bases. They are about 4 in. long, with tails and manes "antiqued" and bodies tinted to a warm brown by smoking in incense. *BOTTOM*—Peking horses about 4½ in. long, each integral with its base. Finish is a high polish. Note that there is no upset horse.

HEAD #1 FORWARD   HEAD #2 RAISED   HEAD #3 TURNED BACK

TOP - #2

TOP of HEAD #4 at RIGHT ANGLE to BODY

HEAD #4 - ALTERNATE SIDE

TYPICAL BASE

BASIC BODY AS ABOVE OR ALTERNATE AT RIGHT. HEAD POSES VARY AS IN NOS. 1,2,3,4

PEKING HORSES in ROSEWOOD

TOP VIEW

TOP VIEW

ROSEWOOD

FRONT

PEKING HORSES in IVORY
ROSEWOOD BASES as ABOVE RIGHT. 4" HORSE

FRONT   TAIL from TOP

ITALIAN CARICATURES of THE PEKING HORSES

WORKHORSE & DROVER - U.S.S.R.

REIN

PRIMITIVE HORSE - I.I.S.

INSERTS

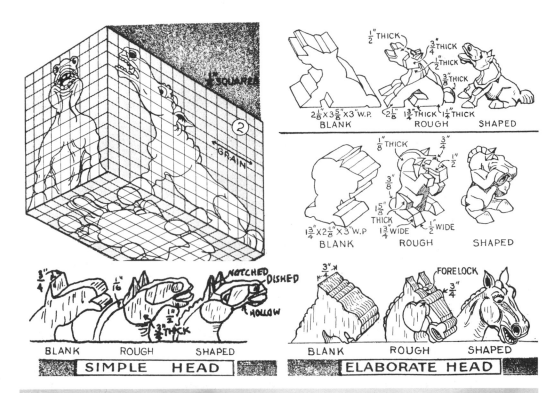

RIGHT—This set of Italian ponies seems to lampoon the Peking horses. Poses are absurd and heads too large for the bodies. Details are extremely important in carving these figures. Included in the sketches, from *Popular Mechanics,* September 1940, are designs for a simplified head as well as an elaborate one, and three steps in making a simple and a difficult pose. Block layout includes a bottom view, which is rarely necessary. Here also are three of Eric Zimmerman's best. *BELOW*—A Lipizzaner stallion in Philippine mahogany, with marble base to support the cantilevered weight. *BOTTOM*—Mare and goat in curly buckeye, an unusual and difficult wood. Wax finish. *BOTTOM RIGHT*—Four racing horses drawing a Roman chariot, each about 6 in. long. The one at left is Honduras mahogany; the second, pine; the third, South American mahogany, and the farthest right is walnut.

✳ Mobile of Bali Birds

Assembly of Eight Ebony Fliers

Although carved in Celebes ebony, these birds are essentially 2-dimensional silhouettes, except that the silhouette is from the top rather than from the side. Except for the two largest, they are obviously made from leftover pieces of wood. But, hung individually or as a mobile group, they show the grace of all Balinese carving. All are long-winged seabirds, and show a good deal of variation, some carrying snakes, butterflies or clams in their bills.

Grain runs with the wings, so designs are often arranged to get long necks and bills turned to the grain line as well, or to support them with a snake, for example. Occasional, more elaborate pieces are desk ornaments, several birds with intertwined bills or joining wings, as we do ducks here. But I selected the simplest ones, with this mobile in mind. Its only peculiarity is that it is not affected by side drafts, as most mobiles are, but by *up*drafts, so a lone candle burning well under it will cause constant movement.

Designs are cut out with a scroll saw and finished with small chisels and a light club or hammer—very few Balinese carvers have conventional mallets. Lines representing the feathers are incised with a knife or firmer; most carvers have no veiners or V-tools because they are too hard to make and too costly to buy. Several of the birds have expert carving of eyes and beak lines, suggesting finishing by a skilled carver. All are carefully hand-sanded, then finished with shoe polish, and they have meeting holes drilled in their backs so a string can be threaded through. The center of gravity of a bird can be found easily by testing with a straight pin on a string, stuck into the bird's back. For more elaborate balancing, two pins can be used, in opposed positions flanking the back. In my sketches, I have indicated where final holes were drilled, but these will vary slightly depending upon how thin you make the wings, neck and bill. On all but the flattest birds, the carver has given the wings graceful arch and sweep, even to having the wingtips curve upward.

The mobile must be built progressively, each pair being balanced as you go, starting with the lowest birds. When the assembly is balanced and hung, you will find it necessary to shorten or lengthen some cords, so the birds hang in "steps" and clear each other, and so total depth of the mobile suits you and the clearance where it is to hang.

Thread lengths will run from 2 to 6 in. in normal circumstances, but can be longer if a deep mobile is preferred. Overall height of mine is 30 in. and it hangs in a bay over a coffee table. Depth could be shortened somewhat by lengthening the whiffletrees so the birds could be hung nearer the same level. Or the whole problem can be minimized by carving only your favorite bird and hanging it alone.

To assemble the mobile, weigh birds on a postal scale and juggle them to obtain approximate balance. My birds weigh 1½ oz. each, except Nos. 3 and 5, which weigh 3 oz. Bottom whiffletrees have two birds, but intermediate ones have one bird on one arm, two and a whiffletree on the other, and the top one (made of coat hanger) must have two loads that approximately balance. Top whiffletree eyes are 18 in. apart, all others are No. 18 piano wire (0.041 in. diameter), the top pair 8 in. long, the intermediate ones 6 in., and the bottom ones 4½ in. These dimensions are *after* eyes are formed and include natural curve of the wire. Length need not be exact. Cords are monofilament nylon thread except for the main support of nylon fishing leader.

THREAD HOLES

CLAM

SIDE of BODY

#1

LEG POSITION

SIDE of BODY

#2

LEG POSITION

6"

18"

4"
8"

8" 3"

MOBILE ASSEMBLY
NOT to SCALE. BIRDS
IDENTIFIED BY NUMBER

6"

5"
6"

3"
6"

4"

#5

#7
4"

4 1/2"
4"

3"
6" 3"

4 1/2"

3"
#1

#3

#8
6" #6

3"
#2

3"
#4

4"

BUTTERFLY

#3

SIDE of BODY

#4

SNAKE

HEAD from FRONT

#5

#6

NOTE HOLE LOCATION
TO BALANCE HEAD

#7

#8

43

❋ Basics in Carving Birds

Realistic, Stylized, Caricatures, Details

Bird carving probably dates back almost as far as animal carving; birds are a familiar and accepted subject for the primitive, the whittler, the carver, and the sculptor, regardless of country. But the rise of bird-watching or "birding," the current ecology "kick," and the affluence of Americans which permits collecting have combined to make the production of bird models a profitable business, whether they be wood, china, porcelain or other materials. As a consequence, there are bird "carvers" in many vacation and resort areas, even plastic birds. There are several specialized books on bird carving, as many more on the carving of decoys—although the emphasis or real skill and art in both instances is not in the carving but in the painting and mounting. (I

know of at least one book on the making of eagles.) There are even commercial sources for a variety of glass eyes and cast feet.

Bodies for birds have also been mass-produced with power sanders, rasps, and other tools designed primarily to remove wood and produce a silhouette that is not a great deal more important in the finished bird than is the canvas in a painting. When I wrote about bird-model making in the mid-forties in a now-defunct magazine called *Science Illustrated,* most of the questions were from ornithologists, several of whom indicated that they were having bodies turned out by manual-arts shops and were therefore primarily interested in how to duplicate the soft sheen and texture of feathers. They wanted true models, more

BELOW—Chickadee has brads for legs, set into a piece of driftwood in which feet are carved. *CENTER*—Female cardinal, also by the author. Tinted. *BOTTOM*—Realistic bird models often require more painting than carving. Canada goose below had carved feathers; another did not. A close look was required to tell them apart.

BELOW—Life-size wrens in walnut, slightly stylized and not detailed. Foot problem is avoided by flowing bird into mount. Carving planes remain. Finish flat varnish and wax. *BOTTOM*—Pete the Pelican is a caricature. Simplest pose *(RIGHT)* is in alabaster, could be soap or plastic.

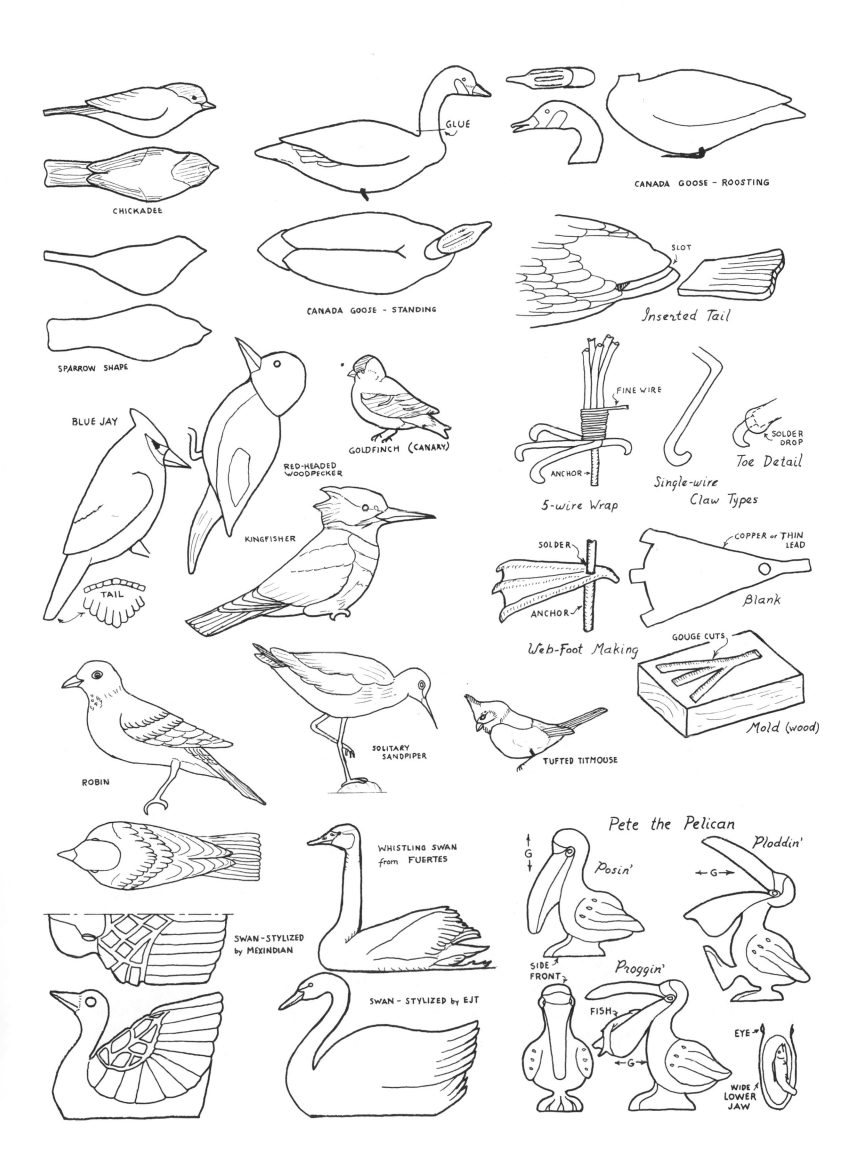

CHICKADEE

GLUE

CANADA GOOSE - ROOSTING

SPARROW SHAPE

CANADA GOOSE - STANDING

Inserted Tail

SLOT

BLUE JAY

RED-HEADED
WOODPECKER

GOLDFINCH (CANARY)

FINE WIRE

ANCHOR

5-wire Wrap

Single-wire
Claw Types

Toe Detail

SOLDER
DROP

KINGFISHER

TAIL

SOLDER

ANCHOR

Web-Foot Making

COPPER or THIN
LEAD

Blank

GOUGE CUTS

Mold (wood)

ROBIN

SOLITARY
SANDPIPER

TUFTED TITMOUSE

Pete the Pelican

Ploddin'

Posin'

G

G

SWAN-STYLIZED
by MEXINDIAN

WHISTLING SWAN
from FUERTES

SIDE
FRONT

Proggin'

FISH

G

SWAN - STYLIZED by EJT

EYE

WIDE
LOWER
JAW

durable than stuffed and mounted birdskins.

Primitive bird carvers tried for a good silhouette of a bird in a characteristic pose that helped to identify it; they varnished and/or polished their products rather than painting them, and often only suggested the feathering. Paradoxically, sculptors and artists who specialize in birds tend in the same direction: Their birds are shapes suggesting flight or other characteristics of the subject; no accessories are added and the only approach to color may be toning of some areas—just as they would do in carving an animal, a man, or an abstraction.

For the simplest bird models, white pine, sugar pine, or basswood is the accepted material, because they will be painted anyway. Even balsa can be used and some decoy makers have worked with styrofoam and papier mâché. Patterns for almost any bird can be found in the books previously mentioned, bird guides, nature magazines and the like. The silhouette is sawed out with bandsaw or coping saw, sometimes in parts which are then assembled. Thus a long-necked bird like a swan or goose is usually two pieces assembled at the base of the neck to save wood and complication. Sometimes

FAR LEFT—Lamp base from Bali, in ebony, a network of birds and vines (sketches).

LEFT—Duckling and warbler from the Southern Highlands, both with limited detailing of pinion feathering and no color. Warbler is mahogany; duckling is maple. *BELOW*—Stylized pine swan by Mexican Indian, 4 in., has planes replacing feathering.

BELOW—Contrast in nesting birds, one a Mexican Indian carving in pine, with burl nest in which are two whittled eggs; the other a Danish pair of swallows, with composite bodies of teak and maple, pinned to a solid nest of highly figured wood. No details except eye indications are on the swallows; the nest is a stylized block. Mexican bird has geometric "feathers."

BOTTOM LEFT—Horn birds, the two OUTER ones from USSR and the CENTER one from Indonesia. Parrot at LEFT is on horn base, involves both carving and heat-forming of the horn. Crane at RIGHT is carved to flow into its base, with all lines faired by sanding and polishing.

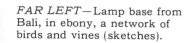

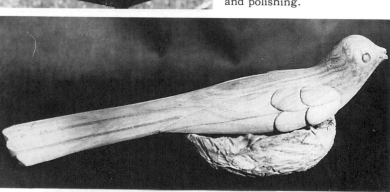
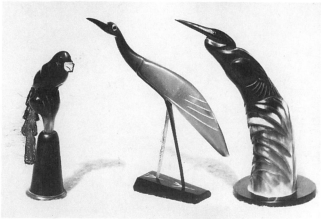

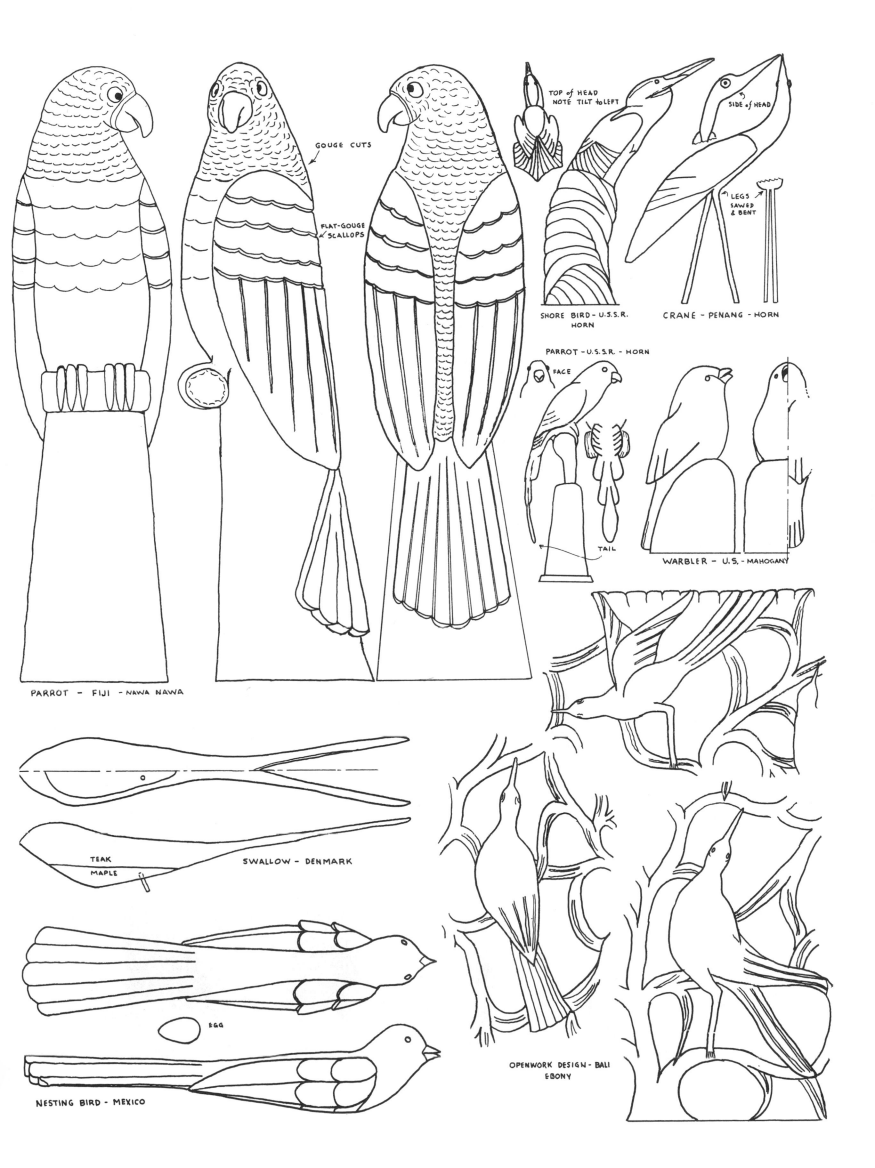

GOUGE CUTS

FLAT-GOUGE SCALLOPS

PARROT – FIJI – NAWA NAWA

TOP OF HEAD NOTE TILT TO LEFT

SHORE BIRD – U.S.S.R. HORN

CRANE – PENANG – HORN

SIDE OF HEAD

LEGS SAWED & BENT

PARROT – U.S.S.R. – HORN

FACE

TAIL

WARBLER – U.S. – MAHOGANY

TEAK
MAPLE

SWALLOW – DENMARK

EGG

NESTING BIRD – MEXICO

OPENWORK DESIGN – BALI
EBONY

the top or bottom silhouette is also given and sawed as well, although in many cases it is practically as fast to whittle. Elements like spread tails and opened wings are made separately and glued into slots, and the bill may be a separate piece glued in a hole.

Legs can take many forms. On small birds, they can be brads or pins, straight or bent to shape. Some birds may have pointed pins for legs so they can be stuck into a surface —like a nuthatch on vertical paneling. They may have a small magnet set in the body so they will cling to a steel surface like a fire-screen, or the bird may be set on a surface on which the legs are carved or just painted. However, in most cases, legs are made of wire and glued into holes after forming. Two forms are sketched, one a single wire and the other five wires bound together by wrapping with very fine wire; the five wires become the bird's four toes and a center support set into a hole in the base. For large birds, like the predators, the upper leg or thigh may be carved from the blank and drilled for a central wire or group of wires. These wires are shaped and completed at the ends by soldering on an arc of smaller wire to form the claw, leaving a blob of solder on the bottom to form the pad beneath the claw base.

Webbed feet can be more elaborately made by forming a thin sheet of copper or lead in a mold made with a gouge. The metal is simply pressed or hammered into the gouge lines, then filed to shape and drilled at the apex of the V for a wire "leg" to be passed through and soldered in place. The leg may be finished with clay, plastic wood, or some similar material over the central wire.

A number of bird silhouettes are sketched here, each at about one-quarter size. The chickadee and sparrow shapes can be used for a number of other small birds, with slight modifications, just as the blue jay can be converted to a cardinal or cedar waxwing without too much trouble. These are one-piece blanks, as contrasted with the 2-piece poses of the Canada goose.

By slight distortion, a bird can become a caricature, as in the case of "Pete the Pelican," which I described in *Popular Science Monthly* back in February 1940. His legs

BELOW—Stylized Swiss eagle about 2 ft. high. Overall pattern of gouge marks, plus a few lines on wings and tail. Eye is darkened, outlined in white. *FAR RIGHT*—Antique 3-ft. conventional American eagle, from Maine, has stylized feathering. It has been on our Great Seal since 1782, when John Adams and Thomas Jefferson outvoted Ben Franklin, who preferred the turkey.

CENTER—Fiji parrot carved in nawa nawa wood by Isimeli. He is the father of ten children, three of them also carvers. The youngest had his first exhibition at 11 in the Suva Museum. Feathers are stylized (see sketch) but not detailed. Eye has blackened pupil on yellow-white bone insert. Height 13 in. This is an example of styling by a primitive carver.

add a bit of complication in two of the poses because they are cross-grain, overhang, and are grooved to simulate toes. Also, in the third pose, I added a fish, which can be carved separately and glued into place. The original Pete was carved from 1½-in. pine 2½ in. square.

In recent years, the popularity of Americana generally has led to a revival in the carving of spread-wing eagles, usually as relatively high-relief plaques rather than as in-the-round figures. They may also have symbolic accouterments like the arrows and olive branch. Patterns are easy to come by—any Federal building, stock certificates, even sources which will sell blank and instructions.

Birds need not, of course, be entirely true to life. Some examples are pictured here, ranging from primitives to sculpture. They are alike in three characteristics only—no painting, no special legs, no glass eyes. Like other carving subjects, they are primarily the product of the carver's skill and imagination. I have tried to make the point more strongly by drawing three swans (page 45), the first from a bird-book painting by Louis Agassiz Fuertes, the second as I stylized it for a panel carving, and the third as a Mexican Indian far surpassed me in stylizing. Somehow he got more feeling into his swan, more virility and life, than my more conventional treatment did. He suggested the feathering with deeply outlined diamonds and angled planes—and got something special into his basically angular design.

An Ark for Noah Preserves More than 60 Pairs—see next page.

✳ Noah's Legendary Ark

A Tradition in Many Lands

Greeks, Hebrews, American Indians, Polynesians, Maori, Lithuanians, Tibetans, and the tribes of Kashmir and India all have legends of the Great Flood. Geologists have found evidence of one between the Tigris and Euphrates about 4000 B.C. which was described in the Epic of Gilgamesh and later in the Bible. Noah's Ark has various dimensions in Jewish lore, but the Biblical ones are $300 \times 50 \times 30$ cubits high, or $450 \times 75 \times 45$ ft., with three stories and nine compartments, drawing $22\frac{1}{2}$ ft. and with a roof $1\frac{1}{2}$ ft. higher in the center.

Traditional arks, so familiar as a child's toy during the last century, were of wood, as were all the animals, and both were rather blocky and crude; the painting usually identified animals that were otherwise sawed silhouettes slightly chamfered. This made a sturdier toy, but arks were already so expensive, and animals so easily lost or destroyed, that arks were stored most of the year, being on display only at Christmas. Peregrine Pollen, president of Parke-Bernet Galleries in New York City, has one containing some 145 pairs, made by a Dutch whittler over 100 years ago; that one comes out only at Christmas for obvious reasons.

When arks were made in quantity in Germany, each animal silhouette was made on the cross-section of a doughnut of soft pine turned on a lathe, head inward. Then wedges were cut from the doughnut, smoothed, and edges shaped. This produced an animal smaller at the head end, but most animals are, so it saved finish-shaping. There was little effort to maintain any scale, because a rooster or hen, for example, would be almost too small to see compared with a horse only $1\frac{1}{2}$ or 2 in. long. Scale really doesn't work out very well anyway; an ark at 1/240 scale would be $22\frac{1}{2}$ in. long, a reasonable size, but a horse to the same scale would be less than $\frac{1}{2}$ in. long! In the designs given here, the ark is approximately 1/240 scale but animals are roughly ten times that, some even larger. Also, details are carved in, legs are separated and shaped (although not to precise proportions with the body in all cases because of resulting fragility). Most animals are, however, reduced in thickness so they will not occupy so much space in the ark when packed. Thus an elephant is 1 or $1\frac{1}{4}$ in. thick (both thicknesses are sketched for comparison), a giraffe only $\frac{1}{2}$ in., a lion $\frac{1}{2}$ in. through the shoulders (although the male's ruff is $1\frac{1}{4}$ in. through). On this basis, about 60 pairs of animals, plus Noah and wife, Og and an archangel can be stored inside the ark in padded layers. Small animals and birds must be placed between the legs of, or between, animals even so. Animals are

The 3-part ark (see previous page) stores Mr. and Mrs. Noah, Og, archangel, and 30 pairs of animals and birds, laid in layers separated by padding. Poses in pairs vary in most cases, avoiding traditional stiff, static, saw-cut silhouettes. Sex differences are shown—male may be bigger, have a longer horn (rhinoceros), heavier build (cattle), or differ as radically as a rooster from a hen. Animals also vary in scale to give sensible sizes. This will result in some disproportion when animals are set up in "parade" formation, as shown here, but gives more interest both to the carver and to the viewer.

DOVE

NOAH & DOVE

MRS NOAH

OG

HALO IS A GLUED DISK

ARCHANGEL

HANG by SCREW EYE

WOLF DOGS

DONKEY

ZEBRA

COCK

HEN

PLATE

DUCKS

SWALLOW

SCARED CAT

SEATED CAT

MONKEY

WALKING MONKEY

SQUIRRELS

TURTLE

GEMSBOKS

RAM

SHEEP

EWE

WILD BOARS

RAVEN

OSTRICH

FOOT PLATE

THIN for BETTER PACKING in ARK

POLAR BEAR

CARVE HEAD & TAIL LIFTED

SNAKE

CHIMPANZEE

LEMUR

FLAMINGO

TOM

TURKEYS

HEN

PENGUIN

PELICAN

COCKATOO

PANGOLIN (SCALY ANTEATER)

CAMEL (2-HUMP)

PANDA

DOE

DEER

REINDEER

HIPPOPOTAMUS

DEER MICE (Full Size)

LEOPARD

BEAVER

CROCODILE

protected by pads of felt, leather, or non-fraying soft cloth between layers. Fragile pieces like the archangel, birds, and people can be stored in the upper section and separately padded. The entire "cabin" is removable, and is floored by a removable ply-wood slab which is also the ramp by which animals enter the ark. The slab is painted to match the hull on one side and sand covered, so animals posed on it will not skid or slide. Og is a seated figure, so he can be perched on the rooftop, and the swallows are equipped with pins and the "arkangel" with a wire for posing on the cabin roof.

Poses may be static (as ark figures have tended to be), or dynamic (some animals running, walking, sitting up, etc). Pairs vary, even if only in a leg or head position. Some characteristic poses are used—howling dog, scared cat, elephant trumpeting.

Because the material is in most cases bass-wood, grain is not too vital, but usually runs in line with legs and horns. This limits poses to some degree, of course, and results in elephant tusks and tails on many animals with weak cross-section. Fragility may be reduced to some degree by carving the tail joining the hock on a hind leg. Heads are usually dead front; if they are turned to the side, the animal becomes monodirectional, and this severely limits the setup of the parade. Animals usually hold their heads sideward because of their nonconverging line of sight, but here it makes trouble.

Incidentally, in carving animals as small as these, a helpful tool is a piece of broken coping-saw blade. It will work wonders in cutting out the filament between legs, or between tail and leg, or between horns.

Because this ark was intended for display rather than play, the animals are realistically colored with oils. They are first flat-varnished (to avoid grain troubles with colors), then tinted and revarnished for protection. In varnishing and painting, work bellies and areas between legs, etc., first, then the body can be touched up if smeared slightly while drying. The ark interior and cabin trunk are white enameled, the hull varnished (to take color evenly), then painted a dark red, as is one side of the ramp, and the roof is stained dark. Roof boards are grooved like thatch.

RHINOCEROS

CAMEL

BISON

FRONT

GIRAFFES

KANGAROOS

COWS

BEARS

TIGERS

NOTE ELECTIVE THICKNESS
(SAVES PACKING SPACE)

PIN

BREAK & PIN
HERE for PACKING

ELEPHANTS

HARES

LIONS

HORSES

✳Miniatures and Models

Weapons, Trains, People, Animals

Miniaturization has always been fascinating, whether the product is a nutshell containing 100 ivory elephants, an ivory camel going through the eye of a standard needle, or simply a little piece of furniture. One man carves a chain from a matchstick; another beats him by carving it from a toothpick. Oberammergau carvers make Nativity scenes and Last Suppers in a walnut shell, but Chinese carvers beat that in ivory (with more detail), even make a sampan with windows that pivot out of an "olive pit" (really more like a thick pecan shell).

What is the limit? No one knows, but it probably is the cell size of the particular material, coupled with the skill, patience and tools of the carver. I once got three links of a

chain into a matchstick before the knife slipped. I know carvers who can make wooden pliers less than an inch long; I've watched Orientals do shell inlay of almost microscopic bits in teak, matching the colors as they worked. You can go as far as you like, but you'll probably want special tools like bits of broken razor blade gripped in lengths of dowel, and steel wire ground and honed to a cutting edge. Ship-model makers use engraver's burins for lines and grooves, and special miniature chisels with burin handles to fit the palm for cutting. Such tools can be made from bits of hacksaw blade or other tempered steel. They are a nuisance to make, because of the danger of burning tempered steel on a power grinder, but they

BELOW—Rural scenes in cedar from Colombia, 4 in. wide, show huts, peasants, and pigs. Trees are shaved sticks. *CENTER*—Miniature trains, the passenger train 7 in. long by under ½ in. high. The 5-in. old-fashioned train can be made in varicolored woods, varnished, and assembled with gold or silver couplers to make the bracelet *(BOTTOM)*.

BELOW—Pistol models (*UPPER* 7½ in. long) are carved from basswood and tinted. *Bottom* ones are pocket types. *BOTTOM*—Revolutionary musket, with bayonet, powder horn, shot pouch, and ax, whittled by my son at about 14 as accessories for a miniature room. The carving of a pistol model is described in detail on the next page.

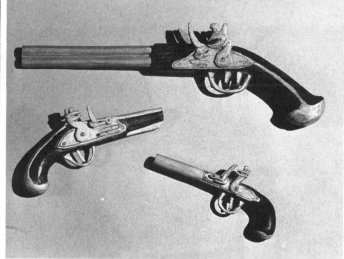

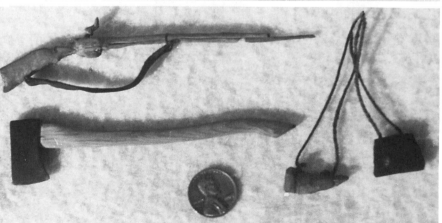

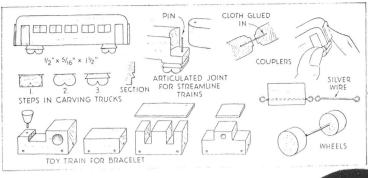

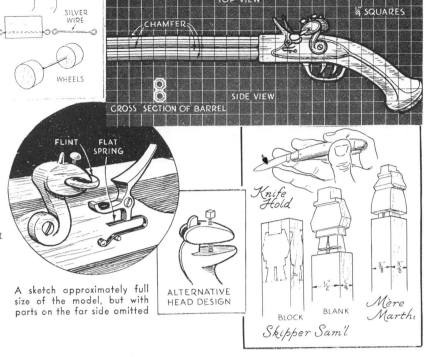

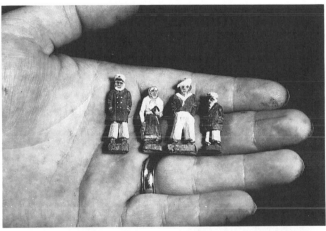

A sketch approximately full size of the model, but with parts on the far side omitted

ALTERNATIVE HEAD DESIGN

Knife Hold

BLOCK   BLANK

Skipper Sam'l

Mère Marthe

ABOVE—Details and patterns for miniature-train models. *RIGHT*—Patterns for a Revolutionary War pistol model, half size. *FAR RIGHT*—Whittle miniature figures or parts on the end of a holding stick. In carving details in miniature, it is helpful to hold the knife as sketched, with the little finger against the piece to steady the cut. For very fine detail, hold the blade like a pen, near the tip. *BELOW*—Skipper Sam'l in two sizes (larger 1½ in.) Mère Marthe and Gaspard models (patterns pages 68–72). *BOTTOM*—Miniature animals in fruit and nut woods, mostly from the Southern Highlands. All are sanded and waxed. Deer at top has a safety-pin backing; others are in-the-round. In ivory or dense woods, animals of the size shown (about half actual) are much easier.

How to Carve a Flintlock Pistol Model

This "over-and-under" Revolutionary War holster or belt pistol was probably brought to America by a British officer between 1756 and 1783—or by some wealthy civilian.

Study relative proportions of barrel, trigger mechanism, and handle before you begin whittling. Thin the barrel portion to a bit under ¼ in. and the chamber behind it to ⅜ in. Mark in the trigger mechanism, noting that the roughly S-shaped hammer, J-shaped spring and long-eared spring project on each side. I have drawn them in slightly different positions to emphasize the double trigger. Score with a penknife tip along each line quite deeply and shave off the wood around the escutcheon plate. Score along the bottom of the plate and shave off from both sides to make the ⅛-in. trigger-guard blank. Now round up the handle, allowing for the decorative ridge down each side and forming the bulging butt. Grip cross-section is really not a circle, but a square with bulging sides.

In all this cutting, go slowly and do not grip the piece around the trigger guard, flashpan covers or hammers. Also, be careful in shaping the butt, so you don't split off the cross-grain sides. Carve the triggers by deep scoring and shaving out chips, a little at a time. Shape up guard.

Begin flashpan covers by V-notching down between them until they are separated. Shape up the foot of each, outlining the pivot, and cut out the wood around the pan. At the same time, cut out between flashpan and hammer and shape the escutcheon plate so it is about 1⁄32 in. above the surface of the grip and body. The sketch in the circle gives details of the hammer, although you may use the alternate elaborate design shown near it. Shape up the hammer head and flint, starting with a V-notch between hammers. Finish-shape the mechanism.

Draw a line down the center of the barrel on each side and V-cut; then chamfer top and bottom edges to form a double octagon. Smooth it up. With a sharp, hard pencil or fine pen, draw in the fine outlines on hammer, escutcheon plate, and butt. Draw in pivot screws. Finish the flat spring that holds the flashpan cover open or closed—or insert a piece of paper or metal to simulate the spring. The pistol may be painted with silver or aluminum for metal parts and dark brown or black for the wood. One may be mounted alone, or two crossed on a plaque. (Gun models from *Popular Science Monthly*, January 1935; miniature figures, May 1937; trains and bracelet, September 1937.)

permit the user to get his hand closer to the work and still retain power and control, which bigger tools do not. Such equipment is for real miniatures in woods like box, which is hard, dense, and brittle when cut. What I show here is more familiar things carvable with a small blade on a penknife—if you keep it razor sharp. It takes delicate, painstaking work, but results are worth it.

Another similar project is the making of model furniture, guns, or even people, all to scale for miniature scenes. I've made guns, pistols, axes, chairs, tables, trains (for a bracelet!), boats, sometimes striving for accuracy in detail like the Chinese, sometimes for the effect like the Germans, and sometimes just for the challenge. I recommend it, particularly the carving of small human and animal figures. Carvers in the Southern Highlands make a lot of domestic animals an inch or so long out of fruitwood, correctly proportioned and nicely finished. German and Russian carvers make them in walrus ivory and very hard and dense woods; Chinese and Indian carvers use elephant ivory and even tint the product. It is for you to select, and a number of examples are pictured (patterns are in other parts of this book), but don't forget that you may have to make tools as you go, and in the harder materials like ivory use files instead of knives. Also, don't miss the point of carving the piece on the end of a handle, then cutting it loose.

LEFT—Chairs are about 4 in. high, made of packing-box pine, and copied from those at the New Hampshire fireplace where I sat. The ivory tea set is from India—mostly turned. *LEFT CENTER*—Rocking chairs and a 4-in. working desk, made in New England, as were the reed-seated chairs, 3-in. Windsor chair and stool *(BOTTOM LEFT)*. *BELOW*—Oberammergau Nativity and Crucifixion scenes in a hinged walnut shell. With them is a wooden hinged almond shell from Latin America containing two human figures under ½ in. high, one with neck yoke. *BOTTOM*—Birdseye maple chest and wooden bucket for a doll house. The bucket is separate staves, assembled with withes, and is 1 in. high.

✳ Articulated Caricatures

How to Get Movement into a Figure

Articulated dolls date back to Egypt, and even early Indian and Pacific Island toys have movable arms and legs, held by a cord or sinew passed through the body and knotted at both ends. But the Tyrolean figures add such refinements as elastic cords and beaded joints, ideas which have also been adopted for modern wooden (plastic and rubber in the United States) toys operated by plungers. Such toys usually have a spring-loaded plunger in a drumlike base. The plunger holds tense cords threaded through the legs of the multipart figure; but when the plunger is pushed, the cord is relaxed and the figure slumps into varied laughable positions.

The Italian figures pictured below have a somewhat standardized caricatured face: button nose, chubby cheeks, double chin, partially closed eyes, that will serve as a simple lesson. (It is interesting to compare this face with the types used on Scandinavian, German, Russian, and other caricatures, most of which are much more lean and drawn and which undertake a greater degree of eye modeling.)

To make this head, whittle a rough sphere 1¼ in. in diameter at the end of a white pine or basswood stick (the stick provides a convenient handhold). Draw a center line across the clearest surface; this will be the line of the eyes. Below it ¼ in. draw a parallel line; the bottom of the nose. Sketch in a vertical center line and draw in the nose, ⅜ in. wide at the nostrils and ³⁄₁₆ in. wide at the bridge or eye line. Cut in ⅛-in. notches at each side and across the bottom (Step 1, sketches). Cut away the wood all around to make a plane around the nose, sloping the bridge of the nose from the tip toward the eye line to make this possible. Cut a deep V-groove along the eye line on each side of the nose for an eye socket and the top of the cheek. Notch a V between nose and cheek at each side, to make the nose still more prominent, and cut a shallow U at the top of the nose to complete the eyebrow-forehead line (Step 2). Shape the nose, flaring the nostrils and cutting in little holes in each.

Now comes the mouth: Cut away a deep crescent below each cheekbone from a line at the bottom outside corner of the nostril to a similar distance below the mouth center line. Sketch in a straight line for the mouth a little over ⅛ in. under the nose, then alter it to turn up in a smile or down in a frown as you will (Step 3). Cut out a narrow V along this line, then shape the upper lip toward the nose. It should be a slightly concave surface, deeper at the outside corners, and there

THREE MOVABLE HEADS on an integral ¾×1×6-in. shoulder piece come from the Italian Tyrol. Behind them are two unarticulated low-relief silhouettes. I wrote of them originally in *Popular Science Monthly*, October 1936, and have since analyzed and made caricatures with articulations like those sketched. Figures like these are pine, with strong outlines made by simply V-grooves and dependence upon painting for characterization. Planes and sharp angles give the pieces individuality and hand-crafted appearance. Head and shoulders have hemispherical sockets in which is a mating wooden bead, the three held together by an elastic cord.

should be a shallow groove from the edge of the upper lip to the base of the septum. Cut a shallow groove following the line of the lower lip and enough below it so the pouting curve of a full lower lip can be formed, and the bottom rounded off into the chin. (Italian caricatures commonly have a full lower lip and a jutting chin.) The nose also curves up slightly from lip to tip; it is not Roman at all.

Cut away the lower end of the cheek crescent at the side of the mouth and put in a radiating line or two to represent laughter lines or a dimple. Shape the chin and fair or smooth the arcs at the top and bottom of the eye. Extend and fair out the outer end of the eye socket and cut two or three radiating lines from the eye position (Step 4). Cut along the original eye line and remove a shallow crescent at the bottom to show an upper lid. (The eye iris itself is done with paint or ink.) In other faces from the same area, the top crescent is removed, to show a lower lid; suit yourself. The head will now look like the right-hand side of the one on this page. Thin the sphere at the brow line on each side, round up the facial lines and accentuate wrinkles as needed.

FIRST STEPS in whittling a face. A 1¼-in. sphere is whittled on the end of a stick which is left to provide a grip. Here the left side of the face is merely roughed out, while the right shows eye, mouth, and cheek shape. Note double chin.

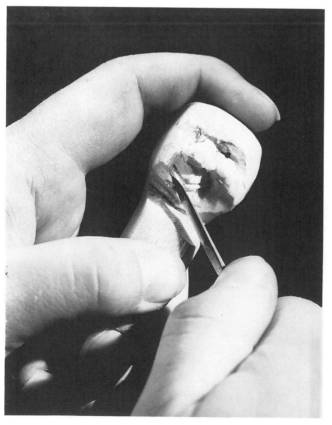

The ears are simple V-shaping of a question-mark shape with a dot cut out in the center. Be sure they are spotted far enough back on the head and line up with the nose. Normally, they are about the same height as the nose, but they can be bigger in a caricature. The head can now be cut off, drilled in the center of the neck for the cord and a locking plug, and a socket shaped for the bead neck. Or, if it's easier, thin the neck down and paint it with oils before you finish the bottom. Brown hair and eyes, bright red lips, and red tinting on nose and chin help the comic effect. It is usually easier to whittle the hat separately and glue it on a flat spot, but a woman's head scarf is simply outlined with a V-groove, then the face side of the groove faired into the face and the scarf shaped with a wrinkle or two rather than the lines that denote hair. Hats can be lathe turnings if desired. A pair of glasses is just a twist of wire; the ends of the bows can be glued into holes in the head for security.

With this much background, you can attempt the faces on caricatures in succeeding pages, and a variety of expressions as well. Or you may be impelled to try something like the political cartoon sketched and pictured here. This started out to be simply an endgame setup in chess, but grew into a political commentary, because the black knight became a jackass head with academic cap and gown, carrying a pen for a sword and a book for a shield, while the black queen became a militant and the white king looks a good deal like President Nixon in a real dilemma.

Figures of the Italian caricatures are basswood or pine, and gain strength from planes and sharp angles. The body for the three heads is simply a ¾ × 1 × 6-in. piece with three pairs of shoulders on it, each with a socket for a bead and head and a hole from below for the knotted elastic. Shoulders are blocked out quite crudely; details like lapels, neckties and wrinkles are simple V-grooves. The kissing couple is a similar carving, with clasped hands and clothes details made of V-grooves. The others are somewhat more elaborate—you will find suggestions for such figures in the chapter about Skipper Sam'l, page 68.

The figures on page 61 show a number of types of articulation, ranging from simple levers to elaborate multiple-string controls. Simplest is probably the cord to connect

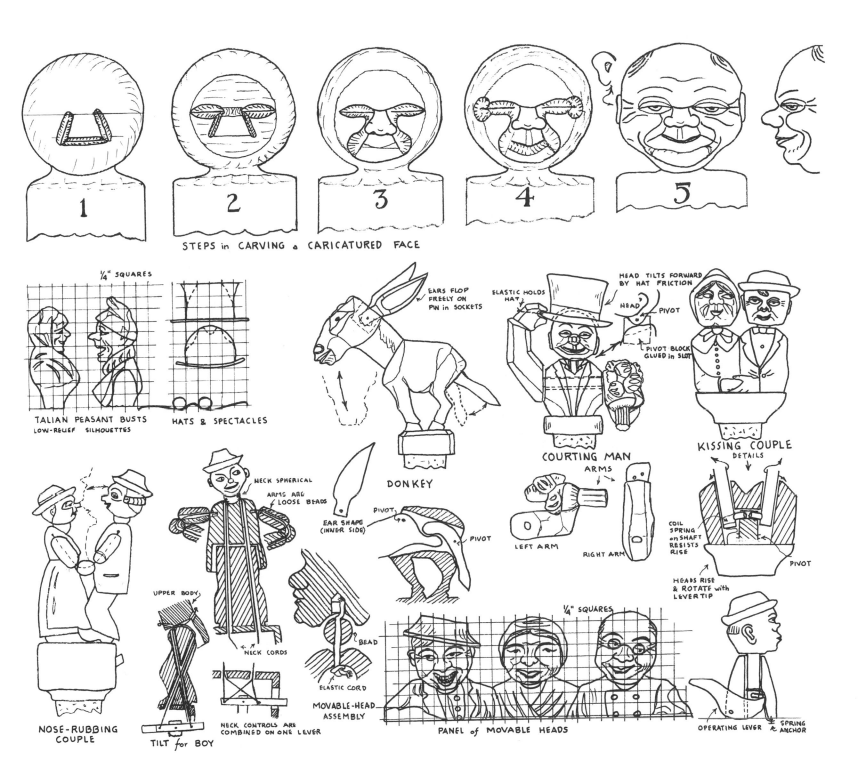

STEPS in CARVING a CARICATURED FACE

1   2   3   4   5

¼" SQUARES

TALIAN PEASANT BUSTS
LOW-RELIEF SILHOUETTES

HATS & SPECTACLES

EARS FLOP FREELY ON PIN IN SOCKETS

DONKEY

ELASTIC HOLDS HAT

HEAD TILTS FORWARD BY HAT FRICTION

HEAD   PIVOT

PIVOT BLOCK GLUED IN SLOT

COURTING MAN

ARMS

LEFT ARM

RIGHT ARM

KISSING COUPLE
DETAILS

COIL SPRING on SHAFT RESISTS RISE

HEADS RISE & ROTATE with LEVER TIP

PIVOT

NECK SPHERICAL

ARMS ARE LOOSE BEADS

EAR SHAPE (INNER SIDE)

PIVOT

PIVOT

NOSE-RUBBING COUPLE

UPPER BODY

NECK CORDS

TILT for BOY

NECK CONTROLS ARE COMBINED ON ONE LEVER

BEAD

ELASTIC CORD

MOVABLE-HEAD ASSEMBLY

¼" SQUARES

PANEL of MOVABLE HEADS

OPERATING LEVER

SPRING ANCHOR

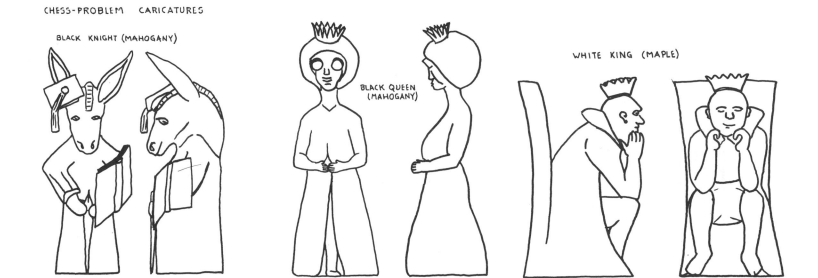

CHESS-PROBLEM CARICATURES

BLACK KNIGHT (MAHOGANY)

BLACK QUEEN (MAHOGANY)

WHITE KING (MAPLE)

GERMAN WHISTLERS, 13½ in. tall, have bodies whittled from the same block as the base. They are hollowed from the back so that each encloses a music box, with a bellows and reeds so it whistles a recognizable tune. An interlock between the two permits only one to play at a time, and each mechanism includes a shaft that rotates the head slightly during the tune.

ABOVE—Four typical Tyrolese articulated bottle stoppers, a beau who offers flowers and his hat in turn, a dancing couple, a kissing couple, and a donkey who lifts and lowers his head, waggling his ears, when his tail is pumped. Each has a different actuating device.

arms or legs to a body. This allows rotation but only in a plane and it is hard to pose the figure. Elastic cord—the cloth-covered round type found in notions stores—will last even longer than ordinary cord and has sufficient tension to cause a limb to stay where it is set. If the limb or head must tilt as well as rotate, it is preferable to form a half-bead on a necked section at the base to fit into a matching socket, or to use two sockets and an intermediate bead.

The donkey illustrates a simple double-lever motion. The tail is actually a cam, so that when it is lifted, it pushes down the extension of the neck to raise the head, as shown in the cross-section. Such a motion will lift the head, but will not lower it, so the donkey must be vertical and pivot positions should be as far apart as possible. (To control the opposite member positively, the end of one cam would have to fit into a socket in the other.) The donkey's ears simply rotate loosely on a through brad. A center post between the ears keeps them separated so they can act independently, and they flop realistically when the head moves.

The man with the bouquet has a positive

motion in that the dowel connecting his arms is fastened only to them and is loose through the body. Thus, when the arm holding the bouquet is moved, the other arm moves with it, taking the hat off or putting it on. The head is also pivoted on a center post set into a neck slot so it can tilt forward and back. The hat is held to the hand with an elastic band so it can move slightly up and down. Thus, when the arm holding the bouquet is moved down, the other arm takes off the hat, in the process tilting the head forward. Raising the left arm withdraws the bouquet and scrapes the hat over the head to tilt it back and seat the hat. The hat, by the way, is a lathe turning with a hollowed bowl socket to fit the head.

The kissing couple have holes drilled through their necks downward to the base, so dowels put loosely in them will flank a lever between them. Each dowel carries a head, and is of such length that it normally seats on the base with the head fitting snugly against the body. But each dowel has a small-diameter pin in it in such a position that the pin rides on the cam surface of the lever, so when the lever is lifted the heads also lift and rotate slightly at the same time. The heads are kept tightly in contact with the cam by small springs wound around the dowels above the pins and fastened at the base. Note that the heads are forward of the normal center-neck position for a dowel, so when the heads rotate, the faces are thrust together. This stopper suits the name in more ways than one, because it requires careful setting of the heads on the dowels so they meet but do not interfere, and because the lips are carved to project in a pouting position.

Most elaborate of these figures is the dancers, in which the boy tilts forward and back and both heads tilt side to side, providing a kissing or nose-rubbing action. Also, the controls must be set so the heads tilt in *opposite* directions. In this case, each head has a half bead carved at the end of the neck, which rotates in a socket in the body, and control is by lever through nylon monofilament fishline or the equivalent. Also, each body is a network of nonintersecting holes, and the boy's body is two pieces, a leg section carved integral with the girl's body and an upper torso with a flat-topped socket in it to fit over the rounded tops of the legs.

Each head is controlled by two nylon cords running up through holes in the body and emerging at the sides of the neck socket. In final assembly, these cords are fastened to a lever in a base, then drawn taut and plugged into holes at the side of the neck, just under the ears. The upper part of the base is a drum shape; it can be turned and glued on or carved integral and the interior bored with a hole large enough to clear the levers, but in either case it should be added before the bodies are drilled, so the holes carry through the upper part of the base. In drilling the holes through the lower part of the boy's body, it is advisable to make them somewhat larger than necessary, so there are no problems of alignment with the upper holes and clearance is provided for tilting.

The two sections of the boy's body are held together by an interesting device which doubles as hinge and control. Holes, diagonal from front to back, are drilled at the center of the boy's leg section so they do not intersect the vertical holes leading to the neck. Through these, from another base lever, nylon cords are run, carried over atop the curved section of the legs and plugged in a hole in the upper torso as sketched, so pulling the rear cord tilts the body forward, and pulling the front cord tilts it back.

With all these elements readied, the base plug carrying the cork must be prepared. It has two posts, one on each side, to each of

which is pinned a small lever that projects through a slot in the side of the base proper. One, which operates the tilt, has a nylon cord at each end—simply passed through a hole and knotted at the end and a bit longer than the body of the figure. The other has two cords at each end. Now the cords are passed up through the holes in the body, the single ones through the leg holes of the boy, and the double ones through the neck holes. This last is a bit tricky, because one cord from one end will go through the left-hand hole in the body of the girl, the other through the right of the boy, and vice versa. When the cords are through the proper holes assemble the base and test the levers to see that they move the cords properly. Now assemble the boy's upper torso, crossing the cords over the leg ends as previously described and plugging and gluing them in the holes of the coat. Assemble the heads by plugging in the same way; tweezers will be a help in this operation. The arms, as shown, are simply beads, two long ones to represent arms and one short one between to represent hands, held loosely on a string pinned into the shoulders, so the arms can flop when the levers are operated. If the test works, the figure is ready for painting in bright colors. And you're ready to automate —or at least, articulate—other carvings you may design.

CHESSBOARD section illustrates an endgame in which a king is checkmated by only two opposing pieces, the 5-in. queen and knight. Somehow, in process, this became a political cartoon. Black figures are walnut, the white king maple, the board $\frac{3}{16}$-in. plywood, with one set of squares stained dark.

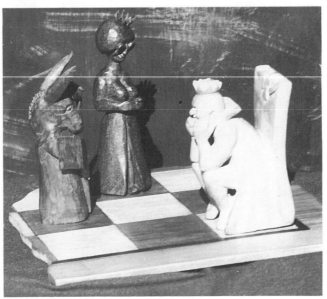

✳Masks for Wear or Decoration

Fun with Faces Is Good Practice

Face masks, for protection or disguise, originated as ceremonial or religious accessories; man made gods in his own image and added the mask to represent a mood, difference, or simply to inspire terror and respect. The face was recognized as the symbol of intelligence even thousands of years ago. Later on, masks were applied to the mummy to simulate and perpetuate the appearance of the person, and in secular, dramatic, and festival representations to make the size, shape, or appearance of the features expected of the subject.

Early masks were wood; it could be worked and would hold a desired shape relatively well, was light, and could be colored or covered to suit. Later ones were sometimes metal—like gold for a king's mummy or bronze or iron to front battle

helmets, or canvas in the Greek plays. Terra cotta, papier mâché, shell, ivory, bone, and other materials have been used. The 100 or more character masks which are the feature of the 250 Noh plays revived in Japan about 100 years ago date back to masks brought there from China with Buddhism in the seventh or eighth century. They are wood, finished with plaster, paint, and gilt. Tibet, various African tribes (Congo and adjacent Nigeria and Liberia), Bali, Java, Ceylon, Papua, Slav and Tyrolese peasants, Guatemalan and Mexican Indians, and North American Indians (Iroquois, Hopi, Zuni, Tewa, Apache) still carve wooden masks for dancers. Many other Indians, like the Inca of Peru and the Maya of Mexico, formerly made them.

Thus it is obvious that the mask is an old

BELOW—Balinese mask of the Barong, good spirit who looks like a dog with a big neck ruff. It is carried by the man who is the forelegs in the many Hindu plays in which this character appears. Parts are not movable, but ears and tusks are separately carved and attached.
CENTER—Typical Fiji decorative mask in nawa nawa wood, designed so nose and mouth are lighter-toned. About 2 ft. high, its decorations are a few simple lines. It is hollow, but only eyes are cut through.

BELOW—New Zealand's Maori were students of the face, which they tattooed with line patterns. This is suggested in the mask below, as well as in panels (page 113). Central exposed tongue is a challenge, to one side means welcome, forked means duplicity. Mask (7½ in.) and man's club ("patu"-17 in.) are both totora wood, with paua-shell eyes, as is the 6-in. fishhook *(BOTTOM LEFT)* with bone point and shank mask. All three are by William Redman, a white man taught carving by a Maori chief.

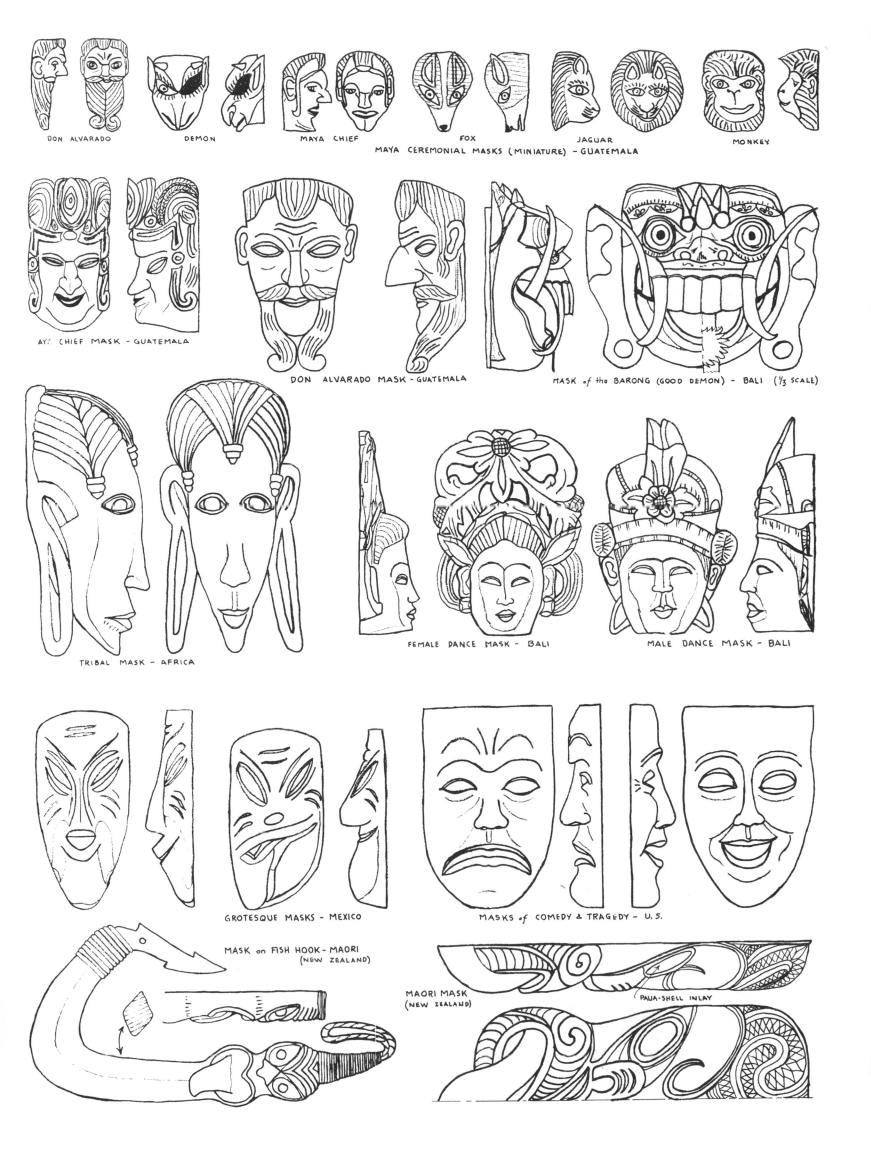

DON ALVARADO   DEMON   MAYA CHIEF   FOX   JAGUAR   MONKEY

MAYA CEREMONIAL MASKS (MINIATURE) - GUATEMALA

AY. CHIEF MASK - GUATEMALA

DON ALVARADO MASK - GUATEMALA

MASK of the BARONG (GOOD DEMON) - BALI (⅓ SCALE)

TRIBAL MASK - AFRICA

FEMALE DANCE MASK - BALI

MALE DANCE MASK - BALI

GROTESQUE MASKS - MEXICO

MASKS of COMEDY & TRAGEDY - U.S.

MASK on FISH HOOK - MAORI
(NEW ZEALAND)

MAORI MASK
(NEW ZEALAND)

PAUA-SHELL INLAY

BELOW—Miniature ebony masks of Balinese male and female headdresses flank one from the Congo, with elongated chin and ears. LEFT—Mexican caricature masks in pine (about 3 in.). LEFT BELOW—Comedy and tragedy are familiar U.S. masks. This is one design; another is sketched, and dozens more are on jewelry, theater marquees, etc.

and respected art form. It is also an interesting one because it teaches the carver so much about the human—and inhuman—physiognomy. It compels analysis of the subtle elements that differentiate your face from mine, and what changes as a face laughs, scowls, frowns, sneers. It lends itself to the grotesque, to caricature, to refinement—note how rubber masks are still used in Hollywood and on TV. The great virtue of mask-making is the basic training it provides in carving the human face, the hardest single thing to learn. (Next hardest is hands.) You must carve dozens of faces to overcome that stiff "wooden" look that characterizes so many carved faces. They show the skill —or lack of it—of the carver very clearly.

Most masks are made of light woods that cut easily—pine, basswood, aspen, willow. Purely decorative masks or funerary ones, those to have heavy usage or not to be painted, are harder woods, sometimes making use of the "figure" in the wood or natural blemishes like knots and worm tracks. Because Americans, in particular, are great collectors of travel souvenirs, many countries now turn out quantities of masks in miniature from wood scraps, like the row of six at the top of the sketch (see also page 130). These are only about 1½ in. high and depict the leading characters of a dance-drama about the conquest of the Maya by Don Alvarado 400 years ago and still danced in the high mountains of Guatemala for tourists. Larger ones, 4 or 5 in. tall, show more detail and skill.

Carving masks can be a great deal of fun, and the product, even if it isn't what you had in mind, is still usually acceptable.

Start with small masks that can be whittled in pine or basswood scraps, to get the "feel." Then try larger ones, working either from a block or from a glued-up "box." Interior hollowing, unless the mask is to be worn, can be quite rough, simply to lighten the weight and allow the eyes, mouth, and sometimes nostrils to be cut through. It will also reduce checking, if the wood is so inclined. A couple of such masks, made into wall sconces in a game room, can produce an eerie lighting effect; I've seen a collection of masks mounted on study walls, with such lighting. Such a mask can also be used on stage for a "disappearing" demon. Another trick is to add a cobalt magnet on the back, so a mask will stick to a fire screen, letting the light of the fire through it.

Larger masks are best made with carving tools, because most of the lines of a face are curves and there are so many hollows and inside corners. Unless the mask is a portrait of a living person, accuracy is not too vital; many of the masks and heads of Presidents Lincoln and Kennedy, in particular, are really caricatures, recognizable only because the dominant facial characteristics have been exaggerated as they are in cartoons. In the human face, the two side are *not* exactly alike. That's why your photos may look a bit strange to you, or a friend's face takes on a different appearance when you see it in a mirror, and why a carved head sometimes just misses the look of its subject. So, unless you're making a portrait, slight variations in the anatomy of a face will serve to make it more lifelike and interesting.

Knots and flaws and errors of cutting are easily corrected with plastic wood or plaster of paris if the mask is to be painted, so you can dare to experiment. If the mask is not too detailed and delicate, the hollowing can be done after carving is finished, so you have some way of holding the piece until the end. Grain normally runs with the nose, which makes hollowing easier as well as giving greater strength to horns, goatees, fangs, and ears. Carving is done just as any other head would be. The silhouette is cut out and the face lowered around the nose. Then eye sockets are cut (unless the mask has bulging eyes), the cheeks rounded, and the hair and ears roughed in. The mouth comes last, except for very delicate details.

The two South Pacific masks below are interesting because of their emphasis on the eyes. As Galsworthy said, "One's eyes are what one is; one's mouth what one becomes." One design emphasizes the eyes with inserts, the other with radial lines. Also, they suggest the possibilities for decoration of staffs, batons, or other objects— as the Indian head mask is used on a bellows. These three photos are thus examples for both the preceding and following articles.

Gadgetry

Bellows, Nutcrackers, Cord Pull

Some of these pieces are in-the-round, some in relief, but all have household applications and offer opportunities for your variations.

The bellows below and in the sketches is 18½ in. long and involves two matching silhouettes of an Indian head and a beaver pelt, carved in ¾ × 8-in. white pine. The beaver's tail and the Indian's feather are the handles, and the Indian's mouth is puckered to appear as if he were blowing, but this ⅝-in. hole is actually the air inlet, covered by a thin leather flap inside. Air is blown out through the bear's mouth at the bottom. The Indian's neck is glued to the bear's head, while the end of the beaver side is hinged to the bear with either a piano hinge or just the surrounding leather. The inner edge of the bear's mouth and the lips of the Indian are flared out slightly to improve air flow; ⅛ × ¼-in. filler blocks each side of the hole in the bear help. Carving is done in very low relief, consisting largely of V-grooves made with a pocketknife. Rib cuts in the feather, markings on the tail and toes, and eye openings are narrower V's. Fur is simulated on the beaver pelt by gouge scalloping.

Suede is best for the bellows, but imitation leather, plastic, or canvas can be used, as

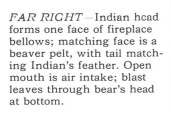

FAR RIGHT—Indian head forms one face of fireplace bellows; matching face is a beaver pelt, with tail matching Indian's feather. Open mouth is air intake; blast leaves through bear's head at bottom.

RIGHT—Marquesan war club, found by Cook's companion Sparrmann in 1774. *CENTER*—Easter Island staff head, collected by Hjalmar Stolpe in the 1880s. Both courtesy National Museum of Ethnography of Sweden, Stockholm. Photos by Bo Gabrielsson.

FIREPLACE BELLOWS

SIDES SLOPE from RAISED CENTER RIB. GROOVE SIDES

CROSS HATCH w VEINER

GOUGE-SCALLOP SURFACE

LEATHER FLAP VALVE

5/8" AIR INLET

GLUE

HINGE

1/2" BORE

BEAR SPOUT

COW SPOUT

CHIEF PONTIAC & FOX BELLOWS

GLUE

GOUGE-SCALLOP SURFACE

5/8" AIR INLET

HINGE

BEAR

PONY

SPOUT SHAPES

IGUANA

CHERUB or BOREAS BELLOWS

HINGE of MOUTH

SPLIT

LEFT-LEG PIVOT

LOW-RELIEF DESIGN

SAW

PIN from REAR

FILIPINO GIRL NUT CRACKER

POINTER

SETTER

DOOR FLAP

JAW OPENS

SLOT

PIVOT

OPERATES JAW

MONKEY NUT CRACKER

FRONT of HEAD

CLEARANCE for SPOON

DOWEL PIVOT

HEAD LIFTS & ROTATES

SEPARATE SPOON AS TAIL

SALT CAVITY

DUCK SALT CELLAR (GERMANY)

FORCE WIRE INTO GRAIN

HANDS on "IRONJAW"

"IRONJAW" CORD PULL

long as it is thin and flexible. Make a cloth pattern for the bellows first; you'll find it is about 25 in. long and 9¼ in. wide at the center, and in the form of a long oval. It is tacked on with carpet tacks, leaving a small flap all around which is then folded back over the carpet tacks and held down with ornamental brass tacks (*Popular Mechanics,* Jan. 1944).

The horizontal bellows is similarly made, but here the head of Chief Pontiac and the curled fox body are inside a 10-in. circle.

The salt cellar at center right in the sketches is an interesting project. The body is a single piece of white pine 1¼ × 2 × 3¼ in. with a cavity near the head end for the salt. A small wooden spoon goes into this cavity with its handle projecting through a slot in the top of the body to form a slightly projecting tail. The head, ¾ × 1 × 2¼ in., is tapered at the top and beak and rounded in back. It also has a small slot in the bottom to clear the inner end of the spoon handle, and rotates on a dowel pivot, glued to the head but looser in the body. The head, when turned back, closes the cavity and holds the spoon in place, but when lifted and rotated, wakens the duck, exposes the cavity, and frees the spoon.

The dog silhouettes at center are carved on a white-pine panel ½ × 2½ × 4 in. They are outlined with V-cuts, the side of the cuts next to the figure being vertical and the other flared out to the surface. Dowels or finishing nails near one end function as pivots. Small blocks with matching holes are put over them, then glued to the guest-bathroom door. Thus the panel becomes a flap, so either side can be exposed. One dog is a pointer, the other a setter, so if the flap is adjusted by a bathroom occupant, others are informed.

Another accessory in our guest bathroom is the 5½-in. "Ironjaw" at lower right in the sketches. With a long wire pushed down into her body through her mouth, she becomes a pull for the light cord—or for any other cord. Ours was tinted, but as the photo indicates has been battered by use.

Nutcrackers of hard, strong wood are carved in various forms in various countries. The commonest form is that of the monkey sketched, about 7½ in. tall and with a lower jaw put through a slot and pivoted in the chest. Such a cracker can be made with any human figure as well, caricatured of course, but is limited in capacity. The female has wider leg movement, thus larger capacity.

BELOW—Filipino nutcracker has a separate left leg, hollow inside thighs, to take a nut. It must be hard, strong wood. *BELOW CENTER*—"Ironjaw" (circus name for an acrobat who hangs by her teeth) has a wire pushed and glued in her mouth for a cord pull. *BOTTOM CENTER*—Duck salt cellar includes rotating head and carved spoon which doubles as a tail.

BELOW—This fireplace bellows combines a head of Chief Pontiac and a fox, each in a 10-in. circle. Air inlet is the hole centered in the fox, outlet a horse head. This bellows is easier to use and has larger capacity than the vertical type, is similarly articulated. *CENTER*—Flap indicator for a guest-bath door has low-relief pointer and setter silhouettes.

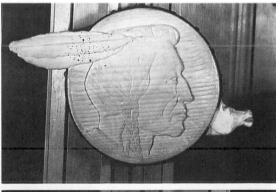

✳ Skipper Sam'l

A Quaint Whittled Figure

Meet Skipper Sam'l, white-haired, square-jawed old sea captain who once trod the deck of a speedy clipper fighting her way 'round the Horn to China. You can bet that one of the gnarled hands thrust deep into the pockets of his weather-beaten old pea jacket is fondling his jackknife, universal tool of sailormen. This genial old salt is French-Canadian, and produced from a white pine or basswood block $1\frac{1}{2} \times 2\frac{1}{2} \times 5\frac{1}{2}$ in. On the front and right-hand side, pencil on $\frac{1}{4}$-in. squares, and with them lay out the patterns of Fig. 1A. Now saw in all the horizontal lines from the sides—tops of shoulders, bottoms of cuffs, bottom of coat. From front and back, saw in under the Skipper's chin, at the back of the neck, front and back of coat, and the slot that divides his shoes from his trousers, $\frac{1}{2}$ in. from the front face of the block. Saw the $\frac{1}{8}$-in. slot between his legs to the bottom of his coat. Shave off $\frac{1}{16}$ in. at the back of his head, round up his back and the tail of his coat, and saw off $\frac{1}{4}$ in. of wood back of his pants.

None of these cuts has destroyed the pattern, but subsequent cuts will remove a part. Saw away the waste wood at the sides of the head and outside the arms down to the elbows. Now saw up the outside of each leg *almost* to the bottom of Sam'l's coat (within about $\frac{1}{4}$ in.). Then stop and saw up the front of his trouser legs until you meet the saw cut which marks the bottom of his coat. Finish the side cuts and both legs are free.

Trim up the sides of the coat to the cuffs, and *down* (that avoids the danger of splitting) from his elbows to his cuffs. Cut away a little at the bottom of the coat as you see in the side view of Fig. 1A. Now all that remains to be done is to slope Sam'l's chest. Measure down $1\frac{3}{4}$ in. from the point of the chin, and from this horizontal line sketch a liberal curve up each side to the inside end of the saw cut marking his chin. Cut away the wood outside this line with knife or saw and your finished blank should look like Fig. 1B.

Lay out the patterns (templates) in Fig. 2 on heavy paper or thin cardboard and cut them out with scissors. Take template *A,* line it up at bottom and sides with the Skipper's coat and mark along the sides, as in

Back in July 1935, when I wrote this article for *Popular Science Monthly,* we had no idea that it would launch so many readers into whittling. It was the first of a series, some of which are abstracted here, which were reprinted in kits containing a block or two sawed to shape, paint, and instructions—all for $1.50! Because of this, I was not permitted to republish the articles earlier. The kits and memory of the other articles have faded, but Skipper Sam'l seems to live on, so here is most of the original article —as an introduction to human-figure carving.

Fig. 3. This gives you the line between arms and body. Place and trace sleeve template *B* on each arm in turn, lining up the bottom with the bottom of the cuff and setting the back edge (the elbow) in about $\frac{1}{8}$ in. from the back of the block, Fig. 4. Next, align template *C* on the front of the block and draw up each side as in Fig. 5 to mark the lines between sleeve and body in front.

Score deeply along the template lines you've just drawn. Keep forcing the knife point down and cutting away the little outer sections of wood until your block looks like Figs. 6A and 6B. This leaves the arms roughly shaped and standing out from the body (see also Figs. 7 to 10).

Let's start now on shoes and trousers. Study Fig. 7 carefully first. Fig. 10 will show you how the shoes look. Nick out the heels and round them off in back. Round off the blunt toe and slope the instep of each shoe. Cut out the sliver of wood all around each shoe to show the joint of sole and upper. Then take off the rough corners on each trouser leg, making a rough octagonal section tapering from the shoes toward the coat bottom. Cut *from* the shoes *toward* the coat to prevent splitting.

Now measure down $\frac{1}{2}$ in. from the top in the back of the block, which is to establish the top of the cap. Draw a horizontal line across the back of the block and angled lines to the top of the block at the front corners, Fig. 8. Cut off this wedge. Put oval template *D* in place, pencil around it, and split off the

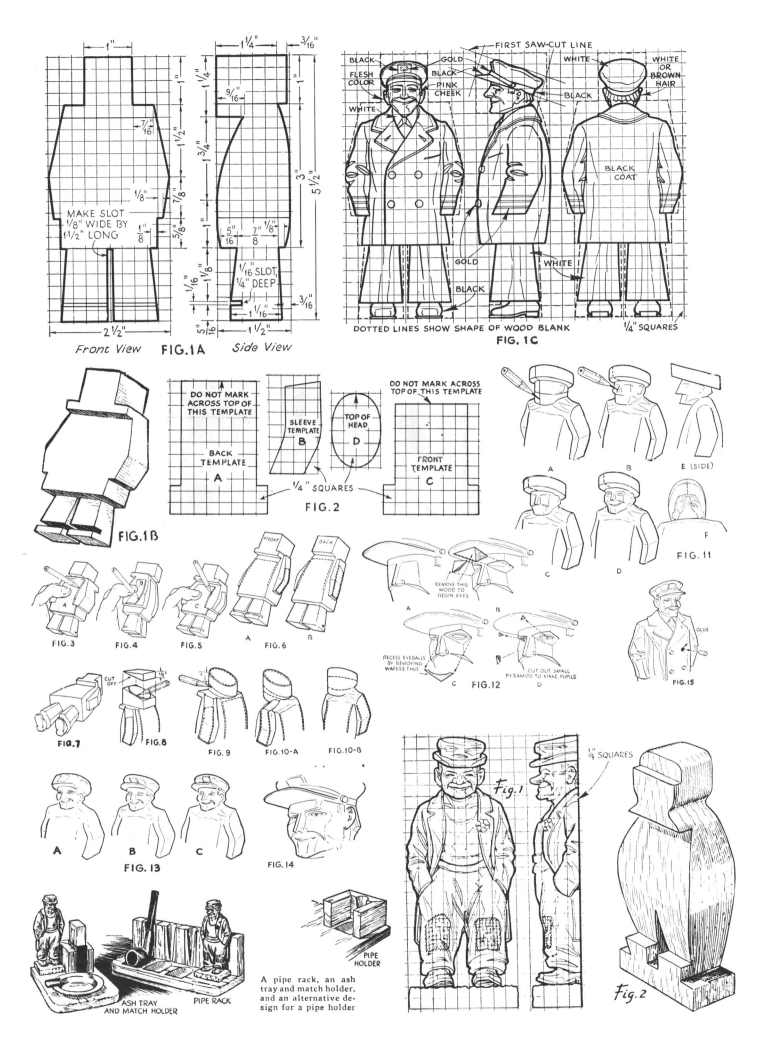

FIG.1A

1"

1 1/4" — 3/16"

9/16"

1"

1 1/2"

1 3/4"

3"

5 1/2"

7/16"

1/8"

7/8"

5/8"

1/8"

MAKE SLOT 1/8" WIDE BY 1 1/2" LONG

1/8"

1/16 SLOT 1/4" DEEP

5/16

7/8

1/8

1/16

1/8

1/16

3/16"

2 1/2"

5/16 — 1 1/2"

Front View   **FIG.1A**   *Side View*

FIRST SAW-CUT LINE

BLACK
FLESH COLOR
WHITE
GOLD
BLACK
PINK CHEEK
WHITE
BLACK
WHITE OR BROWN HAIR
BLACK COAT
GOLD
WHITE
BLACK

DOTTED LINES SHOW SHAPE OF WOOD BLANK
FIG. 1C
1/4" SQUARES

FIG.1B

DO NOT MARK ACROSS TOP OF THIS TEMPLATE
BACK TEMPLATE A
SLEEVE TEMPLATE B
TOP OF HEAD D
DO NOT MARK ACROSS TOP OF THIS TEMPLATE
FRONT TEMPLATE C
1/4" SQUARES
FIG.2

A   B   E (SIDE)

C   D   F

FIG. 11

FRONT   BACK

A   **FIG. 6**   B

FIG.3   **FIG.4**   **FIG.5**

REMOVE THIS WOOD TO BEGIN EYES

A   B

RECESS EYEBALLS BY REMOVING WAFERS THUS
CUT OUT SMALL PYRAMIDS TO MAKE PUPILS
C   **FIG.12**   D

GLUE

FIG.15

CUT OFF   1/2"

FIG.7   **FIG.8**   **FIG. 9**   **FIG.10-A**   **FIG.10-B**

A   B   C
FIG. 13

FIG. 14

ASH TRAY AND MATCH HOLDER   PIPE RACK

PIPE HOLDER

A pipe rack, an ash tray and match holder, and an alternative design for a pipe holder

Fig.1   1" SQUARES

Fig.2

outer corners to round the head, Fig. 9. Shape the shoulders roughly, as in Fig. 10A and B. Draw a line all around the head oval ½ in. down from the top, Fig. 9. This line marks the joining of cap and face, so cut in about ⅛ in. deep all around it and split off the wood carefully all around so that the block looks like Fig. 11A.

Locate the nose by drawing a vertical line down the Skipper's center front. Measure down ⅜ in. from the joining of face and cap, and score 3/16 in. deep straight across the face on this line to mark the tip of the nose. Now cut out the wedge from the point of the chin to the bottom of the scoring cut. Cut away the wood from the tip of the nose diagonally to the joint between face and cap at the same angle. The face will now look like Fig. 11E, with proper chin and nose slants.

Now study Fig. 11F closely to fix the elevations and angles of chin, cheeks, and eyes in your mind. Mark a triangle for the nose, Fig. 11B, about ¼ in. wide at the bottom, and cut away wood at the sides to about ⅛ in. deep, as shown in Figs. 11B, 11C, and 12A, up to the brow line. Now outline the bottom of the cheekbones by cutting a sloping line 1/16 in. deep downward at each side of the nose, Figs. 11C and 12A. Cut up from the point of the jaw to meet this line, and cut along each side of the face to form the jawbone, but don't cut up so far that you remove wood that you'll need later for the ears. Cut a shallow slit for Sam'l's mouth squarely across the face (or tilting up a little at the corners, depending upon how much grin you want him to have), and about 1/16 in. below the nose.

The eyes are started with notches as in Fig. 12B. They are about ⅛ in. deep and down about ⅛ in. from the joint between face and cap. They start at the bridge of the nose and are deepest well out at the sides of the head. If you want to, cut out thin wafers as in Fig. 12C to form eyeballs, and make each pupil by cutting out a tiny triangle as in Fig. 12D; otherwise merely flatten out the base of the eye socket, then cut a slit like the mouth slit across it. Dig a little hole at the middle for the eyeball.

Next, shape the cap as in Figs. 13A, B, and C, sloping in toward the head at the sides and back and cutting in carefully above the cap visor in front. (Be very careful here or you'll split off the cross-grain visor.) Shape the ears as in Fig. 14, and cut away the wood

at the temples below Sam'l's very conservative sideburns. Cut in at the back of his neck as in Fig. 14 and roughen or groove the wood back there to resemble hair. Form the hat strap, side buttons and cap emblem carefully by slitting with the knife point around the outlines and shaving away the outside wood; they're distinctive parts of a seaman's cap.

Now draw on lapels and coat collar, lapel buttonholes, collar and tie, Fig. 1C. Score deeply along these lines and shave wood away outside them (except *inside* the buttonholes) so they stand out. Lower the shoulders a little by cutting away outside the collar, and cut them back a little to show the lapels. Now round up the whole figure, shaping up each part carefully according to Figs. 1C and 15. Sleeve creases are just three notches at the inner edge of the sleeve inside the elbow, Fig. 15. Score the line where the coat laps to button, and round off the coat down to the joint between coat and sleeves. Don't be too careful; a few broad knife cuts will make your Skipper distinctive. Now mark the button positions, drill holes, glue in the ends of kitchen matches and cut them off short. (Or score and shave around them, if you prefer.) If you want the pea jacket strictly "regulation," use six buttons, not four.

Don't sandpaper the Skipper; save the angles and let him look hard-bitten. He looks best painted with oils, in my opinion. Trousers and crown of cap are white, Fig. 1C; shoes, coat, cap visor, strap, and emblem black. His face should be a healthy flesh color with a dash of red at cheekbones, nose tip, and perhaps chin tip. Hair and eyebrows are gray or white, pupils of eyes black with a short white line at the left-hand side. (Don't put both inside or both outside, or the Skipper will look crosseyed or wall-eyed.) Touch up the cap ornament and visor with gold (the ornament is crossed anchors, if you must be exact), and put three or four gold stripes on his cuffs. Your Skipper is done.

This basic pattern can be varied almost endlessly. Change the size of the layout squares and you change his size; change the mouth and cheek lines and you change his expression and age; add a beard. A little work with the pattern will have him sitting, or stooped over, hobbling with a stick. You can even make him into a granny by changing his hat for a bonnet or shawl and his trousers to a skirt—but the later design of Mère Marthe will do that better for you.

✳ Hobo Hank

Mostly Nostalgia

Hobo Hank is largely a memory, as is his Swedish counterpart, page 74. The tramps and hoboes who once wandered down country roads and infested railroad yards and rolling stock are gone, and with them the "tramp art" that they whittled from cigar and packing boxes to pay for a handout or a bed in a hayloft.

Hobo Hank is really a high-relief figure, because he's designed to decorate a book-end, pen stand, or pipe rack. He requires a block $1 \times 2\frac{1}{4} \times 5\frac{3}{4}$ in. of white pine or basswood. Apply the pattern of Fig. 1 (two pages back) as you did that of Skipper Sam'l by drawing squares and copying a square at a time, then saw out the blank to get the rough form of Fig. 2. (It is best to use a scroll saw and cut the front to shape first, then leave the scrap in place to guide you in side cuts.)

Carve off the corners roughly and shape up the trousers and feet. Sketch in the arms and coat lapels (don't forget the flower!), score along the lines, and cut away the waste wood so the lapels and arms are formed. Shape up the trouser top and the sweater, carving in a piece of rope to hold the pants up, the scoop neck of the sweater and the open-collared shirt. Cut the shoulders back and form the arms, then put in the wrinkles in arms, coat, trousers, and sweater. Shape the chin, and mold it into the collar. Shape the top of his battered hat, carrying the shape of the brim down to his neck. Now sketch in the face as done for Skipper Sam'l, locating the prominent nose first, cutting the wood away around it under the hat brim. (The bottom of his nose is $\frac{3}{8}$ in. under the lower edge of the hat brim and projects about $\frac{3}{16}$ in. — study Fig. 1.) Watch that hat brim!

Patches on the trouser knees and a criss-cross pattern on the sweater, as well as details of the flower and hair are optional — they can be painted on if you prefer. You can stain and varnish the figure, or paint it, but in the latter case use faded and subdued colors like grayed browns and blues for his clothes. I whittled mine to go against a shanty wall of $\frac{1}{2} \times 4\frac{1}{2} \times 6$-in. on a base $\frac{1}{2} \times 2 \times 6$ in. and a $\frac{3}{4}$-in. "roof" strip on top. With a little weighting, or a thin metal strip fastened on to extend out the back of the base, it becomes a bookend.

By starting with a block $1\frac{1}{2}$ in. thick, you can carve Hobo Hank in the round. Note that he is wearing a tailcoat, so it would be pinched in slightly at the waist and have a button at either side of the top of the vent — if Hank hasn't lost them. Upright in-the-round figures shown on later pages can also be carved with flat backs suitable for plaque or wall mounting. Simply draw a vertical line at the cut-off point, normally just behind the ears, and lay out your thinner block with the resulting reduced dimensions. Hobo Hank was first described in *Popular Science Monthly* in January 1937.

Hobo Hank stained and mounted for a bookend, unfinished, and painted on a penholder base.

✳ Mère Marthe

Swiss Peasant Woman

This figure originated in Switzerland, adds tilt to the head, hands, a stoop, and a billowing skirt to the problems presented by Skipper Sam'l. She requires white pine or basswood $2\frac{1}{2} \times 2\frac{1}{2} \times 5\frac{1}{2}$ in., laid out in $\frac{1}{4}$-in. squares on front and *left* side (next page). Lay out the outline, then saw all horizontal lines and the vertical ones at the back and side of her head. Next, saw up to $\frac{1}{4}$ in. from the end on all remaining lines from the side, then from the front, with the exception of the lines for the feet, which can be cut all the way in. (Leaving a bit to cut on the other lines preserves the guide lines as long as possible.) Now cut her left side free, then saw out the back lines, the front, and right side.

On the blank, which will now look like Fig. 2, sketch the old lady's face, her kerchief, and the outlines of her arms and apron. Templates drawn from Fig. 1 will help in marking the positions of arms and hands exactly. Round up the head and skirt, but don't forget that dangling right hand and kerchief—leave wood for them. Finish the feet, as shown in Fig. 3. Study the sketch carefully *before* you begin to cut away wood; *both* feet turn slightly outward and the right is forward of the left. This makes the figure more stable and makes it more lifelike— less stiff and blocky than the Skipper.

From now on, it's just finishing details. Groove the skirt into folds, carve the apron, handkerchief, the folds of cloth around the head and at the neck, put in the grooves at the elbows, back, and around the bust. Leave the hands and face until last, if you can. The eye can be simply a convex shape under the brow with the eyelids and iris painted in, or carved in detail.

She looks best in oil colors, muted. To each color, add a little of the complementary one to soften it: a little purple (red and blue) to the yellow for her blouse and skirt; a little orange (red and yellow) to the blue for her skirt; a little green (yellow and blue) to the red for her kerchief and handkerchief. Outline her handkerchief in white, and put narrow, dull red and white vertical stripes alternating about $\frac{1}{4}$ in. apart on her apron. I described her originally in December 1935, in *Popular Science Monthly*.

✳ Gaspard the Sailor

A Breton Figure

Gaspard, originally a Breton made in French Canada, can become a Scotsman with ease— a bit thinner in the face and plaid instead of blue for the blouse and hat pompom. Fig. 1 gives three views; from them you can lay out and cut the blank of Fig. 2. The block is $1\frac{1}{2} \times 2\frac{1}{2} \times 5\frac{1}{4}$ in., white pine or basswood. Saw out around the head and shoulders first, then up between the legs and up from the trouser "cuffs" and down from the elbows on the sides, leaving $\frac{1}{4}$ in. or so to cut in each case to preserve the pattern. Cut in $\frac{3}{8}$ in. at the front between shoes and trousers.

Sketch in the front and back crease lines of Gaspard's trousers on the blank of Fig. 2, and the arm positions. Shape the trousers, being careful not to cut away wood needed for the blouse cuffs and the bulge the hands make in the pockets. Note that the feet toe outward before you shape the shoes; the heels will be at the *inner* back edges of the foot blanks, with wedges of wood cut away at the outside back and inside front of the foot sides. Four radiating grooves at the crotch and a notch or two horizontally in back below the seat will represent the pull of the pants with this hand position.

To finish the arms, it may be best to make a template from Fig. 1 and sketch around it. Vertical lines $1\frac{1}{4}$ in. apart ($\frac{5}{8}$ in. from the

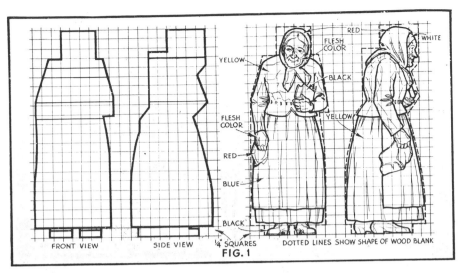

FRONT VIEW   SIDE VIEW   ¼ SQUARES   FIG. 1   DOTTED LINES SHOW SHAPE OF WOOD BLANK

FIG. 2

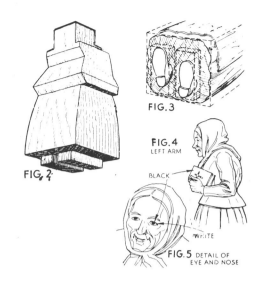

FIG. 3

FIG. 4 LEFT ARM

FIG. 5 DETAIL OF EYE AND NOSE

Fig. 1   ¼ SQUARES

MERE MARTHE above

Fig. 1 left   GASPARD below

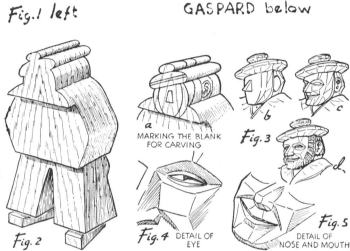

a MARKING THE BLANK FOR CARVING

Fig. 2

Fig. 3

Fig. 4 DETAIL OF EYE

Fig. 5 DETAIL OF NOSE AND MOUTH

center line on each side) will outline his blouse. Score along these lines and cut out the waste wood, then chamfer the outside of the arms as you did the trouser legs, but with rougher cuts to show a baggy blouse. Round up the shoulders and the blouse. Put in the kerchief and blouse wrinkles, particularly those at the inside of the elbow.

Study Fig. 3 before you start on the head. Sketch in the lines of Fig. 3A, then cut away the waste wood, noting that the tam extends as far to the front as the nose and is cross-grain. Be sure to leave stock for the ears behind the beard. Round up the tam and put a slight concave curve on its lower surface toward the head. Shape the pompom round. The head should now look like Fig. 3B.

Round up the plane of the face, and divide it into thirds horizontally, and cut eye notches at each side of the nose along the upper line. Put in a notch angling down and outward from the *top* of each nostril; these will cross your lower horizontal line, if all goes well, and the center of the mouth will be on it as well. Shape the nostrils and mouth

as in Fig. 5, the whiskers and ear as in Fig. 3D, and the eye as in Fig. 4. Note that the lower lip protrudes slightly, so round the surface of the lip, then cut a little groove between it and the chin. Also remember to make the surface from upper lip to chin slightly concave at the center, and put in a small flat area from septum to lip center. Shape the eye as an elongated mound, divide it into thirds from top to bottom, and cut out the outer half of one middle third, the inner of the other, merely outlining the other half. The beard is just a series of radiating notches cut in a flat surface, and the ear can be simply a question mark with a triangular center notch, or can be more elaborate, as sketched. Shape the back of the head and V-notch it for hair, as in Fig. 1.

My colors for the figure were white for the pants and tam, blue for the blouse and pompom, red with white polka dots for the neckerchief, black for the shoes. You may want to add a pipe or cigar and tint the face and hair. I wrote about Gaspard first in *Popular Science Monthly* in December 1936.

✳A Sampler of Caricature

Try Some of These Forms and Techniques

Form and technique go together; the flowing lines of African carvings (upper right) would be out of place on the blocky kings from Mexico (lower left) or the caricatures from Sweden (bottom right). The knife-cut planes of the latter would not suit the curled-up "Yogi" from Bali (center right). Part of the answer lies in the sophistication of the carvers, part of it in the wood—ebony almost cries for a smooth glossy finish and flowing lines, for example, just as pine suggests a surface technique to compensate for its lack of figure and open grain. Pine and other soft woods make detail-carving difficult, while box makes it easy—or easier, at least—as in the William Tell (next spread). Skill is also a major factor; the skilled artist tends to reduce detail, the tyro to increase it. All these elements are evident in this group of carvings.

TOP RIGHT—African figures in ebony (4, 6, and 7 in.) show characteristic flattened heads, large ears, are trimmed with silver wire. *CENTER* is a pregnant woman, *LEFT* a warrior, *RIGHT* a bust of a Coptic. *FAR RIGHT* —Two African paper knives show great differences in design and carving skill. The woman at *LEFT* is stylized, the other figure crude and unformed. *RIGHT*—Fist-sized curled figure from Bali is their equivalent of our worry beads. Lower view is the bottom of the figure. *BOTTOM LEFT*—Mexican Magi (13 and 19 in.) were carved in blanco (white pine) so green the pieces became moldy during shipment. Compare their crude yet powerful design with the smooth sophistication of the cowgirl and cowboy (about 8 in.) carved by H. R. Koob of San Diego, with their effective retained tool marks and coloring. The three Swedish figures *(BOTTOM RIGHT)* are also plane-surfaced and tinted, but much less "real" than Mr. Koob's figures. His are realistic.

TRAMP (8 in.) - SWEDEN

BUNDLE DETAIL

FISHERMAN in TROUBLE (6½ in.) - SWEDEN

PAPER-KNIFE FIGURES - AFRICA

WIRE

EBONY

ICE FISHERMAN (6 in.) - SWEDEN

POLE

TOP   BOTTOM

FRONT

YOGI - BALI

SPEAR SEPARATE

METAL

METAL

WIRE

BOW SEPARATE

WARRIOR (6¼ in.) EBONY - AFRICA - KNEELING FIGURE (7 in.)   EBONY

MAGUS or KING (19 in.) MEXICO - PINE

LEFT SIDE

MAGUS (13 in.) MEXICO PINE

ELONGATED FLAT HEAD IS TYPICAL

METAL

PRIEST (2⅝ in.) SWITZERLAND

BUST (4¼ in.) AFRICA EBONY

ABOVE—These figures are top-quality realism, as compared with the popular-priced caricatures on the *LEFT*. Compare techniques: the plane surfaces and tinting of the Tyrol figures at *LEFT* with the smaller planes and heavier color of H. R. Koob's Plains Indians couple at *RIGHT*, and both of these with the smooth surfaces of the Swiss William Tell and son at *CENTER*. Compare the stern, strong face of the blacksmith with the barely outlined face of the axman and the detailed smirk of the monk. *LEFT*—"Alice in Wonderland" figures from the Tyrol, good-quality caricature, stump figures, painted. *LOWER LEFT*—Three small French-Canadian figures, two tinted and one natural. The little figure at *RIGHT* is from the Congo—a crude figure of a boy carrying a half peach pit which looks like a turtle shell. The elongated monk is my small copy of one 20 in. tall in Mexico. *BOTTOM CENTER*—Little figures are hard to carve (and to photograph). These are Italian *(UPPER)* and Swiss examples, including a Swiss idea of our hillbillies. *FAR RIGHT*—Hand puppets can be carving fun. These by William Gschwind are the king and queen of hearts from "Alice," have hand-carved heads and hands. Below them is his caricature of a concert pianist.

BLACKSMITH (7 in.) – ITALY

WOODCUTTER (7 in.) – ITALY

MINIATURES of VILLAGERS (2½ in.) – ITALY

MINIATURES of VILLAGERS (1¾ in.) – ITALY

TOP VIEWS of HATS

LAUGHING MONK (6½ in.) – ITALY

ALICE (2¼ in.)

WHITE RABBIT (2½ in.)

DUCHESS (3 in.)

LEFT   RIGHT

KNAVE of HEARTS (3 in.)

MAD HATTER (3¼ in.)

QUEEN of HEARTS (3 in.)

KING of HEARTS (3 in.)

"ALICE in WONDERLAND" FIGURES – ITALY

WILLIAM TELL & SON (4 in.) – SWISS

FIDDLER (4 in.) – FRENCH CANADA

VILLAGE MAN (4 in.)

½ PEACH PIT

ELONGATED TORSO & ARM

BOY (3½ in.) – CONGO

MINIATURES (1¼ in.) – SWISS

CHEESE CARRIER

AMERICAN HILL BILLIES (2½") – SWISS

MAN – CANADA

MONK (7¼") – MEXICO

✳ A Study in Contrasts

Eight Figures for Comparison

These eight figures, from as many countries, provide broad contrasts in design, technique, and skill. Four are caricatures; four are realistic. Two are painted; two are in sanded and polished hardwoods; four have standard finishes. Several make effective use of surface textures. The Austrian sea captain (Austria is inland!), the Russian warrior, and the late King Gustav are heavily dependent upon the face for effectiveness, while the Haitian girl is primarily a body caricature—long thin arms and feet, projecting bust and buttocks. She and Gustav are angular and thin; the captain and the butcher blocky and squat.

Both the German butcher and the Jamaican couple are quite realistic, but the Jamaican carver had more will than skill. His faces are poorly modeled, his figures ungainly and stiff, while the others are all of professional caliber. Contrast him with the intentionally stiff Russian figure. Note the distorted faces on this figure and the Amerindian, and contrast them with the almost faceless American woman—her face is a mound peaking at the nose tip. Further, her left hand is just a low ridge dividing into thumb and finger cluster, but her whole figure is dramatic, powerful, unmistakable—eloquent testimony to the importance of form and the sometime distraction of detail.

BELOW, L TO R—German butcher; Russian grotesque, 2 ft.; Sioux Indian, by H. R. Koob, San Diego, California; the late King Gustav of Sweden with my copy.

ABOVE—Austrian captain conceals a bottle with music box below it. Head is the stopper, hence rotatable.

ABOVE RIGHT—Haitian woman by J. Bernard. *RIGHT*—Jamaican couple, 5 in. *BELOW RIGHT*—Female figure, mahogany, by P. D. Woodard, North Conway, N.H.

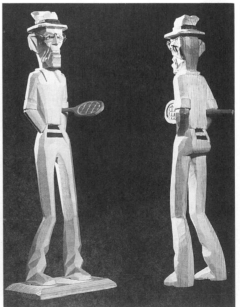

HEAD on STOPPER

SEA CAPTAIN - AUSTRIA - 9¾"

BODY BORED for BOTTLE & MUSIC BOX

FEET TACKED to BASE DISK

ATTENUATED BODY

HAITIAN WOMAN - 10¾"

BUTCHER - GERMANY - 10"

NO FEATURES

TOP VIEW

U.S. FEMALE FIGURE - 8¼"

WIRE & PLASTIC

SEPARATE

KING GUSTAV of SWEDEN - 9¾"

✳ Latin American Indians

Some Self-Portraits

Latin American Indian carvings tend to be simple, softly curved forms, without extraneous detail, usually in soft woods. The usual Indian carver works at home, with a limited number of tools, in local woods, often still green. A common wood is blanco (white pine), although occasional pieces are in woods as hard as mesquite, cocobola, and lignum vitae. Near Guanajuato, Mexico, the village of Paseo el Alto does much commercial carving, some quite large, in a wood like balsa, but stained and painted almost out of recognition. I did the Juchitán woman (bottom right) in a piece of guanacoste, an open-grained wood used primarily for furniture. And the village profile below was carved in thick bark! Mexico has set up state handicraft shops and Guatemalan priests have established cooperatives which provide some training, but many carvers carve primarily to feed their families. More sketches on page 82.

RIGHT—Two figures from Ecuador show superior quality. Compare them with the Mexican figures in blanco *(BELOW)*, by a self-taught guard at a historic site. *CENTER RIGHT*—Doll figures were probably designed by an artist, are now made in plastic.

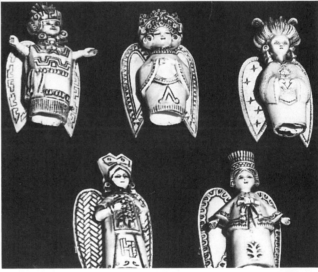

BOTTOM—Guatemalan couple were carved in a cooperative. The *viejo* (old man) from Pátzcuaro *(BOTTOM CENTER)* is also obviously the work of a trained carver. Compare him with the woodcutter *(CENTER)* from Pátzcuaro or the feather dancer *(BOTTOM RIGHT)* from Oaxaca. (The *viejo* has become popular because of the Pátzcuaro Dance of the *Viejos*—actually done by agile young men imitating age.)

NOTE: ALL FIGURES *from* MEXICO; AREAS SHOWN

SLEEPING PEON - OAXACA

REAR VIEW

RESTING PEON - OAXACA

SEPARATE PIECE

SERÁPE & SOMBRERO - OAXACA

MOTHER & CHILD - JUCHITAN

HEAD CLOTH

REBOZO

FEATHER DANCER - OAXACA

STAMPED DESIGN

PADDLE (INSERTED)

RATTLE

STAMPED

VIEJO (OLD MAN) PATZCUARO

WOODCUTTER PATZCUARO

INSERTED

PIPER - ECUADOR

PEON - ECUADOR

HOODED PADRE - MEXICO

INDIAN WOMAN - GUATEMALA

INDIAN FIELD WORKER - GUATEMALA

VEINER PATTERNS MAKE PRE-COLUMBIAN MEXICAN COSTUME DOLLS

MAYA

ZAPOTEC

TOLTEC

TOTONAC

MIXTEC

✳ From Scandinavia

Farm People, Fishermen, Lapps, Trolls

Verve and vigor characterize Scandinavian carved figures. Subjects are usually farm people in characteristic dress and occupations, and the execution is blocky, angular, and retains knife marks. Of the many pieces I have, the Norwegian ones seem to have more color and action than the Swedish, particularly in carvings of Laplanders and farmers, but this may be co-incidence. I have selected a number of these figures for sketching, because they provide strong silhouettes, are easy to duplicate, and can be tinted in bright tones to provide a spot of color in any setting. The third panel features trolls, those delightful Scandinavian elves who some people say were the result of seeing a bear in dim light. A Norwegian engineer in Stavanger gave me his design of the latter, and a Swedish engineer in Trollhättän passed on the troll with the lantern.

These figures were all made by one man or one group in Norway, although I found some in Sweden and Denmark. They are alike in having vigorous outlines and bright colors. The trumpeter, for example, has a white blouse, red bolero, and black skirt, the latter two with multicolored flowers for trim, the skirt with gray, red, and purple bottom bands. The Lapp's jacket is natural with red trim, his cap black with red and gold trim, pants black. Other colors are indicated on sketches. They are tints rather than solid color; the wood shows through at edges, done by wiping base colors while still damp. Trim colors are solid, of course. Study these dynamic, pert poses for contrast with usual rigid ones. These are all Norwegian carvings, with sketches on the next page.

SAUCY MAID

DANCING COUPLE

WHITE CAP
GOLD TRIM
BLONDE HAIR

RED
WHITE
BLACK

GOLD
YELLOW

GREEN on
BLACK
GOLD
TRIM

RED
GOLD

RED

WHITE
GREEN FACE
GOLD

TAN
GREEN
GOLD

TRUMPETER

RED w YELLOW
NATURAL

SEPARATE

BRIGHT RED
NATURAL

BLACK

GRAY
RED
PURPLE

LAPP with HUSKY PUP

RED w GOLD
BLACK

NATURAL

BACK of CAP

JACKET SKIRT

RED & GOLD

TAIL DETAIL

BLACK

MILKMAID

BLACK w FLOWERS
WHITE
RED & GREEN
OUTLINING

SEPARATE
STOOL &
TURNED
BUCKET

GREEN
YELLOW
RED
BLACK w GOLD BAND

GOAT MILKMAID

RED

SEPARATE
(TURNED)

WHITE
TAN SKIRT

REAR VIEW

TOP VIEW

FRONT END

COUNTRY MAN

WIFE...

...& FISHERMAN

MARKETING COUPLE

FISHERBOY

YELLOW GREEN

BLACK

NATURALS

"LITTLE" GRANDMA

TWO MEN

LAPP LAD on SKIS

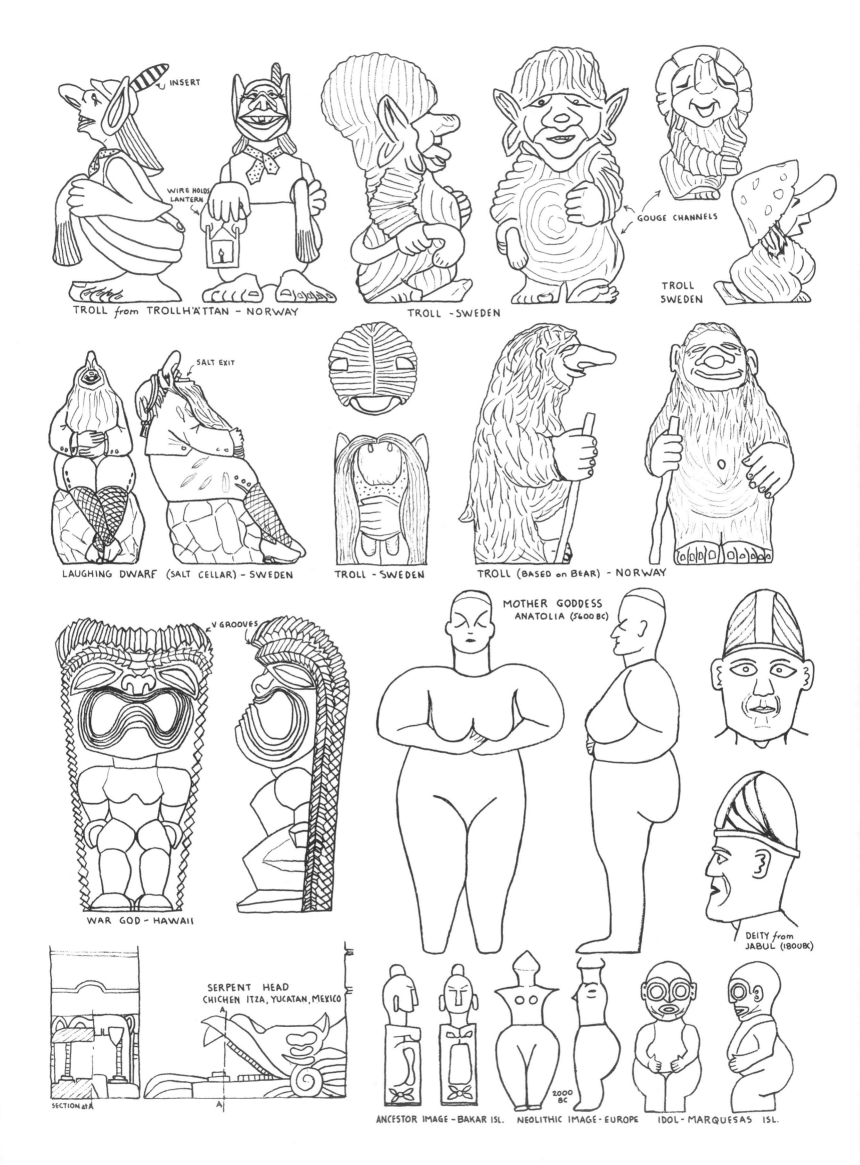

INSERT

WIRE HOLDS LANTERN

TROLL *from* TROLLHÄTTAN - NORWAY

TROLL - SWEDEN

GOUGE CHANNELS

TROLL SWEDEN

SALT EXIT

LAUGHING DWARF (SALT CELLAR) - SWEDEN

TROLL - SWEDEN

TROLL (BASED on BEAR) - NORWAY

V GROOVES

WAR GOD - HAWAII

MOTHER GODDESS ANATOLIA (5600 BC)

DEITY *from* JABUL (1800 BC)

SECTION at A

SERPENT HEAD CHICHEN ITZA, YUCATAN, MEXICO

ANCESTOR IMAGE - BAKAR ISL.

2000 BC

NEOLITHIC IMAGE - EUROPE

IDOL - MARQUESAS ISL.

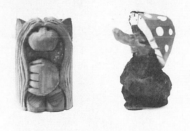

Figures *ABOVE* and at *LEFT* are all Swedish, carved in angles and planes and tinted with dark and dull earthen colors. Several are foreshortened figures, and most seem to be prosaic farm types, except for the three above, which have interesting faces and shapes, as does the old lady at left, who has quite a twinkle as well as an unusual dome-shaped silhouette. Stick, marketing bag, and basket are of course separately carved and added. Note the tendency to pocket hands—an easy way to avoid a carving problem!

Trolls are a Scandinavian tradition, although the Swedes seem to have done most with them. Those shown here are Swedish except for the one at *BOTTOM CENTER*, which is from Stavanger, Norway—an engineer's explanation of the troll. The one at *FAR LEFT* is 2 ft. tall— I carved it from cherry and added a big mahogany nose and tin flower as a garden ornament. The troll *ABOVE LEFT* is a most unusual saltshaker from Sweden.

✳Caricatures Should Be Fun—and a Challenge

For Both Carver and Subject

BELOW LEFT—Priming the pump, another of William Gschwind's assemblies, will be as nostalgic to rural people as my organ grinder is to urbanites. *CENTER*—This Mexican woman seated in a market was carved in mahogany by an Indian. Next to her is a grotesque carved from a suitable available piece of mesquite. It has a monkey's head on a distorted human body. Next to it, in turn, is another *viejo* (old man), this time in mesquite and showing 2-color effects. *BOTTOM LEFT*—These three figures offer interesting comparisons. The bow-legged old man with his stick and the action of the costumed bowler contrast sharply with the static pose of the woman—and take considerably more skill and imagination. *BOTTOM CENTER*—Skiers these days have colorful costumes—but sometimes a rather vacant look. My son carved this 4-in. figure during a Dartmouth ski meet, and got the vacant look. I've sketched a face, however, if you must have it.

RIGHT—The French-Canadian couple—here shown full size—were undoubtedly both fun and a challenge for the carver, who got surprising detail into basswood miniatures. So was the old lady *(BELOW)* who is just about to puff out a mouthful of smoke. *BELOW RIGHT*—The sleeping fisherman, by William Gschwind, a 6-in. figure, is a gentle poke at himself and his friends, as is the Negro couple *(RIGHT CENTER)* who were carved by a Black some years back. The organ grinder *(BOTTOM RIGHT)* I carved from life when organ grinders were still common in New York and nobody worried about whether the monkey enjoyed his role or carried disease. The organ itself is a section of 2×4, bored out to hold a music box. (Such mechanisms can be ordered by the half dozen from distributors in New York.) Of these figures, the first couple was left natural, the old lady is stained and waxed, the others tinted.

TWISTED WIRE

HAND DETAILS

OLD MAN - SWITZERLAND

NEGRO PREACHER - U.S.

FARM WOMAN - CANADA

SEATED WOMAN - MEXICO

NEGRO WOMAN - U.S.

SHOWN ACTUAL SIZE

MINIATURE SEATED FIGURES - FRENCH CANADA

SEATED WOMAN - FRENCH CANADA

FISHERMAN - CANADA

PORTER - ITALY

BOWLER - ITALY

SKIER - U.S.

✳Realistic, Cartoon, Caricature?

More Comparisons

Sometimes, the distinction between caricature and portraiture is narrow—just enough
to make the subject uneasy or critical, or to
make the carver wonder what went awry.
This group of figures was chosen with that
problem in mind. The nude torso by Margaret Brassler Kane and the head of Abraham Lincoln by E. Jerome Frye are definitely formal art, and the nude of the pipe, while
less well executed, is formal as well. The
mountaineers, the Negro group, the hunter,
the fishermen (all three), and the tubby chef
are caricatures, but what of the golfer, the
mandarin, and the penniless "Old Ribs"?
These are cartoons, perhaps, but not caricatures in that body proportions and expressions are not distorted for an effect. The
Amish couple and the boy accordionist are
quite formal as well.

E. Jerome Frye, who made many of the
figures here, is self-taught. A careful crafts-

Except for the fisherman (below left), which is a 5-in.
self-portrait in pine, all of the caricatures on this page are
by E. Jerome Frye. The chef and the two fishermen are
yellow poplar, the chef 13 in. tall, the fishermen 10 in.
Other figures are 8-in. white pine. The mountaineers
were based on Paul Webb's cartoon series, "The Mountain
Boys." Note that the golfer has a fence post here—and
does not in the sketch. Suit yourself. The chef, by the
way, is colored with white shoe polish; the mountaineers'
costumes are blue water color, their hair walnut stain.

GOLFER in the ROUGH

AMISH FARMER at MARKET

BACK DETAILS

AMISH WIFE at MARKET

HAND from REAR

NEGRO PREACHER

NUDE TORSO

"OLD RIBS"

ACCORDIONIST

ORIGINAL BLOCK

PIPE BOWL

TROUT FISHERMAN

man, he takes as much as 50 hours for an Amish figure, and he carried his head of Lincoln to the curator of the Lincoln Museum for criticism—and got it. (The cheeks were originally too fleshy.) He works commonly in basswood, but also carves white pine and yellow poplar—and the Lincoln head is in walnut from an old newel post. The finish he commonly uses is flat varnish and wax. When he tints a figure he has used oil paints thinned with gasoline to make the tone penetrate, but he is currently using a stain of acrylic water colors.

While the figures pictured here have been made by Mr. Frye in a variety of sizes and woods, he has recently carved an ox yoke in full size for a pattern for a plastic sign.

Outside the Negro group (which seemed to belong with Lincoln), these are formal carvings. The mandarin *(BOTTOM LEFT)* is yellow poplar, the Amish man (8 in.) and wife, "Old Ribs," and the accordionist in basswood, finished with varnish and wax. The Negro group are 8-in. figures in white pine, and reminiscent of the work of Leslie Bolling, a Black who carved for the Sage Foundation some years ago, but all of these figures are the work of E. Jerome Frye. So is the formal bust of Abraham Lincoln, 8 in. high, in walnut and finished by waxing alone. This carving was meticulously researched for accuracy, shows none of the unintended caricature of the typical bust of Lincoln. Next to it is a nude mahogany torso 8 in. high by Margaret Brassler Kane (made in multiple in a "limited edition," so I could afford it). The nudes under it are briar pipe blocks which I found more fun to carve than to smoke. (Thick pipe bowls tend to be heavy and get hot.) Pipe bodies, by the way, make excellent surfaces for low-relief and intaglio carving of monograms, coats of arms, even caricatures and scenes.

✳ The Professional Touch

Proved Examples by Skilled Sculptors

What distinguishes the professional from the amateur? Strictly, the distinction is that the former sells his work. Not all professionals are more competent than their amateur counterparts, or better trained, or more inspired. Some, in fact, are merely the product of good management, a fad, or favorable publicity. But the good professional has a uniqueness, a personal style and technique, as well as artistic ability and skill in suiting concept to material and form. Here are examples by recognized sculptors.

The group includes two works by one sculptor, five by another, so you can compare not only different sculptors, but also different works by the same artist. At *BOTTOM LEFT* are two 24-in. figures by the late William Zorach, showing his characteristic slightly distorted style. His daughter was carved in mahogany, his son in maple (photo of son by Peter A. Juley & Son). Similar abstractness is evident in the applewood figure next to them, "Adam's Rib," by Anita Wechsler. (Collection of Mrs. Milton Reiner.) "Young Woman," also by Anita Wechsler, is slightly voluptuous by today's standards as is "Torso" *(BOTTOM RIGHT),* in tulip wood by Margaret Brassler Kane (Photo —Soichi Sunami). These two figures, about 24 in. high, were reproduced in mahogany for "limited edition" sale. The three sculptures *AT RIGHT* are also by Anita Wechsler. "Cassandra" *(RIGHT)* is a 30-in. figure in coca bolo, a wood which has a "figure" that accentuates the curves of the sculpture (photo by Colten). "A Time to Embrace" *(TOP RIGHT*—Bogart photo) is 21 in. high, in prima vera, and "Daphnis and Chloe" *(RIGHT CENTER)* is 24 in. high, in butternut. Of the five, Miss Wechsler considers "Embrace" as most characteristic of her work; it is now in the permanent collection of the Norfolk Museum of Arts and Sciences. "Daphnis and Chloe," which has curves where the other pair has angles, was a most successful composition—it sold almost immediately.

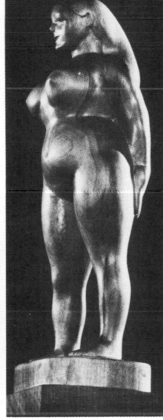

✳ The Human Head and . . .

Related Body Proportions

The human head has been the downfall of artists since art began, probably because so much of the personality of an individual is centered there. Early Egyptians wisely stayed with profile views, and carvers through the ages have tended toward rather chubby faces—probably because they shared my mounting fear that one more cut would ruin the face beyond retrieval.

Since I carved a head of my 2-year-old son —and got a likeness only hours after his normal bedtime—I have been an admirer of those artists who can get a likeness without caricaturing. Racial characteristics, expression, the fact that the normal face is not symmetrical—all of these create difficulties. A face shows fleeting expressions. How do you suggest sight in a translucent eyeball? How do you suggest maturity without suggesting age and worry? These take practice.

The heads sketched here were carved by natives of various countries, so they presumably picture typical local people. But even this is no criterion; there are sometimes

BELOW—Hawaiian heads in driftwood, the male with typical features and the female showing Oriental interbreeding. *CENTER*—"Vera Finger," life-size bust by E. Kapinov of the U.S.S.R. Note finish planes on head. *BOTTOM*—Fijian male (*LEFT*—note check) and female heads in nawa nawa by Isimeli show the large lips and wide nose, as well as the characteristic hairdo.

BELOW—Japanese priest (9 in.) in a yellow pine fragment exhibits excellent design and use of grain. Head elongated to denote wisdom; heavy eyelid is supplemented by slant. *BOTTOM*—Chinese heads of Confucius (*LEFT* —6 in.) and Mencius have the heavy eyelid, but eyes almost turn up at outer corners. These are intended as bookends, carved in a yellowish wood called willow.

CONFUCIUS BUST - TAIWAN

GIRL & BOY BUSTS - FIJI

MENCIUS' EYES - TAIWAN

MAO CHILD - CHINA

BEAM END - POLAND

CRANIUM ELONGATED

FACE IS TWO CHANNELS w/ NOTCHED RIDGE

PRIEST - JAPAN

DRINKING CUP - PHILIPPINES

WOMAN - MEXICO

FISHER-MAN - BALI

WARRIOR PHILIPPINES

startling differences depending upon tribe and race and degree of intermarriage. The Oriental eye is really not at a slant but has a special fold near the nose that creates that effect. The high cheekbones of the Indian, the "Roman" nose of the Italian, the flat, wide nose and thick lips of many dark-skinned peoples, the rounded chubby face of the Chinese—none of these is a constant.

Before you undertake formal heads like these, study again the carving of caricatured ones (page 57), because you may carve a caricature unintentionally. Also, learn the proportions of the head and the body.

Formal body proportions are based on the length of the head. Thus the normal person is seven or eight heads tall, the "fashion figure" nine or ten or even more, the caricature often no more than four or five. A man's shoulders are a bit over two heads wide, his hips about 1½. Women are narrower in the shoulders and wider in the hips. A typical figure of 7½ heads will have the nipples one head below the chin, the navel and top of the hipbone 2, and the crotch and bottom of the buttocks a bit more than 3. From the ground to the crotch is roughly half the height in men, but highly variable in women—beware estimating the overall height of a seated woman! The upper and lower legs are the same length, so the kneecap center is about 4½ heads from the chin. The body overall may be divided as one head for the head itself, 2¾ for the neck and trunk and 3¾ for the legs and feet. The male neck is ½ head long, the female a bit longer. The fingertips come midway between crotch and knee, because the arms are about 3 heads to the fingertips, with the elbow in the middle. (The female upper arm is shorter, so the whole arm is shorter in proportion.) The seated figure is about 4 heads high from the seat and 2 heads to the heel, with 2½ heads from kneecap to back of buttocks and shoulders. Incidentally, a man's knee, calf, and neck are about the same girth if he is muscular, the thigh is slightly smaller in girth than the head, the upper arm is smaller in girth than the calf, and his nipples are one head apart. The latter dimension on a woman is greater because the breasts do not project straight forward but at a diverging angle because of the rib-cage shape. She also has a shorter breast bone, hence a longer abdomen, more sloping shoulders, a forward-thrust neck.

On the head itself, the eyes are in the middle, with the face about ¾ head long (below the hairline) and the mouth about the same distance from the point of the chin as the hairline is from the top of the head. (Remember that an upright hairdo must be added on —it is not considered in these dimensions.) The distance from nose to mouth is about half that from mouth to point of chin.

Children, by the way, have heads disproportionately large. Thus a child a year or two old will be 4 heads tall, with the body center line at the navel. At three years, the child

BELOW LEFT—Filipino mahogany cup has female face with stylized large lips, blank eyeballs, no real indication of race, perhaps because there are so many in the Philippines. Next it is a portrait head of a friend carved in an 8-in. block of Bermuda cedar. Tool marks were left for texture. *BELOW RIGHT*—Polish head from Krakow, copied in maple (?) from a much older one on the end of a cathedral beam. Note the power of the face and strength of the

beard, suggested by a few lines. Eyeballs are blank, but heavy brows accentuate them and add a strong, brooding look. *FAR RIGHT*—Iroquois Indian head in mahogany, 6 in. High cheekbones, strong nose, forehead bulge over brows—all are facial characteristics. Long upper lip and straight mouth line show soberness, almost severity. Carved by my son (when he was 17) in mahogany, it was finished with oil and wax to approximate skin color.

ABOVE—Madonna and Child by José Ramón Trujillo, Jalisco Indian of Mexico. Mesquite, 10. in high, it took two days. The carver, totally self-taught, achieved a very spiritual face on the Madonna, but in common with many primitive carvers, has a 12-year-old face on the Child, so the body appears chopped off at the knees (see page 7).

will be 5 heads tall, with the center line halfway between navel and crotch. The 6-year-old is 5½ heads tall and the center line is approaching the crotch. A child gains one head in height between its first (4 heads) and fourth year, between its fourth and ninth, and between its ninth and fifteenth.

To carve a portrait head, study the person's face. Get nose and eye relationships. Are eyes, nose or mouth oversize? What is the head shape? Can you get front and side photos and photostat them to size, so they become patterns? Can you show a characteristic expression? These are the problems.

TOP CENTER—Filipino warrior in mahogany stained dark, 10 in. high. Head is abnormally large, with high cheekbones and thick lips. Weapon and shield removable.

ABOVE LEFT—Chinese child in yellow wood, 2 in. high, clutches a toy rifle, has Mao's face. Propaganda? *ABOVE CENTER*—Some modern sculptures merely suggest the features, as in this Mexican carving, which has nose and mouth positions indicated by notches on a central ridge between hollowed cheeks (see sketch). Figure is elongated as well. *ABOVE RIGHT*—Ebony figure of a Balinese fisherman, by Kt Gedeh of Sanur. The ascetic face with straggly beard is unmistakably that of an old man, but it is sympathetically done. About 15. in. high, this figure is strong and yet light. Note the delicate pierced carving of the net and entrapped fish.

Four heads from the U.S.S.R, "Man" and "Stenka Razin" at *LEFT* by Vera Sandomirskaya. Women and man at *RIGHT* are lifesize busts, merging into the block shape at the base. All show gouge marks except in the face.

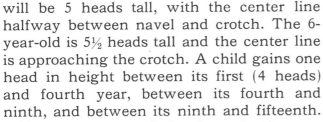

*Tradition Shapes These Figures

Some are Almost Symbolic

RIGHT—Small Chinese figures are delicate and light in feeling, even the Happy God at *LEFT*. He and the differing poses of a lady (6 in.) are foreshortened in thickness and barely carved in back, a common Chinese habit probably based on carving elephant ivory, as is the curve of the body. This is particularly evident in the tall fisherman sketched, where the third dimension is neglected (see photo on page 166). But the mandarin at *RIGHT* and the little bust at top are fully in the round. The three right-hand figures are tinted, the others lacquered and polished.

RIGHT—Lithuanian figure (2 ft.) of a weary peasant resting on her mattock is blocky and strong, as contrasted with the seated French girl *(FAR RIGHT)*, a 2-ft. figure in ebony by Arnel Beaufils, "Nu Jour de Pardon." Both were at the New York World's Fair '39.

BOTTOM RIGHT—The Cossack was a symbol of brutal repression under the Tsars, but also a fun-loving, simple person. I tried to get this combination into my rough-cut "Balalaika Player," which is blocky and surfaced in planes. It is mahogany 6 in. high, and the base houses a music box.

BELOW—Spindly Don Quixote and resigned Sancho Panza, either like this pair or with Quixote in broken armor on a decrepit Rosinante and Panza on a tired donkey, have been carved in Spain for over a century almost without change. These are 10½ in. and 8½ in., slightly antiqued.

BELOW RIGHT—The Chinese like humorous carvings, as these squatty (and squatting) old figures attest. One is apparently a boy at stream edge (see sketches), the other a fisherman with his catch. Both are blocky, yet detailed.

BOTTOM CENTER—Korean figures (4 and 5 in.) do not have the flowing finish of Chinese ones, tending to be planes and angles, but they show great strength and vigor. Both the village elder and the carrier are finished a very dark, glossy brown. Staves are separately carved and inserted, as is the old man's hat.

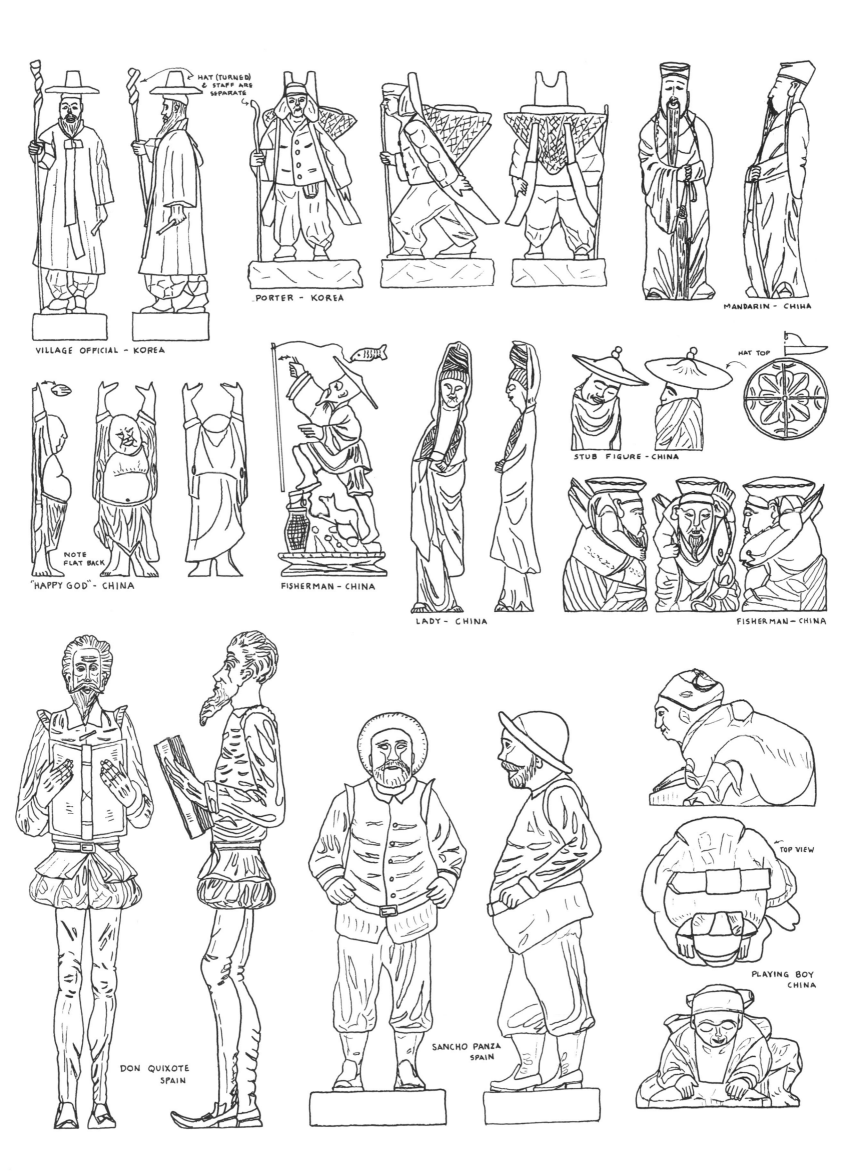

VILLAGE OFFICIAL - KOREA

HAT (TURNED) & STAFF ARE SEPARATE

PORTER - KOREA

MANDARIN - CHINA

NOTE FLAT BACK

"HAPPY GOD" - CHINA

FISHERMAN - CHINA

LADY - CHINA

HAT TOP

STUB FIGURE - CHINA

FISHERMAN - CHINA

DON QUIXOTE SPAIN

SANCHO PANZA SPAIN

TOP VIEW

PLAYING BOY CHINA

✳ How to Carve a Nativity Scene

Crèche, Krippe, Nacimiento, Praesepe, Jeslicky

Saint Francis of Assisi originated the Nativity Scene in 1223 when he set up, with Papal permission, a Holy Family in a stable in the churchyard at Greccio, a small town near Assisi. The figures were surrounded by live animals. Saint Francis was surprised by the success of the scene in conveying the story of Christmas to these largely illiterate peasants, and a friend reported a dream in which the child in the manger reached out to Saint Francis as he sang the service. (This singing, incidentally, was adapted to the Christmas carol, and the scene itself was one of the origins of the Christmas mystery play which was used so successfully during the Middle Ages to convey the concepts of Christianity to the untutored.)

The scene was on display from Christmas Eve to January 6, and villagers promptly attributed magical curative powers to the residue of food for the animals. The custom was continued, and as the years passed, more and more churches took up the idea. The scenes became more and more elaborate and competitive. Shepherds and Wise Men were added, as well as images of such animals as camels and elephants. Then individual families had their own, some including highly imaginative additions like musicians, a gypsy group, or even card players at a table! Goethe reported in 1787 that Neapoli-

tan houses had these scenes, decorated in evergreens, on the flat roofs, some including such costly costuming for the figures that the families were almost beggared.

This was probably the peak of competitive showiness. Gradually, the scenes became smaller and were moved inside the house, there serving somewhat the same function as a Christmas focal point that the Christmas tree serves in northern Europe. Surrounding countries took up the custom as well, so you will find the *Krippe* in Germany, the *crèche* in France, the *nacimiento* in Spain and the *Jeslicky* in Czechoslovakia matching the Italian *praesepe*. Oberammergau is now a center for the carving of figures for such scenes of all sizes, as is the Italian Tyrol. There is a museum of such groups in Munich. Some figures are now dressed in *Lederhosen and Dirndls* instead of the more traditional Holy Land or early Italian costumes. Figures are made in plastic, in china, and in other materials as well as wood.

A complete Nativity scene can consist of a great many figures, and they may, or may not, be to scale. Sometimes the Holy Family is made larger than the others. Mine originally included 26 figures and the stable. It is now 30—two camels, a driver and a "little drummer boy" ordered by a six-year-old.

The background, incidentally, should prob-

Nativity scene is based on a Joseph 5 in. high. Included are Mary, Joseph, manger and Babe, donkey, star, 4 sheep, goat, 3 shepherds, 2 cows, cow boy, angel, 3 cherubs, 3 Wise Men, one attended by a slave boy, camel and driver, resting camel, drummer boy, 2 doves, and a stable background with a rock wall. Patterns for figures are sketched. All figures are basswood. The rock wall is ¾-in. plywood, V-grooved into a rock pattern, with a tile roof carved of a piece of redwood and set on twig posts. All figures are flat-varnished to prevent end-grain soaking of color, then tinted and varnished again. Kneeling and standing camel, driver, and drummer boy (sketches) were additions to the original scene.

SHEEP

BABE in MANGER

CAMEL ₩ PANNIERS

CAMEL DRIVER

DONKEY

SHEPHERD BOY

SHEEP

HORNED COW

CUSHION

MARY

JOSEPH

THE MAGI

HORS D'OEUVRE STICK
with WOOD BEAD

GOAT

ATTENDANT
for MAGUS ₩ STAFF

RUMINANT CAMEL

CORD

"LITTLE DRUMMER
BOY"- A MODERN ADDITION

Mary, Joseph, and the Babe are the crucial figures *(TOP LEFT)*, thus should probably be done last, when you "have your hand in." Mary rode the donkey into Bethlehem. Oriental Magus and his slave boy *(TOP)* are on a thin base for stability, permitting dynamic leg positions. The staff is a cocktail pick from Japan with a wooden bead on top. Sheep and shepherds *(ABOVE LEFT)* in several poses lend interest. One shepherd is ancient and stooped, another is carrying a lamb, the third is a boy with a gift box of wool. I also included a goat. Surface texture on the animals is gouge grooving. Grain runs with the legs, for strength and easier gouging. Wood for some figures was too thick, so the silhouettes, carved in low relief, made plaques *(ABOVE)*. Cow horns are plastic knitting needle. Mexican Madonna *(LEFT)*, also sketched, is carved in mahogany, 6 in. tall, flat-backed.

ably be a rock wall. While the story in the Bible speaks of an inn, there is some evidence that this was an early mistranslation, and a more proper one would be "living room." If so, it refers to a private house, which usually consisted of an outer room where the animals were stabled in inclement weather, with a few steps up to an inner room where the family lived. This seems more logical as a resting place in a very crowded town and for humble people. Some of these houses still exist in Syria as caves hollowed in the rock. If this is true, the manger was simply a pit in the ground into which food was put.

Have a clear idea of the pose of the piece when you start—Mary is traditionally shown kneeling, and some of the others may be as well, depending upon the ultimate arrangement of the scene. Costumes are usually flowing robes such as desert people wear.

You may want to have finer costumes for the Wise Men, who are traditionally kings or kingly advisers from afar—and in some cases are not placed in the scene until a week after Christmas because of the travel time supposedly involved. I made one black, one Oriental, one aged, bearded, kneeling.

Some figures should be mounted on thin-wood bases for stability, particularly if they lean or are massive compared with their foot area. Also, I added a tube light hidden by the sloping roof of the shed so the Holy Family is clearly shown. The shed roof, by the way, is redwood, with the tiles carved all in one piece, as well as the roof beams. Figures like the angel, doves, and cherubs can either be glued in place or supplied with pins in sockets of the wall so they can be removed for storage. When set up, the figures are surrounded by white sand or by a mixture of cereals or cornmeal to simulate it.

MORE NATIVITY FIGURES

ANGLE CUT MAKES FIGURE STOOP

SHEPHERD

SHEPHERD with LAMB

COWHERD

SEATED CHERUB

STAR

DOVES

ANGEL with SCROLL

VOTIVE ANGEL

ANGEL DESIGNED for STYROFOAM

MADONNA
NOTE EXAGGERATED HEIGHT. - GERMANY

FLAT BACK for WALL MOUNTING

MADONNA & CHILD
CARVED in a CYPRESS KNEE
(SEE "ACCIDENTALS" for PHOTO)

COPPER TRIM STRIP

MADONNA
LOW RELIEF with
STAMPED DESIGN
CEDAR - MEXICO

Nuestra Señora de la Soledad

✳The Angels Sing—and Play

Three Types and Three Scenes

RIGHT—Oberammergau angels have billowing robes, spiked wings, and tightly curled edge hair—all quite standardized. They play various tiny whittled instruments, so arm position and facial expressions vary. These, about 4 in. high, are typical of the dozen or so sketched. Wings and hands are very long, thin, and delicate (see enlarged sketches), are separately made and glued in place, as are some heads. They have no feet. (Overseas shipments customarily include extra parts to restore broken parts.) Angels are mass-produced, with apprentices doing rough work. Curls and eyes are made with the veiner. As compared with Tyrolese angels *(BOTTOM)*, these are elongated and mature. The Tyrolese pieces are one-piece, tend to be chubby and tinted in soft tones, with more-rounded baby faces and figures. They are less dependent upon planes and angles for effectiveness, but do not have the delicacy of the German angels. Hands, in particular, are made with a few cuts, but may have curled fingers and bent wrist while under ½ in. long. I found them hard to duplicate. *CENTER*—Traditional blessing angel about 4 in. high, made for me in 1935 by Susan Collins of New Hampshire. It is pine, carved with chisels and burins.

BELOW LEFT AND RIGHT—These three pieces are all from the Oberammergau area of Germany and are alike in that figures are very much simplified, yet dramatically effective. The "Last Supper" *BELOW*, for example, is less than 1 in. high, in a 2×3-in. walnut box with folding doors. The Nativity is in a turned walnut dome about 3 in. high, shows shepherds on one wing, the Magi on the other. Figures are an assemblage of planes (see sketch, next page). The larger Nativity scene *(BOTTOM RIGHT)* is about 8 in. high, has 1½-in. major figures with veiner hollows for eyes and mouth area, curled shavings for music in 1-in. angels' hands, etc.

SEVEN ITALIAN ANGELS *from* THE TYROL

SEE TOP VIEW BELOW

TOP VIEW of KNEELING ANGEL

SEPARATE WINGS GLUED IN HOLES

THIRTEEN GERMAN ANGELS *from* OBERAMMERGAU

DRUM & CYMBALS TURNED PIECES

TYPICAL HANDS, SEPARATELY CARVED, ARE GLUED ON. (4X)

HARP ASSEMBLED *from* WOOD PARTS

NOTE SIMPLIFIED FIGURES & FACES

WINGS

CRECHE DETAIL - GERMANY (MUCH ENLARGED)

✳ The "Exaggerated Realism" of Emil Janel

An Album of Figure Ideas

Emil Janel, born in Orsa, Sweden, began carving at four, beat 250 sculptors for first prize in Stockholm at 24. He was a woodsman in Canada, then an accordion player in San Francisco in 1917. Most of his figures are in alder because it holds its color. Each is about a foot tall, made from a single block which he holds on his knees and carves with mallet and chisel. He has no pattern, works entirely from a mental image to produce his "exaggerated realism." The accordionist, man on bench, blacksmith, man with peavey, and fisherman appeared in *Westward*, Kaiser Steel. All photos by Fran Jones.

*How to Carve in Low Relief

Design, Techniques, Procedure, Finishing, and Mounting

Carving in relief is distinctly different from carving in the round, as many carvers have learned to their sorrow. In three-dimensional carving, it is possible to have all dimensions correct—either those of the original or in some fixed relationship to them. The finished carving can be viewed from any position or any angle and will look as correct as it was made. Light direction and intensity do not make too much difference.

When the third dimension is foreshortened, as it is in relief carving, some elements must be altered so they look as they should from a particular point of view. Thus a curved surface may become almost angular, or a given line may be shorter or longer than it is on the original or on its mate. A near cheek may be almost flat; a far one almost angular. The third dimension is always shortened, and planes or locations which may actually be at different depths in the original may be at the same level in the carving and made to appear to be at differing depths by the way in which the area between them is treated. Thus, in a relief carving of a face, the cheeks, nose tip, chin, and lips may all be at almost the same level, or in a landscape a distant object may be at the same level as a near one.

This sounds complicated, and is—at first. It accounts for some of the portrait panels and other carving that looks flat and lifeless. It takes practice and experimentation to learn how to subordinate a background and how to make an area or point stand out. It also often involves careful design, to arrange the picture or pose the subject so the illusion of a full third dimension is created. In terms of lighting, it is a matter of shadow effects.

Study of examples here pictured will help to show you how to defeat the problems. Many of them can be used as patterns; they are the equivalent of front-view drawings.

Traditional relief carving was frequently quite deep, some almost in-the-round, like Grinling Gibbons' swags and panels. Also, the entire area of a panel was "busy"—spaces around the key figure or central element were filled with intricate leaf and vine patterns or some repeated design. Often, the design became so intricate that it was a real exercise to find the subject or subjects—which led some medieval monks to produce liturgical carvings that contained somewhat irreverent, even bawdy, elements.

In recent years, this intricate carving has gone out of fashion. Furniture and moldings are mostly quite simple or "carved" by machine. An entire panel may be blank, or the grain of the wood accented. Fashion is only one reason; others are prohibitive cost, common use of plywood paneling, inability

Swiss students at the State Woodcarving School, Brienz, copy these panels to learn techniques, patterns ranging from lines (bottom) to floral figures in high relief (top).

Delta Queen, Ohio River steamboat, a presentation panel in teak 1 × 12 × 12 in. "Figure" in lower left corner suggests churning water from the sternwheel. By author.

to find skilled carvers, difficulty of maintenance, and reduction of clutter. A modern carved panel may simply have the subject carved into or projecting from a flat area, even glued on, and carving tends to be in low relief. Wood paneling, if used, stresses the wood figure and the moldings rather than a carved design. Also, we are in an era of color, so walls are painted in bright tints and liberally bespotted with paintings, prints, and photographs, most framed in rough wood that an old-time craftsman wouldn't have allowed near him. Furniture may be a mixture of styles and involve explosive colors or shapes. Against such competition, the warmth and quiet elegance of carved wood may appear anachronistic.

In the past several years interior decoration has been turning more and more toward three-dimensional free-standing elements—in other words, sculpture. Some of these may be assemblages of scrap metal and the like, of course, but wood is finding an increasingly important place. Shapes are often simply silhouettes with subtle shading. Backgrounds may be darkened to increase the contrast and illusion of depth, and lines may be "antiqued"—emphasized with dark color—so the real shadows of high-relief carving are replaced by an effect. This also permits the use of thinner panels of costly woods, with less carving, again reducing cost. An exception may be the appliqué carving, in which pieces of wood of contrasting color and/or texture may be carved and glued to a background panel. Each piece may be carved in low or high relief, but the panel is flat. Familiar for years as a way of mounting ship models, the technique is now used for figures and as a way of adding height for projecting elements in an otherwise flat panel.

In planning a panel or other low-relief

Presentation panel in primavera ("white mahogany") 1½ × 13 × 18 in. for Fred Annett, who had been a woodcutting champion in his youth, later a railway signalman and electrical maintenance man, ultimately a magazine editor and writer. A brass engraved plate on the lower rectangle included inscription and facsimile signatures. Note conventionalized trees, background "well" with pattern of tiny scallops. Finish was flat varnish and wax.

Blacksmith panel carved in 1¼-in. white pine for a magazine. The low-relief figure is stylized, with right arm almost double the size of the left for emphasis and perspective. Background was sunk an extra ¼ in. for better shadow effects. Figure was tinted and reproduced in color, approximately 9 × 12 in., with lettering stripped in as shown. These panels are an unusual overlap between my hobby and my business as a magazine editor.

subject, it is best to keep in mind the basic rules for picture composition. You can find them in any text on drawing or painting.

Elements should not be of the same size, or repeatedly in the same pose, unless you are producing an all-over or "diaper" pattern. One element should not simply touch another; it should either not touch at all or should overlap slightly. A line of the subject should not be paralleled by an adjacent line in the background. Extraneous detail should be eliminated: the nails in a fence, the veins in leaves, even the leaves themselves unless they are quite large. Background detail only serves to detract from the subject, and often requires a disproportionate amount of carving time. If your subject is a bird, avoid branches, leaves, nests, berries and the like unless they are essential to the idea you are trying to convey. It is not necessary to have interlacing vines to tie elements together except in pierced carving; even in nature there are blank spots in a view—like the sky, or a meadow, or a placid lake. A telephone pole or two will suggest the wires,

without your attempting to carve even the insulators; particularly because they are almost certain to be out of scale as well as irregular anyway. Perspective and proportion are much more important. Bear in mind that good photographers tend to throw the background out of focus in portraiture, so it doesn't compete with the subject; suggest the background rather than carving it in intimate detail. You'll be surprised at how frequently it can be left out with no loss.

In a single-subject design, simplicity requires a minimum of background, not only in absence of detail but in reduction of background area. This helps in another way: It reduces the difficulty of obtaining the effect of a third dimension in low relief. The painter can gray his background tones, or make outlines less distinct; this effect is hard for a carver to achieve.

In a multiple-subject design, like a flock of birds, it is mandatory to show perspective, of course, and also vital to vary the pose. Even a line of West Point cadets will not be identical, in hand or head position, leg angle, body carriage, let alone shape and size. Birds will have different wing and head positions, will not fly exactly in line. Some variety is a must.

It is important to have a dynamic pose, so the subject doesn't appear stiff or stilted. And try to select a characteristic pose, one that will help to identify the subject at first glance.

Ship's-clock bases (BELOW) I designed and carved for company executives, the upper in teak butts from the deck of the USS *North Carolina* with a wave pattern, the lower in oak with initials and a rope pattern. Note carved rope-coil feet. *Grandfather clock (CENTER)* with motto and simple incised dial and base design, from the State Woodcarving School, Brienz, Switzerland. *New England scene (RIGHT)* was designed around a traveling clock. Tower incorporated two music boxes for my daughter. White pine, about 1½×10×15 in. Grillwork slant-cut to pass music but stop dust.

The subject should fit the shape. A tall subject will look lost in an essentially wide panel; a free-form shape may look peculiar in a rigid panel. And, strange as it seems, it is easy to design a panel so a rear element looks too large for a forward one; the bird in back may be too big by comparison, or the wrong wing may be on top. I have seen carvings in which the far hand was bigger than the near one; one I have has the thumbs on the wrong sides of the hands, another has six fingers. (Mention should be made here of deliberate distortion for emphasis. In the panel of the blacksmith (page 109), the right arm is almost twice the size of the left, so the viewer's eye goes immediately to the dominant and active arm.)

Straightforward panel carving may be varied in many ways, some of them hundreds of years old. There is the pierced carving, in which the design is cut through the panel, so light from the back changes the effect. There are insertions of metal, contrasting wood, ivory, jewels, bone, shell, etc.

Indian and Chinese carvers have made pierced carvings in wood, ivory, and other materials for a very long time. The Chinese, in fact, have developed a whole special skill in pierced carving of ivory. This sort of thing makes our ball-in-a-cage look like kid stuff. The Chinese also carve the surfaces of what they refer to as an olive, but that seems to be a thick-walled nut, so that it adds tricks like swinging doors and idols behind them—all out of the shell wall—to surface decoration.

These require special tools, techniques, and time, but pierced carving itself does not. It's just a matter of selecting parts of the background to be drilled through and cut away with a keyhole saw, carving tools, or even a router. As a result, the panel becomes a screen, and can be very dramatic against a wall of lighter color or a light. The carving seems to have added depth. Obviously, the openings must be separated by membranes of sufficient size and strength to hold the piece together, and usually evenly distributed over the surface.

A shaped silhouette carved in low relief is another possibility—a letter opener, bellows, bread and cheese boards, free-form figures or plaques. It is also possible to apply low-relief to a three-dimensional object, like the "Man for All Seasons" head (page 14).

Another example of the two-dimensional becoming almost three-dimensional and utilizing pierced carving ideas is the planetary mobile (page 14). The central element is a two-sided sun-moon combination, in which a mahogany sun upper half and a

LEFT—3-panel low-relief door frame in the peasant-craft museum, Zhagorsk, U.S.S.R. Motif is hunters in a forest, with stylized trees framing hunters, horses and dogs. Lintel is two sections. *CENTER*—Door of nine vertical panels, each depicting a different trade or craft, carved in Poland. Outside each low-relief figure, the surface is faired to the panel edges. *RIGHT*—Low-relief double doors in teak in the compound of Ida Bagus Tilem, master carver of Mas, Bali. Intricate floral pattern is matched by designs in the teak frame and carved lintel.

maple half-moon lower half are joined so one eye of the sun becomes the eye of the moon as well. The stars, comets and "little black cloud" are all basically two-dimensional with surface carving; only the Saturn is in-the-round. But the mobile arms help add a third dimension.

I usually begin carving at the bottom of a design, and work up. My reasons are purely practical. It assures a well-planned and well-spaced bottom or base for the panel, and it avoids erasing any drawn-in elements of the design by rubbing with arms and elbows. Some carvers lay out the design for an entire panel before they start; I often do not, unless the panel features only one subject. Also, they lay out the design in India ink or fiber pen; I usually do not because of the necessity of removing stains after the carving is

finished and the difficulties of changing a design to suit wood peculiarities or for some other reason (like breakage).

BACKGROUNDING

The first operation is to ground the carving —to remove the background to a desired depth. Depth is largely a matter of choice. On a relatively simple panel, it can be relatively shallow. On a panel a foot or two square, I tend to ground to a depth of $\frac{1}{8}$ to $\frac{1}{4}$ in.; on wooden shoes, I ground to $\frac{1}{8}$ in. or less; on the "bug tree"—a relatively large piece—I ground to about $\frac{1}{2}$ in. Depth is governed by panel thickness, by how many overlapping elements or planes of depth are involved, and by how much shaping of design elements is intended. If fairly large heads or other elements are to be carved al-

BELOW—Modern Tudor Rose carved in maple drawer pulls and antiqued with gold. *BOTTOM*—Photo of local school principal's retirement home, "Fo'Rest" (sic) and plaque $\frac{1}{2} \times 6 \times 6$ in. carved from it and framed in pine twigs. Finish is eggshell varnish and wax.

BELOW CENTER—Indian-head medallion in Honduras mahogany, carved with a jackknife. Background is haphazard grooves. Tinted. 6-in. diameter. *BOTTOM CENTER*—Caricatures of skiers in white pine, 6 in., framed in miniature skis. Eggshell varnish.

BELOW—Cartoons in low relief for a guest bathroom. Small boy racing for a huge backhouse; small girl seeking information for same reason. From magazine cartoons. All by author.

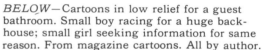

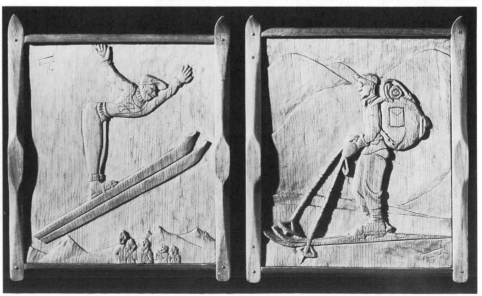

most in the round, the ground may have to be sunk an inch or more.

To gage background depth, you can make a gage—simply a pin projecting from a crossbar—or mark the desired depth on the firmer or other tools you are using for stop cuts and outlining. Or you can rout to the desired depth with either a hand or power router. I find that I can gage accurately enough by eye in most instances. I don't want the ground table-top flat anyway because I want it to be subordinated—by staining dark, roughing, grooving in patterns, scalloping, or some other similar device.

Grounding is begun by outlining the design elements with a veiner or V-tool. The veiner usually does a better job of this, and is easier to keep sharp. The outline should be along the line of the actual design, but not following each tiny detail, particularly if they are across grain. Once the outline is in, it is extended downward into the wood by driving a small firmer or flat gouge in at right angles. On ordinary-size panels, I find myself using a ⅛-in. firmer and a ¼-in. flat fishtail gouge. These are driven down about half the intended grounding depth and the ground wood cut away with flat gouges, then they're driven to the desired depth. This 2-step grounding reduces the crushing of fibers at the edge of the design and also provides an opportunity to evaluate the surface of the wood in that particular area, so the grounding will not produce a hole or split. Also, it is less likely to split off narrow sections, like an insect leg or antenna, which stands up unsupported from the ground. On deeper grounding, take three steps.

I ground with a light mallet; it gives me better control. And I set in along the side of the veiner line closest to the drawn outline. This reduces the time required to come to the correct outline later, but it involves constant care to avoid crushing the edge fibers while wedging out a chip by pressing against the outline with the tool, cutting into the design itself, or the like. Also, on occasion, I set in with larger tools, but I find them harder to place accurately and am impatient at the time involved in switching tools every time I reach a complex area. Also, large and high-curvature gouges tend to crack out the arc of wood within them at this stage.

Once the ground is roughed out with a flat gouge, you can go over it carefully with a firmer to smooth out the hollows and make a square edge with the design. You may also find a ¼-in. offset or dogleg tool very helpful in tight spots. At the same time, you will want to smooth up the outlines of the design; there may be a step between your first and second setting-in cuts, and details to ground.

BELOW—Filipino tray, ¾ × 12 × 18 in. plus molding and handles, of farm couple with house and water buffalo. Low relief with deepened background. Mahogany, varnished. RIGHT—Maori bird pattern with paua-shell inserts, part of a temple pillar, shown at New York World's Fair, 1939. RIGHT CENTER—Maori panel about 7 ft. tall there. FAR RIGHT—Totora-wood Maori panel by William Redman, 9½ × 19 in. Both show a full Maori Teko (god) showing defiance (straight tongue) conquering a bad Teko (only head shown—split tongue indicates lying). The 3-fingered hands are characteristic, indicating long life span. Both have paua-shell eye inserts.

In all these operations, you will find yourself adopting a certain rhythm, which can be both good and bad. You may find that to set to a desired depth across grain with a particular tool takes three light mallet blows—but with the grain it may take only two. You'll develop patterns and rhythm in your mallet strokes, which makes the work easier, but beware of letting this make you overconfident in the tight corners. The intricate areas may require hand work, even with a penknife, to avoid overstressing thin elements of the design. In setting in and grounding also, you may want to slant the tool away from the design at first, thus cutting a slope but avoiding stress. Then you can come back and cut it vertical as you clean up the ground. In a really tight corner, a penknife tip is my safest tool.

You will discover certain basic rules as you work. You'll ground out the big areas first, leaving the intricate ones for more careful attention later. When you set in an outline, you'll set the lines across grain first, so these cuts will stop any tendency toward splitting when you set in with the grain. You'll learn to use the firmer very delicately in grounding, both because it may tend to dig in tight areas and because it may slip and shear off a part of the design. You'll probably also find that you want to vary the routine occasionally by doing some finishing on the design before all the grounding is done—even though the old books insist that all roughing be done first. Just between us, I often ground an area, then work on the design itself for a change of pace, so I may have a panel which is in four stages at once, part blank, part laid out, part grounded, and part finished. The other virtue, besides relief of boredom, in carving as you go is that your hand and arms will help to rub a patina into the carving under them. Also, you can relax still more on occasion by cleaning up small areas and splinters on the finished portions, so there isn't so much of *that* to do at the end, and you have something to show to the questioner sooner or later who comes up with, "What on earth are you doing?"

When the inevitable occurs and your tool slips, breaking off or shaving a section of the design itself, stop and fix it. You thus avoid

BELOW—Free-form panel in conacaste wood by Alberto Chuc-Orozco, Guatemala. It is 24 × 32 in. and depicts the Maya god Kukulcán, always shown with a decapitated bird. The panel was made for presentation to a foreign dignitary, but was rejected because of a minor check at the top. Note finishing with gouge lines.

BELOW—Mahogany panel depicting guitar players, from Poland. About 2 × 3 ft. and mounted on a base. *BELOW RIGHT*—*Tortillería* or tortilla stamp from Jalisco, Mexico. Wood probably mesquite, 1½ in. thick by 7 in. diameter. Crudely carved by an Indian, it stamps its pictures in red dye on tortillas produced for fiestas.

TOP LEFT—Honduran peasant figures in mahogany—very simple, except for face detail. *LEFT*—Head in mahogany, from Haiti, about 7 in. high. *ABOVE*—Two pairs of peasant Filipinos. Carved in mahogany only ½ in. thick, but 16 to 18 in. tall, they are strong, supple figures which can be silhouetted against any desired background, like other figures in this group. Note that one couple are profile silhouettes, the other full-face. They sell in Manila for a dollar or two each, finished with shellac (unfortunately) and with a tendency to warp.

losing the chip and you get an immediate lesson in care. You can repair the break and work somewhere else on the panel while it dries. I use Elmer's Glue-All or the equivalent on carvings which are not to be exposed to the weather. It sets quite quickly, dries transparent, holds securely. (One professional I know thins Elmer's Glue-All with water in a 50-50 mix and uses it to appliqué surface blocks and slabs and has no difficulties. It goes on more smoothly and easily than the pure glue, saves glue, penetrates better and dries faster.) For outside carvings, better repair with a 2-element or other dependable plastic cement. In either case, cut or sand away any spillage because it will affect the finish later if you don't.

Gluing is not all repair work. It can save you money. High spots and bosses in a carving can be glued on, so you don't need such a thick panel to start with. Besides, a thick panel may be hard to find. On my walnut mailbox, I used ½-in. wood because I had a length of that dimension available, and glued on wood in which to carve the shield, helmet, and lion head. In another case, I saw a carver making a large memorial plaque which had a raised carved design only in one corner. By gluing wood on there only he saved not only the cost of wood twice as thick but also the time and trouble involved in thinning most of the surface and getting it smooth again. With this technique, it is also possible to add decorative or design elements in contrasting-color woods or other materials, like ivory, shell, and metal.

If, as you carve, you find a knot, wormhole, crack, or soft or discolored or rotted area, cut it out to the necessary depth and glue in some of the same wood as a replacement. The cut-out area need not be rectangular or circular; with a little extra trouble you can follow grain lines or figure of the wood and make the repair less noticeable. A long crack can be filled with chips—if you don't dispose of all your chips as you go. The chips should be wedge-shaped, of the same color as the area into which they go, and with the grain running the same way, of course. I have done a number of pieces in black walnut and filled cracks this way.

If you must sand during carving, incidentally, do it with care and clean the wood afterward. There's nothing like sand to take the edge off a tool—and most modern abrasives are much harder than sand. Basically, however, sanding should be considered a necessary evil, only to be done when a high polish is sought. Actually, no matter how carefully it is done, it will roughen the surface more than a honed tool does, so sanded areas will look dull by comparison with cut ones. Instead of sanding, you may want to try the old trick of rubbing with a piece of smooth stone like agate, or a whale tooth or a "pencil" of buffed metal. This will lay the fibers and produce a sheen.

If the design will include a great many large and relatively flat areas, the background will have to be subordinated. This can be done in many ways, and of course is done after the design itself is completed, but we can speak of it here while discussing backgrounding. In some relatively crude work, the background may be covered with a pattern made by stamps. A simple type would be a spike with the point ground off and filed into a cross or a star. These have a tendency, however, to crush the wood fibers and generate splinters in the background, which I find undesirable. It is also

RIGHT—"King Midas," in primavera, 7½ in. Eyes are gilt-plated plastic buttons, cut to fit and inset. *LEFT*—"Angel Fish," in mahogany, 7½ in. high. Horizontal grain gives trailing fins strength. Spots in coral are veiner holes. *LEFT BOTTOM*—Intaglio fish, 6 in. long by ½ in. deep, a test piece in pine. This is good exercise, if you can think "inside out," and necessary in mold-making. All by the author. *BOTTOM RIGHT*—"Angel Fish," a 16 × 25-in. mahogany panel by Margaret Brassler Kane.

possible to make a criss-cross pattern of parallel lines with a veiner or V-tool, but these tend to be difficult to bring close to the edge of the design and also may cause breakouts and uneven spots difficult to repair. Better is a pattern of small depressions, such as can be made with a spoon gouge, a dental burr or a hand grinder with a ball cutter. I prefer to leave the background fairly smooth and flat and to stain it darker than the wood itself. This is time-consuming, exacting work, because it must be done accurately with a small brush to avoid getting stain on the design, but it makes the grounding appear deeper than it is by intensifying the shadows. Thus, on the "bug tree," which was apple, I used mahogany stain; on the teak panels I use walnut stain; on willow shoes, I used a thinned mahogany stain with better success than thinned walnut color, which proved to be too dark and "contrasty." On walnut, I add a little black to walnut stain. (Don't use black alone; it is "dead.")

It is preferable to ground out a figure and the elements nearest it before any shaping of the surface is attempted. Otherwise, there may be inconsistencies in carving depth and differences in relationships that make recarving necessary.

A practical procedure in carving is to put in stop cuts and cut to them, just as is done in backgrounding, except not so deeply, of course. The usual feature will not be over one-third background depth, if that. But to carve surface shapes first helps to establish the general shape of the piece, and avoids the common error of chamfering all edges initially—the way some whittlers start a figure by rounding all the edges. Taking off a square edge may destroy a sharp shadow or line that later you'll wish you had. Also, some fine definition of things like hair, scales, buttons, and such may be needed in edge wood. It is always advisable to know, before you cut, what will have to project and to allow the wood for it. It isn't easy to add a beard to a figure after an angular jaw has been shaped, or to provide buttons, moustache, or something in a hand; this must be done in wood left for the purpose.

It is possible, however, on occasion to correct a mistake or to add a feature, simply by recarving at a lower level. This should not be done until you're convinced that the lowering of that particular portion of the carving will not spoil the rest of it by creating a depression. With arms, legs, and other elements that project into the ground anyway, it is relatively easy to make such corrections, but on a broad flat surface, excessive depth will show. The heights of adjacent elements may have to be cut back a bit to avoid the appearance that the recarved section is behind the rest of the carving, particularly when side lighting hits it.

It is also possible to invert the level of a small feature like an eye, a button, or a whisker or two, actually making them depressions instead of projections. On fish and birds, for example, I often make the iris of the eye as a drilled hole, although in actuality the iris is flush with the surface. The drilled hole will look black and accent the eye or supposed button. It is also possible to suggest hairiness, such as a beard, with scratched lines on the surface, even though the silhouette will not look quite natural.

Low-relief carving requires intelligent distortion anyway, so the carving will look natural from the intended point of view. A carving to be placed well above the eye, for example, can actually have sloping planes for what would normally be horizontal surfaces, and relatively sharp edges on the upper side may look like rounded corners. Such problems can best be handled by setting the carving in place after it is carved but before it is finished to see how the light affects it. I know of one case in which a carver of eagles actually had one of his carvings removed from a pleasure-boat counter so he could do deeper carving on some portions when he saw how daylight affected elements below the viewer's eye.

Also remember that one feature may be behind another in appearance and yet not actually be so. This can be achieved by the relative angles of the surface cuts. A sharp outline on one section and a sloping outline on the other, tend to put the latter visually behind the former. This is important to remember in carving something like a face, in which most contours are soft in life, and the nose is nearest the observer, with the cheeks on a level definitely behind it and the ears farther back still. In a good low-relief carving, the cheeks may be as near the observer as the nose—but are separated by soft cheek contours from a relatively sharp nose to give the appearance of being set back.

Surface textures are of course extremely important. The suggestion of sand or roughness can be made by leaving the surface slightly rough. A pattern of cuts across the surface can subordinate it, make it appear uneven or darker. A series of gouge depressions or small planes will break up the light and avoid shine, as well as giving a "hand-cut" appearance to the piece. Some carvers actually achieve the desired shape, then go over the surface with a flat gouge to leave a hand-carved appearance.

There are a great many devices and techniques in surface carving which you will discover as you work. Some will work better

BELOW LEFT—Polish ecclesiastical figures in oak, stylized. *BELOW*—High-relief panel of the U.S. privateer brigantine *General Armstrong,* which figured in a naval action against the British off the Azores, September 28, 1814. It was carved in 1940 by Robert Petscheider, who learned his trade in Innsbruck. It was presented to Sperry Gyroscope Company, source of this photograph. Ropes and standing rigging are detailed, men are shown on deck, and sails are free of the background.

BELOW—"Cap'n Bob" Bartlett, study in maple 4 in. wide by John T. Tangerman, copied from a photo. It was planned as a decoration for the wheel of a yacht named after the Arctic explorer.

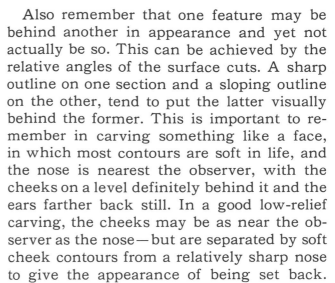

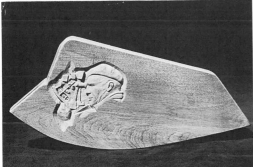

PEASANTS in Eastern Europe once used paddles like these to beat and press dirt from clothes washed in running water. A handle was set in the squared opening. Simple chip-carved and line patterns decorated them — still popular and easy. Peasant craft museum, Zhagorsk, USSR.

for you than others; I use some that other carvers disdain, and vice versa.

To "lower" the background and to accent eyes, buttons, grooves, and the like, I apply woodstain after all carving is finished. In general, I use a stain darker than that of the wood itself. It can be done in either of two ways, depending upon the result desired. Stain will of course be more heavily absorbed by end-grain areas — including those at the sides of the design, so if a fairly uniform background color is desired or necessary, it is best to give the piece a coat of flat varnish first. This will prevent excessive stain in cross grain, but of course the stain will take longer to dry and must be varnished over in its turn. Applying the stain directly to the wood may cause some spatters and

touches in the wrong places, but these can usually be wiped or scraped off if caught before they're dry. Also, when the varnish is applied over this stain, the varnish will tend to carry the stain into tight corners which couldn't be reached with the brush. A good technique is to varnish after the stain has dried for four or five hours, so the varnish brush will spread it into corners, but to be careful that the varnish brush doesn't pick up enough stain to tint the top surfaces of the wood.

"Antiquing" of the carving can be done to good effect — but *always* over a varnish coat. This is a tricky business of brushing thinned stain into the deeper parts of the carving itself, to emphasize desired lines and crevices, just as dust and other accumulations would emphasize them over the years. The effect is the same as that theoretically created by brushing a dark color over the entire surface, then wiping it all off the higher surfaces. This latter technique I do *not* recommend; I've had no luck with it on most woods. Antiquing will be found particularly useful in making one element of a design separate from another where they cross. It is painted in a thin band along the line, then wiped with a cloth or tissue at once to fade or thin out the edge away from the cut. It is sometimes helpful in intricate areas to follow such outlining with a larger brush dipped in turpentine or mineral spirits; this will do the same blending job as wiping does.

FINISHING

There are as many ways to finish carvings as there are carvers. A tavern sign is obviously painted, while a wall panel may be finished only with oil or wax. One professional carver of tavern signs, after carving is completed, goes over the surface with a blowtorch to remove small chips and give an antique look, and he sometimes precedes this with sandblasting to round exact corners and increase the apparent age. He hasn't used a piece of sandpaper in years. A friend in England writes of an aged carver there who has made a gold mine by producing tavern signs on pieces of old boards and shipping them to the United States. He gets $500 apiece and turns out two or three a week. They're sold in art galleries in the United States — and if the gallery owner suggests that they're authentic English antiques, the carver claims that isn't his fault, because *he* makes no such claims.

My own experience with painted panels has been limited. Paint holds up quite well, but varnish offers problems. For pieces to be outside—a mailbox or a door or door frame—even the best marine varnishes last less than a year. Many successive coats of varnish build up in the carving and can't be removed except by recarving the piece. Also, only high-gloss varnish will last any time at all—forget trying for low-gloss finishes to be exposed. The best solution for a natural-finish outside carving seems to be either to leave it unvarnished or to use one of the newer finishes, which are a combination of oil, a penetrant, and a thin plastic. Several coats of this will fill the surface and protect it against sun, wind, rain, and snow. I have used it with success on two teak doors, one of which required varnishing every six months for 30 years because of its southern and unprotected exposure. Several companies make such preservatives for decks.

My favorite finish for carvings to be displayed inside is flat varnish, followed by waxing. This provides protection, gives a soft sheen, and makes cleaning easier. However, two carvings in mesquite which I brought back from Mexico and finished in this way later developed woodworms. The remedy is to put the carving in a freezer for a few days if you see the dust boring insects make.

MOUNTING

Thin panels that are to be free-standing or simply hung on a wall may show a distressing tendency to warp. What's more, they may twist and change with the season and the humidity. This can be controlled in various ways. The ancients did it by hollowing out the center of the back of the panel, by putting bolts through it across grain, or by invisible framing at the ends. I have used ordinary aluminum angle to good effect. This is available in many hardware stores because it is used in framing cabinets and the like. It is commonly $\frac{1}{2}$ or $\frac{5}{8}$ in. on a side. This can be cut slightly shorter than the width of the panel, the ends of the upstanding leg chamfered to reduce the likelihood that it will show on the ends, and the angles screwed to the panel back at intervals of 1 ft. or so. It is important to get screws as near the outer edges as possible, to hold the edges securely, because most panels tend to curl outward—they generate a concave face. This is probably the result of the greater surface exposed on that side by the carving.

Panels can be mounted against a surface in a variety of ways. A convenient one is adhesive—either Elmer's Glue-All for inside service or plastic cement for outside, provided there is no intention of ever removing the panel in one piece, and provided also that the panel and background do not differ too greatly in expansion rate under changes in humidity. When I made panels to be applied to an existing plywood door, we selected teak both because of its excellent weathering characteristics and pleasing color, and because it has very little tendency to warp or change shape under exposure. But there would be some differential expansion between panel and door, and the owner might at some time wish to move and take his panels along. So we mounted the panels with 1½-in. brass screws set in countersunk holes. The holes were somewhat larger than the screw shank, to permit some relative movement with weather changes, the screw bearing only on the countersink. Holes were spaced 6 to 10 in. apart all around the panels, and filled with cross-grain teak dowels.

"COAL" and "SALT," two of a series of five 3½ × 6-ft. panels assembled of yellow poplar, carved by Seth M. Velsey for the U.S. Post Office, Pomeroy, Ohio, in 1937. Simple figures are outlined with deep V-cuts, with the side of the V adjacent to the figure vertical. Lighter V's, plus a little modeling, develop figures and perspective.

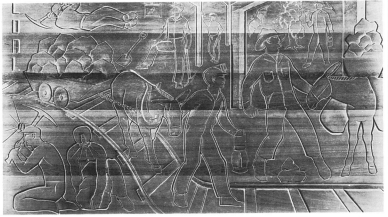

✳ Mahogany (in part) Rocking Horse

Panoply Saves Wood, Avoids Leg Problems

Familiar since the days when a carved wooden horse wasn't prohibitively expensive, the rocking horse may be due for a comeback because of recent discoveries showing the value of the rocking motion for soothing children. This horse is a modern version with plywood "panoply" or skirts, so it does not require a large piece of good wood, difficult to find, expensive to buy, and hard to work. Elimination of the legs makes this a good basement project.

The head and rump are mahogany (from a World War II airplane pattern, incidentally), and only they, a stretcher, and the edges of the seat are carved. The horse is about 21 in. high (excluding ears) and about 28½ in. long, with seat height 12½ in. above the ground, but these dimensions can be increased for an older child. In the interest of safety and softer "feel," the ears are leather and the

Two blocks of "good" wood and some scraps of pine make this horse. Chief mane and tail maker at left also tints carvings. Note mailbox (page 125).

mane and tail are wool yarn (avoid the flammable synthetics!). The bridle is also leather, glued tightly in place to discourage juvenile fingertips. Lettering and decorations are painted on; carving pine plywood is difficult and unrewarding. Bosses on the tassels are decorative brass tacks, and the tassels themselves can be thinner yarn if desired.

My horse is provided with movable wood stirrups with leather toe pockets, but these are not strictly necessary if the child's legs can reach the floor. I found also that the elaborate shaped and belled reins were frequently discarded in favor of a handful of mane.

My original intention was to carve a spirited Arab charger, but somehow he became a snub-nosed pony as I worked. The head block is 10 × 10 in. and a bit over 4 in. thick, the rump block 3 × 4 × 6 in. Carving is relatively crude and blocky, and is done with fairly large tools except for detail around the eyes and nostrils and the mane portion over the eyes. This section of mane and the roach (along the back of the neck) are unnecessary, but do help when the wool mane shows wear — as it promptly will. The rump block is simply rounded and drilled for the tail. The head can be fully formed except for the sides of the neck, which are later notched to fit the skirt boards. Sawing out the head blank is a large part of the work, especially if you do it by hand, as I did. Grain can run either in line with the head or in line with the neck, but the former is slightly preferable for easier carving and absence of end grain on the face. Skirt boards are sawed from ¾-in. white-pine plywood. Remember that the rocker surfaces must be slanted so contact with the floor occurs all across rather than just on the inner edge. Upper surfaces can either be squared or fitted to the head and rump blocks. Thus the rockers are right- and left-hand rather than exactly alike — important to remember anyway, because usually one surface of plywood is better than the other. The head and rump blocks are notched to take the skirt boards full depth, but the notches will slope up toward the bottom because the rockers or skirts flare outward to 10½ in. at the floor. Angle in the blocks should be precise for sturdiness, so must be cut carefully.

The easiest way to measure it is to set up the skirt boards so their *inside* rocker edges are 11 in. apart, then place the head and rump in position and measure the space between the bottom of the block and the skirt. If the *top* of the notch is cut to precisely this depth and the sides sloped smooth, then the depth of cut increased until the top of the notch is ¾ in. deep, the skirt boards should fit in so their lower *outer* edges are 10½ in. apart and the upper ends flush with the block.

Blocks and skirt boards are assembled with glue and long brass screws (at least 1½ in.) which can be countersunk and hidden by pine disks glued over them or a mixture of glue and pine dust used as filler. The seat boards are simply cut to fit the space atop the skirt boards and between head and rump. Either ½- or ¾-in. boards can be used, and they should be a little wider (say ¼ to ½ in.) than the space they cover. The job looks better if three pieces are used, one for the bottom, and the other two lining the rump and head blocks. Upper edges are carved half-round to a ½-in. cross-section, and the roundness carried into a groove at each side, achieving about a three-quarter–round cylinder. This can be carved into a rope molding and colored or gilded. Seat parts are held with finishing nails, which are easier to hide than screws. There is also a stretcher between the skirt boards at the front, and one at rear as well if you like. The stretcher also has rope moldings at top and bottom, plus a center emblem simulating the martingale brass that a harness horse wears. The stretcher is ¾-in. white pine, and mine had a central heart with Gothic initial and date.

Lettering along the bottom, done with a brush pen and India ink, is a rebus of the old English quatrain:

Ride a cock horse to Banbury Cross,
To see a fine lady on a white horse;
Rings on her fingers, bells on her toes—
She shall have music wherever she goes.

Figures are "illuminated" or tinted in color, or provided with tinted background. The quatrain, by the way, is said to refer to Lady Godiva's ride in Coventry. Banbury Cross, at Banbury, was destroyed during Cromwell's time, rebuilt later and damaged during World War I because the German eagle was shown among the arms of the royal family carved on its sides. This cross is perpetuated in so-called "hot cross buns," called Banbury buns

in England. A cock horse was a spare horse stabled at the foot of a hill in the coaching days; it was added to those pulling a coach to help over the hill, then stabled on the other side. Here again the phrase is retained to describe the wooden horse head on a wheeled stick that English kids once rode. I pictured the latter, of course. (By the way, be sure to paint the final horse in the rebus white—or precede it with the word "white.")

The ears can be made from any leather available, although it should be about ⅛ in. thick at least to provide a little perkiness. Curl the bottom into a tight roll and bind it with thread, then glue it into a hole in the head. The tail and mane are of two-tone wool yarn (brown and beige) of variable

Hobby-horse head is the key to its appeal, so eyes should be large and contours well-rounded. Here the bit ring has been applied, but bridle, reins, and wool tail and mane are still missing. Note elaborate Banbury Cross.

Give us our daily bread this day

OFFSET
or BOTTOMING
TOOL SHAPE

OUTLINE LETTERS with
VEINER, THEN SET IN on
UNDER EDGE of VEINER CUT

BREADBOARD - MAPLE or WALNUT

LETTERS
HERE

VARY in LENGTH or
DESIGN to FIT SPACE

UNDERSIDE RELIEVED

HOBBY HORSE - MAHOGANY & PINE
(¼ SIZE)

ROLLED LEATHER
for SAFETY

ANGLE
IRON

STIRRUP

MAHOGANY

BIND YARN STRANDS
BEFORE GLUING IN

ROPE MOLDING

LEATHER REINS
& BRIDLE

COUNTERSINK
& MASK SCREWS

¾" PLYWOOD

BRACE

on her ⚬⚬⚬ , ▒▒ , she shall have ♪♫ wherever she goes

Ride a 🐴

REBUS PATTERN
for OPPOSITE SIDE →

to Banbury ✝ , ∐ c a fine 🧙 on a 🐴

thickness and fairly heavy weight. Lengths of this are bound at one end with thread, then the resulting tail is glued into a hole and trimmed as desired. The mane is lengths of yarn sewn to a leather strip in the middle, the strip being tacked to the head in turn. The rein is leather, scalloped and with little spherical bells sewed on, and is fastened to rings at the "bit." The rings are available at hardware stores—the kind that have a knob-and-screw head and are intended for opening small drawers.

Before these finishing touches, however, make sure the rockers contact the floor solidly, then chamfer their edges slightly. Upper portions, where the edge is visible, can be covered with the glue-on wood strip, obtainable in rolls 1 in. wide. Trimmings of the panoply can be colored as desired, as well as the seat, eyeballs painted dark brown, inner nostrils darkened, and the entire horse given several coats of good hard varnish. I prefer eggshell, but gloss varnishes are sturdier. Then brace yourself for the battering the children will take falling off initially, then the greater battering the horse gets when it becomes a dragged-around and made-to-sleep-and-eat household pet.

❋ Antique Breadboard

Maple or Walnut, Prayer or Word

About 30 years ago, I saw a maple bread-board like this hanging in an old Vermont kitchen. It turned out to be a *real* antique—over 100 years old—so I made a rubbing of the lettering and a sketch of the edge cross-section (left), and duplicated it for my wife and sisters. In due course, I made others for my children. Two or three years ago, when one brother-in-law cleaned out the family farm in Indiana, he found a similar breadboard in walnut, but somewhat thinner and carved economically with just the word "Bread" (photo on next page). When I showed this to a friend from Buffalo, he laughed and brought from his kitchen a board like the Indiana one—but this one came from his ancestral home in Nova Scotia! All of which indicates that good designs do get around, even if the copyist sometimes is too lazy or too unskilled to copy the entire idea precisely.

Note that the Vermont board, as well as its counterparts, have exactly the same letter forms in the word "bread." What's more, all three are bastardized Gothic, indicating that they are themselves all copies of copies of a remote original. Indeed, the lettering varied so much in the board I made the rubbing from that I found it necessary to "restore" the shapes so the same letter had the same shape each time it appeared.

This board is a good practice project in that it demands care and attention and ability to follow an outline under changing conditions of grain, ability to produce a fairly level and constant-depth "ground"—and delivers a utilitarian object at the end. The original was a trifle over 12 in. in diameter, but this can be altered somewhat by varying word and letter spacing and closing or opening up the gap between ends of the phrase with more wheat, or just a dot or a diamond. Also, lettering size can readily be changed to fill a larger-diameter board; just be sure you draw all the letters out and cast a good eye over the result before you begin to carve!

An excellent element of this design is that the lettering is on a bevel, so it is protected

12-in. breadboard of rock maple with deep-carved Gothic lettering on beveled edge.

by the top and the rim and also sheds crumbs easily. I prefer maple—and rock maple at that—for the blank because of its hardness and denseness and clean color, but you may want the greater figure of walnut or butternut, or the really tricky effect of birdseye maple. Just rock maple is trouble enough for me—and I've made six or seven of these.

The blank is turned on a lathe, including the grooves above and below the lettering, so the primary job is just to cut the wood away around the letters to the level of the grooves—a very convenient guide. I also have the latheman turn the bottom of the board to give clearance at the outer edge as well as in the middle and thus reduce scratching potential on a tabletop. Lettering is put in a band 1⅜ in. wide and ⅛ to 3/16 in. deep.

Begin by outlining the letters of one word with a very sharp veiner. With a larger gouge, cut away the waste wood between words. Then outline each letter by setting in with a small firmer (preferably about 3/16 in. or ⅛ in. wide) and small gouges of suitable shapes. Do not attempt to outline to full

Two versions of the same 100-year-old idea, rock maple carved all around at *RIGHT,* walnut with just one carved word and a wheat stem at *LEFT.* Don't mind the grin. Recently, in Oberammergau, I saw the same boards except that the lettering faced outward and was in German, of course. Some were flat and/or octagonal in walnut or maple.

depth the first time; take it in at least two steps. The firmer or other tool is placed, as in the sketch, along the *inner* edge of the veiner groove near the letter, and it is driven by a light mallet. (You'll bruise your hand if you try to do this by hand force alone.) Cut away the waste wood around and within the letters with a small flat gouge. The ground can be flattened with a small flat gouge, firmer, or double-bent firmer (called a "grounding tool"—see sketch). Don't make the ground too smooth; it is better somewhat rough so it contrasts with the smooth upper surface (we hope) of the letters themselves. Also, do not make the letters too precise or the board will look as if it were machine-made— or plastic. It should have an antique flavor, because who slices bread anymore?

Be very careful as you work around the board. Grain direction is constantly changing, as you'll discover. If you break off a part of a letter, glue it in immediately with a good waterproof glue and lay off that letter until the glue dries. Slight splintering or roughness on the top of a letter is easily taken care of later by just shaving the top of the letter down a little; that's the beauty of carving the lettering deep. When the lettering is finished, clean up the sides of the lettering with the small firmer and gouges, making sure chips are removed where letter meets ground. If you prefer, a dental drill or hand grinder with a small cylindrical grinding wheel can be used at this point, but they tend to tear and blur outlines. A ball cutter in a dental drill will, however, make interesting patterns on the ground, if you want to go over the whole job later and extend those patterns by hand up to the bases of the letters.

I finish these boards in a rather unusual way—with mineral oil. Linseed or vegetable oil will have, or will develop, an odor and taste and affect whatever is cut on the board. Also, they tend to oxidize and darken. Mineral oil gives a good, water-resistant finish which is not ruined by knife cuts on the working surface. Of course, if the board is to be merely a wall decoration recalling a former era, then varnish it or wax it as you will—but I warn you that someone will eventually ruin such a finish for you by using the board. One friend, more pragmatic than religious, suggested that I replace the word "bread" with "cheese"—but we still have home-baked bread and slice it thick!

✳ Fun with a Coat of Arms

Plaque, Mailbox, Statuette

Coats of arms are a dime a dozen these days, so you should have at least one in your family. They make up into impressive plaques to hang in the hall, besides being challenging things to carve. I had a piece of well-seasoned mahogany 9½ × 13 and an inch thick, so I did mine. My original coat of arms is German, so relatively simple, a shield halved diagonally, the upper right half gold, the lower left black with a gold arrow. Above it is the crest—a gold lion's head with extended tongue. Students of heraldry add a helmet over the shield and some decorative vegetation at the sides.

As a project, it is a straightforward low-relief job, done with ⅛- and ½-in. firmers and equivalent gouges flat and curved, with a little knife work on the helmet and lion's head. The black portion of the shield is grooved vertically with a veiner to provide a texture behind the arrow. In this case, I also applied green highlights to the foliage, silver to the helmet, and gilt paste to the arrow, upper quarter of the shield and the lion. Colors were essentially pigment in oil, and rubbing them down with a soft cloth left

some color and an antique effect. The lion's tongue, however, is a good, solid red. After tinting, the entire plaque was flat-varnished and waxed. It is necessary, incidentally, to be careful in varnishing over the gilt and silver because the varnish tends to pick up the pigment and spread it. It is best to varnish other areas, then do the metallic areas last and by patting rather than stroking.

Later on, I decided to end my problems with rainy-day mail and designed a mailbox in black walnut, using the crest again. I had a length of ½-in. wood, barely enough for the exposed portions of the box, so it has a back and bottom of ¾-in. white pine and the carving, rather than being made solid, is partially appliquéd. This is a common professional technique when a limited area of a plaque or other piece is elevated above the surface. It saves wood and time, and simplifies the retention of a flat surface for the body of the work. In this case, it avoided the purchase of a 1-in. walnut board, still gave me a

Family crest is a lion's head with pendant tongue, and coat of arms a shield, half black, half gold, with a gold arrow in the black *(RIGHT)*. Mantling and helmet are decorations. I reproduced it in 1 × 9½ × 13-in. mahogany, routing the background to ½ in., so the shield is ¼ in. thick, the lion's head and helmet ½ in.—almost in-the-round. Foliage and scroll are carved about ⅛ in. deep in background. Mailbox *(BELOW)*, in ½-in. walnut, has crest, shield, and helmet portions appliquéd, foliage cut into surface. Box has 8 × 16-in. top, is 8 × 15 in. outside and 5 × 14 × 3 to 6½ in. inside, so can handle largest magazines. Back and bottom are ¾-in. white pine, and the box is bolted to the wall in back.

shield ¼ in. above the surface, and a helmet and lion's head ½ in. above. Blanks for these portions (the helmet and shield as one piece) were cut out and glued with plastic glue before carving. The foliage trim around the coat of arms is carved into the lid itself and about ⅛ in. deep, sloping up to the surface.

On the front of the box, which is narrow and long in this design, is a flat oval with my name incised (V-grooves) Old English lettering. On one end is an open jackknife and on the other a flat gouge. Along exposed edges and corners is carved a rope molding with a veiner groove ⅛ in. inside it to set it off. Surfaces inside this groove are textured with a flat gouge to give a scalloped effect. I find the rope molding is most easily done with a knife because of the curving surface. (If a three-quarter round surface is created on the edge of the board and the first curve of the rope molding drawn in at about 30 degrees from the axis of the rope, successive lines can be drawn quite easily, gauged by a strip of ½-in. paper wrapped around, as sketched.) Note that the molding is on the front of the box body, and only on the bottom of the sides, because the box is assembled without mitering. I used sections of ½-in. aluminum angle in the inside corners, to

Lion 2 ft. tall fits into a triangular walnut section, 11 in. wide and 8½ in. at its deepest. To fit into the triangle, lion's back is twisted so hind feet can straddle shield and tail carried around to right and up into blank area between right hind leg and belly. He varies coat of arms somewhat in that tongue is not protruding and shield is elongated. Paper templates aided in shaping head and forepaw on shield.

stiffen the box, avoid screws or nails from the outside, and to combat warpage. There are also two strips of the angle inside the lid top to prevent it from warping, as well as a piano hinge its full length to combat lengthwise warpage. (This kind of angle, if not available at your lumberyard or hardware store, can be gotten at a shop that makes displays or at a maker of aluminum windows.) Finish is marine gloss varnish; nothing else will stand the wind, rain, sleet, and icicles that this box must.

Postmen have been quite complimentary and found the box adequate for my mail, even allowing for today's junk. A friend from Buffalo liked it so well he has duplicated it in ¾-in. mahogany, but his is under cover so the bracing isn't necessary. He's Scottish, so his end designs are thistles; and not much of a carver, so his coat of arms, which includes dogs supporting the shield, is largely scroll-saw work, appliquéd.

While we're talking about mailboxes, let me point out that this is a whole field for development. Carved wooden mailboxes individualized for the user: a book for the student or professor, a toolbox for the mechanic, a TV or radio for the repairman or ham, a pack for the hiker or climber, even a miniature mailbag. The owner's profession, name, or hobby will suggest other ideas, either for shape or decoration.

Another variation of the coat of arms is the lion, 24 in. tall, who guards my chair by the fireplace. A friend had given me a well-dried quarter-section of a walnut tree trunk from my home state of Indiana. I stared at it for a year, rejecting such ideas an an elongated cat, a nude, and the usual other figures. Then the triangular shape of the piece suggested a lion's head. I carved it with only the vaguest notion of what the lower part of the figure would be, and found of course that the triangular section which made such a good nose would also require back feet that were pigeon-toed or splay-footed—there just wasn't any wood where the paws would normally project. I ended by curving his back and having the hind feet at either side of a shield on one side, with the tail curving up on the other and the right forepaw curving around to support the top of the shield, which makes carving of the legs unnecessary on the left side. He was a fairly lengthy project, and walnut is hard wood, but he has been a very satisfactory household pet, we all pat him.

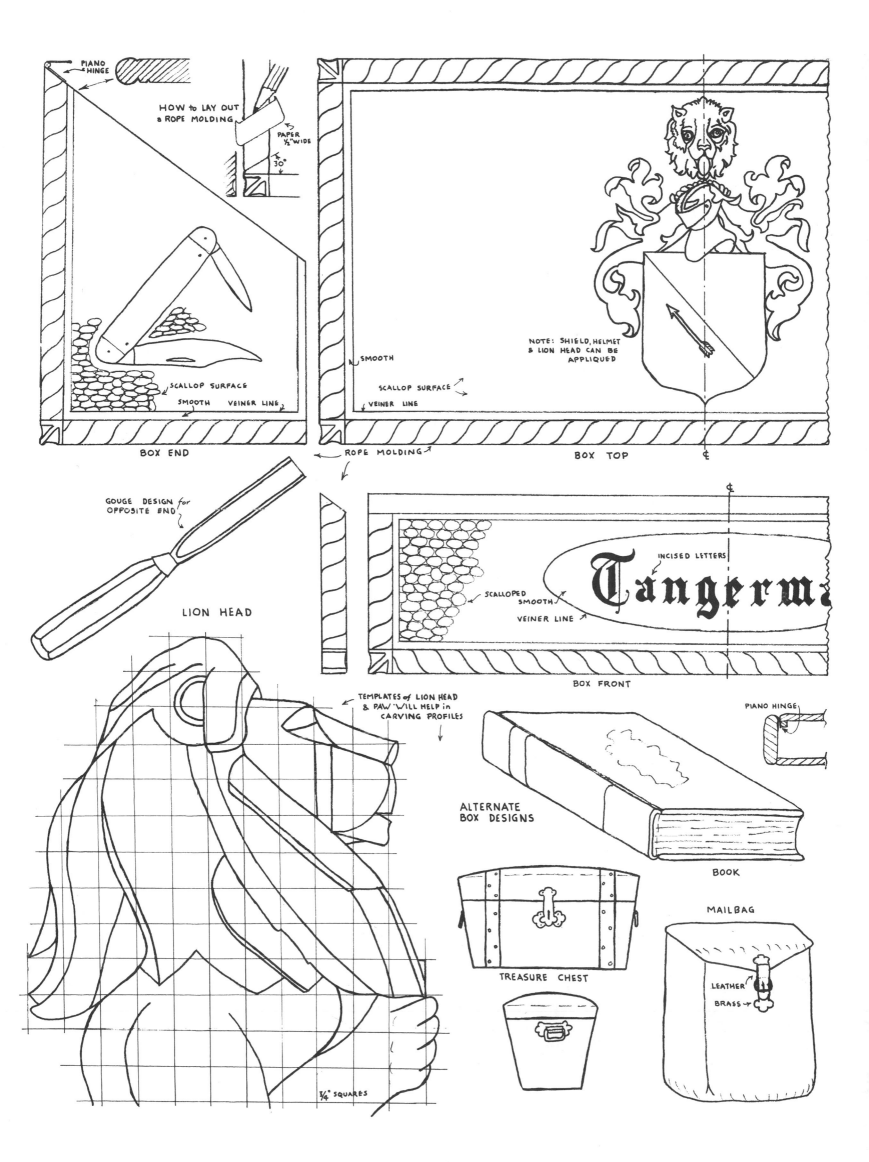

PIANO HINGE

HOW to LAY OUT a ROPE MOLDING

PAPER ⅛" WIDE

30°

SCALLOP SURFACE

SMOOTH   VEINER LINE

BOX END

SMOOTH

SCALLOP SURFACE

VEINER LINE

ROPE MOLDING

BOX TOP

NOTE: SHIELD, HELMET & LION HEAD CAN BE APPLIQUED

GOUGE DESIGN for OPPOSITE END

LION HEAD

INCISED LETTERS

Tangerma

SCALLOPED

SMOOTH

VEINER LINE

BOX FRONT

TEMPLATES of LION HEAD & PAW WILL HELP in CARVING PROFILES

PIANO HINGE

ALTERNATE BOX DESIGNS

BOOK

MAILBAG

TREASURE CHEST

LEATHER

BRASS

¾" SQUARES

✳ Humpty-Dumpty Rocker

A Fairy Tale in Wood

A fortunate visit to the mill at our local lumberyard some years back uncovered several 1-in. white-pine boards almost 14 in. wide, clear and unwarped. The cut pieces were cheap, so this rocking chair was the result. White pine will do the job, although maple might be sturdier and more attractive. Wider sections can be glued up from narrower boards, of course, because of good support.

The back is carved in low relief to be Humpty Dumpty before the fall, with spindly arms forming the chair arms and supported by cocked-up legs. The rockers are solid and also carved in low relief, showing Humpty Dumpty after the crash, with the king's horses and king's men standing helplessly around. The egg white forms a pool that makes the bottom of the runner.

If boards of sufficient width are not available, narrower ones can be assembled with glue and braces in back and under the seat. Rockers can be ¾-in. plywood, but some difficulty will be experienced in carving it with even, very shallow V-grooved lines, and edges should be covered with wood ribbon.

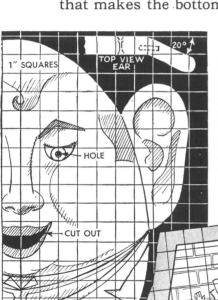

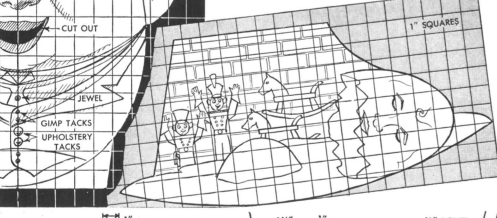

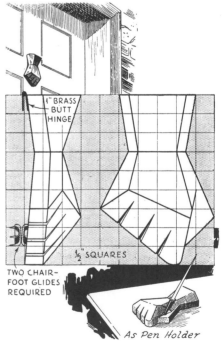

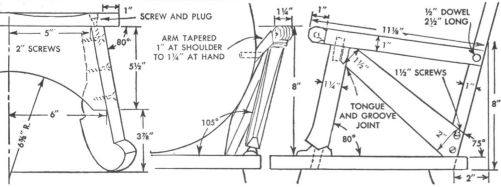

128

Carving on the seat back should not be deeper than ⅛ in. so it causes no discomfort to the occupant. Outlining is done with a veiner, followed by shallow modeling with a flat gouge and firmer. Holes are drilled through for eye pupils and the mouth is also cut out to shape; you'll be surprised at the fun they'll provide. I used gimp tacks for vest buttons, upholstery tacks for coat buttons, and set a small "jewel" in the tie for a stick-pin. Ears are separate pieces, set forward at an angle of 20 to 30 degrees and held there with dowels and glue, then carved on the front and rounded to avoid sharp edges.

Rockers are cut to shape and carved with the veiner alone—no modeling. The front brace is made in the form of an arch, with stone outlines carved and a name and date in the keystone. The seat (12 × 13½ in., tapering to 11 in. at the back) is also hollowed out for more comfortable sitting.

The back is attached to the seat with dowels, glue, and screws, the lower end of the back being beveled so the back tilts about 15 degrees back of the perpendicular. Rockers and brace are similarly assembled to the seat. Put the rockers on first, setting them by beveling their tops so their front tips are separated about 12 in. and the rear tips about 8¾ in. This "toe out" keeps the chair from "walking" across the floor and from tipping easily. The brace is then cut to fit and fastened in place, after which the rocker bottoms are shaped to bear flat on the floor. Screws are set in countersunk holes hidden by dowel plugs.

The three parts of each arm are whittled and assembled to fit, with flared trouser cuff, "crease," and a separate shoe held by the foot dowel. Small fists are whittled on the arm ends. The upper leg section is also whittled with rounded sides and is set in with a tongue-and-groove joint at the knee. Note that the legs tilt outward about 15 degrees on a side, and the lower leg also tilts backward about 10, so due care must be taken in drilling for dowels. (It is easier to glue the shoes to the seat, then drill the angled hole through both, to avoid splitting the shoe.)

The black busbies of the soldiers, and their white gloves, as well as Humpty's black shoes and candy-striped shirt, are painted solid color. Other coloring is pigment thinned with linseed and turpentine, brushed on, then wiped down so only a suggestion of color remains.

❋ Carved Fist

A Novel Knocker

Cast-brass mailed-fist knockers date far back in Europe, but here is a modern, stylized version in wood. It is 3 × 4½ in., in wood 1½ in. thick—choose the wood to suit yourself. The finished fist can be either a knocker, or, with felt on the back and a hole between thumb and index finger, a desk-pen holder.

Lay out and saw the blank as sketched at left. The back face (for the knocker) is tapered from both ends to the line of the wrist, so the latter is ¼ in. below the back surface (side view). Form the fist by tapering from the knuckle line to the middle joints of the fingers until the lower edge is only ½ in. thick, and from the knuckle line back toward the wrist until wrist thickness is only ¾ in. Form the thumb by cutting straight across at the edge of the index finger and notching out so the thumb extends as a ½-in. shelf. Chamfer the sides of the wrist as indicated, and cut in equally spaced notches to indicate the fingers.

Put a 1-in. brass butt hinge at the top and drive in a chair-foot glide at the bottom so it strikes a similar one spotted on the door.

The Humpty Dumpty rocker was first described in *Popular Mechanics*, January 1945, the knocking fist in *Popular Science Monthly*, November 1935. Both articles are extracted here with permission. The photo *BELOW* by Dick De Marsico was published in the now-defunct *New York World-Telegram* in late 1945, showed a member of the "Salvage Program for Men" painting a non-carved copy of my rocker. Photo courtesy Lee B. Wood, executive editor.

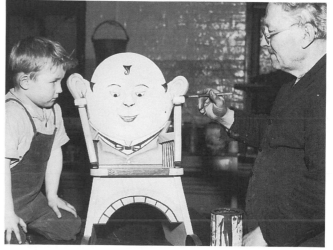

✳ Pre-Columbian Trim Motifs

Trophy-room Furniture in Low Relief

Enthusiastic souvenir buying in Guatemala led us to a refurnished combination guest, sewing, and display room. It is really a stage set, because I made the furniture of ¾-in. white-pine plywood trimmed with 1 × 2-in. pine strips, and two pieces of "furniture" are assembled by nailing to the wall. But motifs are pre-Columbian Maya and Aztec.

The principal piece is the wall cabinet, 53 in. wide by 66 in. high (left). Twin doors (each 12 × 19 in.) on top hide a makeup mirror and light and are flanked by open display areas on each side 11 in. wide. The door (14 × 24 in.) just below drops down to become a tabletop for the sewing machine stored inside. Central doors in the lower portion swing out as spool racks for thread and exposed shelves, knee space, and the control. They are flanked in turn by three drawers on a side, about 6 × 11 in. The tabletop, 29 in. above the floor, projects 17 in. from the wall, the upper portion only 11 in.

While all trim bands are carved, some have simple basket-weave patterns or a "snakeskin" motif (verticals) to make the whole less "busy." All carving is about ⅛ in. deep and background was scalloped with a ⅛-in. flat gouge. All surfaces were stained dark brown, almost black, to resemble Spanish oak, varnished and waxed. Other pieces in the room include a small coffee table (next page), a headbox between the beds (next page, lower left), and a folding X-shaped luggage rack, 19 × 25 × 21 in high.

Cabinet (ABOVE) has 63 ft. of low-relief carving in 1 × 2-in. strip, plus four feet carved on exposed faces and in-the-round snake heads (sketch on page 103) at outer ends of tabletop. Painted Maya panels decorate lower doors, painted masks (page 63) the flanking drawers (BELOW RIGHT). Natural-finished masks of an Indian chief and of the conqueror, Don Alvarado, are door pulls (BELOW). Note snake motif at sides and more elaborate ones on horizontal bands. Bottom band is heads. Motifs are readily available in books on pre-Columbian design, and can be adapted from wall paintings or pottery as desired.

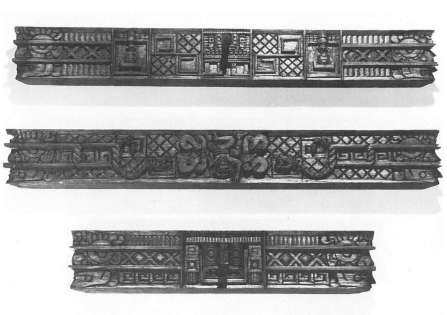

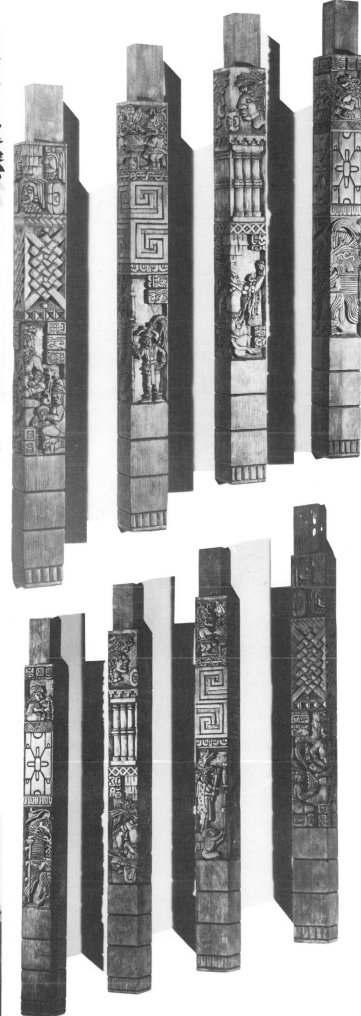

Carved coffee table has leather insert on top, is $13\frac{1}{2} \times 20 \times 22$ in. high. Top band incorporates unusual corner faces from Tulum, Quintana Roo, and band motifs from Uxmal, Yucatan. Each band and each leg is different. Wide motifs on legs *(RIGHT)* also go around the exposed corner. Upside-down or "bee" god, also from Tulum, is shown as center element on two faces of skirt *(ABOVE)*, rain god from Kabah on two others. Projecting nose of rain god requires frequent repair. Finish is dark stain, varnish, and wax. Some designs are from books on Mexican design.

Corner-box cabinet, $33 \times 33 \times 29\frac{1}{2}$ in. high, provides head for beds. Top is piano-hinged at middle for storage of pillows, blankets, etc. Box is built-in but has its own floor supported by a $4 \times 4 \times 6$-in. carved corner post at outer corner. 1×2-in. strip trims the $\frac{3}{4}$-in. plywood top, has low-relief Maya and Aztec motifs.

✳ Pierced or Openwork Carving

Relief—with No Background

Background is not always essential in a panel. Far Eastern carvers have removed parts or all of it in carvings of wood, ivory, and stone to create a delicate tracery that looks unbelievably fragile and usually is not. Sometimes the removal of background is for purely aesthetic reasons; sometimes it is for pragmatic ones. A carving may be designed to function as a screen, passing light, air, and sound, but obscuring sight. Or the piercing may help to attain the appearance of greater depth, to provide a background of contrasting texture or color or brightness, or simply to approach greater verisimilitude. Thus pierced carving has been common in the blades of ladies' fans and combs, in ivory carvings generally, in trivets, screens for window openings, and the like.

One interesting and unusual application of the technique is in the shadow puppets of China, Malaysia, and Indonesia. These are two-dimensional figures of parchment or hide, supported and operated by sections of horn, tinted in colors, and shown behind a screen with light passing through them.

The details of their faces and costumes are created by piercing holes and lines through the material. Some may be as large as 3 ft. tall and very fragile in appearance; others may be only 6 in. tall, painted black, and be designed for use as wall silhouettes. Cutouts are made entirely with carving chisels and mallets on a table like a chopping block. Similar work is done in shell and bone (pages 160 and 161). Balinese bone carving is a particularly good example.

There is no essential difference in design between a pierced carving and a solid one. Many panel carvings have background areas that are relatively thin anyway. The principal need is to avoid, insofar as possible, unsupported carved elements in crucial areas. Most Indian work is done within a sturdy frame for this reason, but the screen panel pictured here from Bali, which has openwork to the edges, was actually damaged in two areas when I bought it.

In most cases, it is easiest to cut through the panel after rough carving of the design is done, but before the finishing. In some

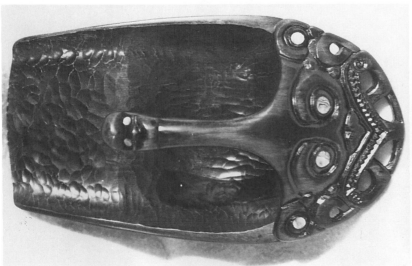

LEFT—Balinese railing of Java teak combines openwork birds and flowers with low-relief medallion of a Hindu god. LEFT BELOW—Handle of 10-in. Maori bailing scoop has 6-hole openwork pattern and four paua-shell inserts at base. BELOW— 12-in. Indian screen, all openwork.

instances—as in the magazine-cover panel I did—the openings are large enough so that they actually make finish-carving and shaping easier, because you can cut from both front and back. I have watched Balinese carvers working on extremely fine pierced carvings. The secrets seem to be two; first that a 3-dimensional carving is supported on the knees so it is not subjected to shock, and second that they use very small tools and light mallets and nibble at the cutting. They seem not to be concerned about the time involved. One recent design of Ida Bagus Tilem, the master carver, is a tabletop in teak about 1 in. thick and in sizes up to about 4 ft. square. This is an ingenious combination of leaves and flowers arranged so a large flat flower is at the center of each side and at the center of the table—where plates would be placed—with smaller flowers for similar solid support under the teacup and salad-plate locations. Thus the tabletop can be used without a covering glass if the buyer so desires.

RIGHT—1-ft. epergne, turned and carved in Switzerland, has a separate base housing a music box. A shallow central pattern of grape leaves and grapes is surrounded by a 4-part pattern of grape leaves separated by a stem with a symbolic 6-grape cluster. *RIGHT BELOW*—10-in. shesham-wood disk by Sara of India has a top pattern of pierced-work leaves and vines surrounding a central circle and spaced around large lobed-leaf outlines. Under the leaves and central circle is a hex pattern like an enlarged honeycomb, probably done from the back. *FAR RIGHT*—Elaborate 7 × 19-in. panel of the goddess Siva made in Bali. See also openwork lampbase (page 46) and fisherman (page 97) for other examples.

BELOW—Ceremonial neck yoke for a span of oxen has surface designs of chip carving with openwork background. Made in Portugal in 1935. *BOTTOM RIGHT*—High-perspective pierced carving depicts the early method of cutting screw threads on metal with a "Fox" chaser. Relatively large pierced areas permitted me to do some of the work from the rear, give greater depth and reality to the carving, which was photographed in color against a fluted-paper background for a magazine-cover illustration.

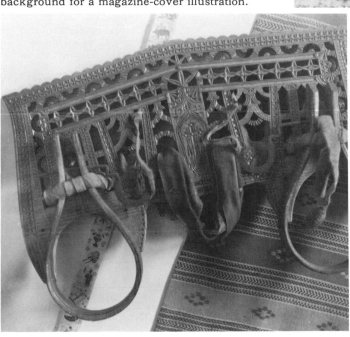

✳ Appliqués and Assemblies

A Background Can Emphasize

Contrast in color, texture, or material can be achieved by appliquéing a carving to a background. It is also possible to cut time and cost by gluing silhouette blocks on a background of the same wood, then carving the whole (page 125), and to assemble carved elements on a background or base. A casein glue, at full strength or thinned 50-50 with water, will do the job if the finished carving is to be displayed inside, but 2-element plastic cements are safer for assemblies to be exposed to the weather. Screws through the backboard, or from the front, countersunk and covered with cross-grain dowel plugs glued in, are also suitable, and allow for differential expansion of carving and background. Shown here are a few examples of appliqués and assemblies; others are shown elsewhere in this book.

ABOVE—Rainbow trout of basswood, tinted, appliquéd on a 5½-in. disk of mahogany. The body, 6 in. overall, is cross-grain to get a pattern through the body, so lips are fragile. The projecting ventral fin is carved separately and glued in a hole. A real trout fly is caught in the lip and the leader carried through the fork in the tail to the back. The fish is about 6 in. long, carved in the round.

"Just Passing Through" *(FAR LEFT)* and "Emerging" are complementary assemblies of mahogany elements mounted on 14 × 31-in. backgrounds of rough pine floorboards 150 years or more old. Each is a vertical slice through an imaginary 24-in. female nude, although the rear view is admittedly somewhat callipygian. The head-basket segment in each case is hollowed and holds several colored-glass marbles. By the author.

Sloop (TOP) is an assembly of four pieces on a 4 × 6½-in. mahogany plaque. Sails are white pine, shaped and hollowed. The hull is maple above the waterline, mahogany below. Contrast in woods provides contrast in color and texture, with flat varnish.

When my son was two years old (1933), I carved a high-relief head as a Christmas present for my father *(TOP, CENTER).* My son carved a matching head of his daughter at two *(TOP, RIGHT)* as a Christmas present for me. The original, carved in white pine and finished with linseed, has since oxidized to a brown almost as dark as the walnut background; the maple head of my granddaughter, varnish-finished, after 14 years, is still its original color. Heads are held by screws from the back and are set off in an oval surrounded by a gouge-scalloped ground.

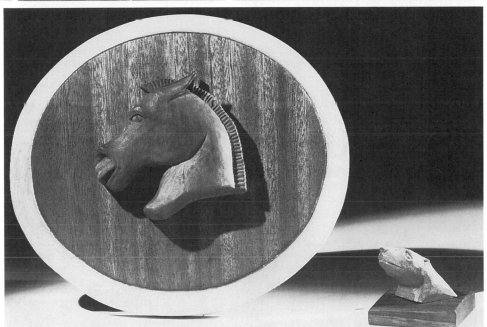

Horse head, in mahogany and about 4 in. long, is mounted on mahogany veneer which is in turn glued to a chamfered oval of white pine (shown before staining). The polar-bear head, also in mahogany, was mounted on a walnut base for a desk ornament for an Arctic explorer. Both were hasty carvings, for the effect.

Neandertal habitat, a display for a grade-school exhibit by the author, combines carved figures, tinted, of a man, woman, child, and mammoth head with other elements like stone, twigs, and sponge. A typed legend is glued to the front of the base, explaining that Neandertal man already knew how to cut saw teeth on his stone ax.

✳ Improvisations

You Carve What You See

African carvers in the old days insisted that they could not carve a block of fine wood until they "saw" both the object to be carved and the "soul" of the owner-to-be in it. That idea seems to have died with the old men, judging by today's repetitive output, and was never very common in the Western world because so many of our carvers and sculptors start with dressed lumber. I see occasional examples here and there, usually done by a nonprofessional in wood found on or near his own property.

Mounting a bird on, or cutting a face into, a piece of driftwood is *not* the same thing, for in this case the rough wood is only a frame or setting for the carving. The basic shape of the wood itself must be involved. Occasionally, professionals produce such a piece, as did Lawrence Tenney Stevens in his "Tree of Life" for the New York World's Fair of 1939. Sixty feet high, it cost the life of a Connecticut elm planted by Hessian prisoners in 1781, but the Dutch elm disease probably would have gotten it anyway—or a new thruway. An entire outdoor chess set in a Stuttgart park is made from selected tree sections and butts about 2 ft. high.

Odd-shaped pieces of wood, with very little touching up, will sometimes produce very interesting sculptures; in other cases—like the walnut gnome—the wood provides merely an unusual shape from which you must dig the figure. The hands and bowl of the miner in the "bug tree" (see page 139) were largely complete (at least the bowl was) in the original apple burl. "Protest" (next article) required only shaping of the hand from available wood; the head I added could have been carved from the original branch if I had thought faster when I started to take the tree down. My son-in-law did better than I when the wind blew the top out of a cedar; he left enough of the branches to make forelegs for the bear (page 138).

Demon grotesqueries carved from hollow tree trunks at compound of Ida Bagus Tilem, master carver of Mas, Bali.

(This, by the way, starts out at top as a totem pole, finishes as an obelisk with surface carving.)

A design is not always immediately evident. The gnome resulted from a winter of staring at a piece of walnut "firewood" brought from Ohio on which the sawyer had left a length of half branch that ran almost at right angles; the carving utilizes the full height of the available piece. This is also true of the 4-way–head coffee table made from the butt of the same tree, but its potential was immediately evident. So was the windswept figure from driftwood, and most of the pieces made from cypress knees. These pieces were brought to me by friends returning from Florida who themselves "saw" in each piece a potential carving. One artist brought me a piece with the remark that she'd be interested in which of the two potential figures she saw in it I'd carve; the Madonna and Child could also have been a nude. In contrast, a 5-ft. length of walnut log I found in Ohio is now a nude torso chained to a tree—there was less choice in that case.

Grain and knots or other distortions of the wood will often provide ideas, just as the basic silhouette does. Thus Balinese carvers have utilized the distortions of dead hollow tree trunks in three interesting pieces reminiscent of Arthur Rackham's drawings. The principal artist and owner of this particular "factory" works almost exclusively in "improvisations," by the way; he no longer enjoys routine carving.

There are no rules and no patterns for pieces like these; they are there if you are lucky to have the wood and the idea come together. But you won't find improvisations —or "inspirations" if you prefer—if you don't keep an inner eye open. If you are designing as you go, or if you have salvaged stumps or odd pieces, keep them visible. If you put them away, you may miss an inspiration. It is, by the way, a good idea to keep visible *any* carving on which you are working. Some disproportion, or some knotty problem, may suddenly solve itself as you look during noncarving hours. If you then drop whatever else you're doing to put into the wood what you have in your mind's eye, that's a hazard of being creative. I recently carved a cypress knee that I'd stared at for ten years.

Cypress-knee improvisations include Rapunzel *(RIGHT),* centaur and oread *(CENTER RIGHT),* Madonna and Child *(FAR RIGHT),* and frog, wading bird, and lion *(BELOW, RIGHT,* from scraps). Rapunzel herself was white pine against gray bark, but exposure turned her dark gray, while the cypress, debarked, is light yellow. The fisherman below, by a Madeiran, is carved from cedar which looks like a crag.

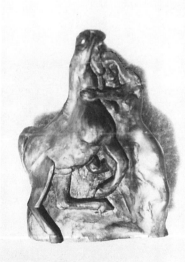

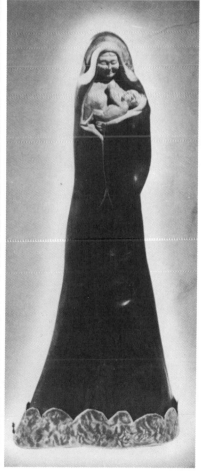

✳ More Improvisations

RIGHT—Sioux head carved by a Jaliscan Indian in Mexico from a deformed tree section *(BELOW)*.

FAR RIGHT—Cedar totem pole, with owl atop a bear carrying a trout in his mouth and seated one-sidedly on a turtle. Lower figures in relief include woodchucks, rabbit, squirrel, chipmunk, skunk, deer, fox, raccoon, and snake, using wood surfaces and shape as far as possible. I'm the man at the bottom, appropriately.

RIGHT, BELOW—"Windswept" is a piece of driftwood in which I carved only hands and feet.

BELOW—Outdoor chess courts in Stuttgart include this one with modern pieces made from planking and another in which carved tree stumps are the pieces.

BOTTOM—Gnome and 4-way head are from walnut "firewood" rescued in Ohio. Legs of the gnome are in a half branch left by the sawyer, and the figure is about 20 in. high. The 4-way head is now the base for a glass-topped coffee table 22 in. high (so the heads can be seen from above), and again utilizes natural bulges of the wood.

138

✳ The "Bug Tree"

A Start for Polyglot Carving

Big apple trees of a former orchard once surrounded our house. From one I cut a big limb or almost fork. Ants and boring worms disregarded my tarring of the scar, which was only a foot or two above ground level, and had a field day in the butt. When I eventually cut away the affected wood, I had a niche 6 in. deep and about 10 × 30 in. Neighbors suggested a Saint Francis, but I wanted something different.

Some years earlier, I had carved from an apple burl a pair of hands holding a shell (the burl). The piece was never a success—somehow it suggested a headstone (see closeup overleaf). So I drew a miner's head and hat to the same scale, and decided I'd have a Forty-Niner panning for gold. The miner's head was carved in end grain of an apple-log section, leaving half the trunk over his head as a shed roof for the niche. There were three reasons: 1. The bark-covered shed roof, which harmonized with the tree itself. 2. The log was green, so by locating the bridge of the miner's nose at the core, any checking as the section dried would cause radial splits that would only enhance his smile. 3. I wanted to work in end grain for a large piece. Reason 2 has been amply justified; the miner now has a big "dueling scar" running from the bridge of his nose under his left eye, which at the back of the block (fortunately out of sight) becomes a ½-in. check. (However, in the drying, the periphery of the "roof" also was reduced almost 2 in., so the head must now be blocked up to fit the top of the niche.)

The back of the niche was an irregular surface which, with a little carving, could be made to look like a miner's shirt, and there were channels from insect activity and a rotted spot through which I could lead a small plastic water tube from the base up to the back of the "pan."

Meantime, the tree itself was succumbing to age, so I topped it at about 12 ft. and began to strip off the bark. Somehow, that led me to memorialize the bugs who had caused all the trouble by carving them in heroic size in low relief. I soon discovered how little I knew about bugs; I needed reference texts. Then I found how little even entymologists know about them, because the same bug was drawn differently in different texts, and the bugs that neighbor kids brought in jars, or that lit on the tree while I was working, often were not identifiable in available references. But some children's books have excellent enlarged drawings, and my schoolteacher daughter had some colored photographic enlargements. All of these made it possible for me to show 176 subjects of 170 varieties in a carved area 9½ ft. high and 3¾ ft. around at its widest. (There are nine amphibians around the base, just for a change of pace, and a cherrywood cardinal on top—incongruous because he doesn't eat bugs.

Carving was done mainly with carpenter's chisels up to 1½ in. wide and big woodturning gouges for roughing, with woodcarver's firmers and gouges up to ½ in. wide for finishing and veiner and V-tool for details and a backbent flat gouge and firmer for grounding. Background is about ½ in. deep, smoothed and stained with mahogany stain which has now weathered to a quiet brown which nevertheless sets off the carvings, which are off-white to light gray.

The finished obelisk includes a cardinal with coat-button eyes atop a melange of bugs with a miner peering from the bottom, but my artist friends seem to consider this all reasonable. I drew patterns for identification after the carving was done, by wrapping acetate sheets around the trunk and copying the carvings with an oil-ink felt pen. These drawings will provide some idea of how the "bugs" are interrelated and drawn directly on the wood "as we go" to suit surface irregularities such as knotholes, bumps, etc.

For several years now, the tree has attracted curious visitors, but these include carpenter ants and worms at the now-dead root, so the next step is to cut the tree off at the bottom, treat it to get rid of bugs and forestall root rot, then mount it on a metal plate.

FAR LEFT—The ant lion, No. 133, and the doodlebug, No. 134, will locate this closeup of a section of the carving. The spider was designed around the hammock hook, which was in the tree first. *LEFT*—Irregular line at top is the end of the first summer of carving. Designs had to be drawn the next spring to make the irregular top line not too evident. Luna moth, No. 114, near lower right edge, will locate this section on the charts.

LEFT—Another dying apple tree bore a striking resemblance to a heroic arm. With a little distortion, the hand *(BELOW)* could be carved on top. The head was added on a stub. Overall height of "Protest" is about 10 ft.

BELOW—The miner fountain in the "bug" tree has separate apple-burl hands and pan, as well as head carved in end grain and set into a shaped socket.

KEY TO THE "BUG TREE"

1. Night crawler
2. Black swallowtail butterfly
3. Tiger beetle
4. Grubworm
5. House fly
6. Underwing moth
7. Citheronia regalis moth
8. Stinkbug
9. Zebra swallowtail
10. Wasp
11. Japanese beetle
12. French bee
13. Tiger swallowtail butterfly
14. Flower grasshopper
15. Cucujo or Pyrophorus
16. Cicada nymph
17. Red admiral butterfly
18. Grasshopper (head on)
19. Yellow jacket
20. Stag beetle
21. Giant water bug
22. Horntail (Siricid)
23. Praying mantis
24. Gypsy moth
25. Carpet beetle
26. Cockroach
27. Atteva aurea moth
27a. Potato beetle larva
28. Spicebush swallowtail caterpillar
29. Beetle
30. Paper wasp eating caddis fly
31. Scorpion (arachnid)
32. Arctic skipper butterfly
33. Flour beetle
34. Gray hairstreak butterfly
35. Brantling worm
36. Katydid
37. Bluebottle fly
38. Froghopper
39. American copper butterfly
40. June beetle
41. House fly
42. Western tiger swallowtail
43. Wartwort sphinx caterpillar
44. Silver-spotted skipper
45. Damselfly
46. Earwig
47. Andrenid excavator bee
48. Beetle
49. Capricorn beetle
50. Giant swallowtail caterpillar
51. Robber fly
52. Clothes moth
53. Water strider
54. Flour beetle
55. Silverfish
56. Fly maggot larva
57. Powder-post beetle
58. Mexican bean beetle
59. Zebra swallowtail larva
60. Mayfly
61. Walking stick
62. Colorado potato beetle
63. Firefly
64. Diving dysticid beetle
65. Nut weevil
66. Lightning bug
67. Bedbug
68. Field cricket
69. Purplish copper butterfly
70. Fall webworm moth
71. Cicada

72. Prometheus moth
73. Firefly (flying)
74. Firefly larva
75. Pearly-eye butterfly
76. Hornworm (sphinx) caterpillar
77. Sphinx moth
78. Scorpion fly
79. Silverfish
80. Anglewing butterfly
81. Aphid
82. June bug
83. Sweat wasp
84. Robber fly
85. Earthworm
86. Io moth
87. Grasshopper
88. Mayfly
89. Praying mantis
90. Click beetle
91. Tsetse fly
92. Hornet
93. Cabbage butterfly larva
94. 17-year locust
95. Carpenter ant
96. Cherry fruit fly
97. Ladybug
98. Dragonfly
99. Flea
100. Monarch butterfly
101. Sowbug
102. Cottonwood dagger moth
103. Wasp
104. Silverfish
105. Psocid (bookworm)
106. Housefly
107. Grub
108. Black beetle
109. Palm weevil larva
110. Ant
111. Bedbug
112. Spring azure moth
113. Cockroach
114. Luna moth
115. Luna moth larva
116. Black pinchbug beetle
117. Black widow spider
118. Carpet beetle
119. Box beetle(?)
120. Beetle
121. Wood tick
122. Silverfish
(10 numbers omitted)
133. Ant lion
134. Doodlebug eating . . .
135. Red ant
136. Grubworm
137. Milkweed bug
138. Katydid
139. Termite (worker)
140. Termit (queen)
141. Goldsmith beetle
142. Honeybee
143. Checkerspot butterfly
144. Luna moth caterpillar
145. Grasshopper
146. Clouded locust moth
147. Ladybug
148. Inchworm
149. Millipede
150. Stag beetle (female)
151. House cricket
152. Monarch butterfly
153. Fly (unidentified)
154. Beetle (unidentified)
155. Io caterpillar
156. Clothes moth
157. Potato beetle
158. Caterpillar hunter
159. Viceroy butterfly
160. Termite (worker)

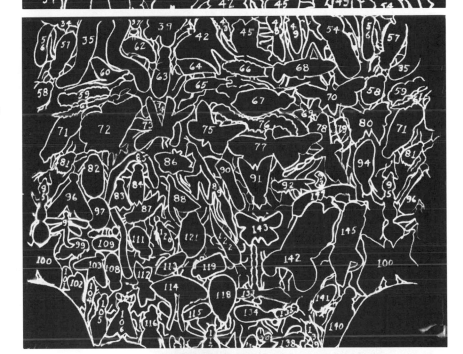

161. Brown spider (arachnid)
162. Spicebush swallowtail
163. Earwig
164. Unidentified
165. Hairstreak butterfly
166. Mosquito
167. Earthworm
168. Japanese beetle
169. Cicada (flying)
170. Colorado potato beetle
171. Anopheles mosquito
172. Click beetle
173. Stag beetle
174. Cotton-boll weevil
175. Damselfly (caught by toad)
176. Tomato hornworm
177. Cicada

AMPHIBIANS
178. Bull frog
179. Tree frog
180. Blue racer snake
181. Snapping turtle
182. Toad
183. Newt or salamander
184. Lizard
185. Garden snake
186. Box turtle

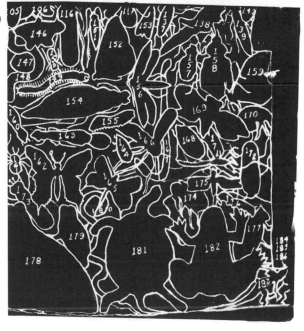

141

❋Polyglot or Montage Carving

Panels, Compound Curves, In-the-round

The "bug tree" project led me into polyglot or montage design, a sort of all-over pattern of elements of a particular class or group. It may not work for others as well as it does for me, but I have found it to be as much fun as solving a jigsaw puzzle—putting a series of odd shapes together to obtain an all-over total result. I have used this technique for surface decoration of wooden shoes, a section of tree trunk, and on candles, as well as on flat panels. A virtue is that it does not require a lot of preplanning and patterning, which are relatively impossible on an irregular surface like a shoe or a log. A pattern may look well in two dimensions, but be much less impressive or balanced in three because of disproportionate spaces between elements or differences in the amount of surface decoration or definition. Further, surface textures, such as checks and knots, may throw a rigid pattern into trouble for the carver. Perhaps some of these problems

could be overcome by shading the pattern and drawing in the detail, but I find it easy to make the design as I go, keeping just ahead of the carving. It provides variety in the work and allows use of elements that may become available after the carving is begun.

I often do the actual design right on the wood itself, and make a drawing for purposes of identification of elements only after the carving is done. This makes it possible actually to incorporate knots or other wood irregularities, as well as the figure or grain, in the design, and not to attempt to place thin delicate elements across a knot. What's more, during the actual carving, if I run into grain problems, breakage, or let the tool slip, I can usually modify the design rather than be compelled to glue in a piece of wood.

The approach to polyglot design is to select a theme—flowers, birds, fish, instruments, animals, monsters, symbols. I gather conveniently available reference books on the subject from my own or the local library. (For many of these fields, children's books are better than those for grownups because they have more pictures. Field guides will provide pictures of birds, trees, or flowers.) From them I make a rough selection; this determines whether or not I'll have enough elements for a panel or to fill whatever space I have available. I usually have at least 25 subjects, and have used more than a hundred.

Then I select a general scale for the elements, one that will make them not too small

FAILURE . . . AND SUCCESS—The 3½ × 16-in. candle at far left was carved with polyglot mathematical symbols ranging from simple arithmetic at the bottom to calculus and geometry at the top. Neither material nor design was cooperative. Wax is translucent, so V-grooves disappear in most light, and the "stickiness" of the chips makes endless cleaning necessary, so a bold, fairly deep, or strongly tinted, design is needed. Further, the symbols and geometric shapes are rigid and lack "sex appeal." A far better result was obtained in the holly stump at right, about 4 × 16 in. From a neighbor's dead bush, the piece was checked and knotty, so a progressive design of 22 dolphins was worked around the cracks, bumps, and knots. This is polyglot design in three dimensions. Finish was flat varnish and wax. Constant requests for permission to pick up the piece and look at the other faces suggested a special base. This is a plastic "lazy Susan" 10½ in. in diameter, made for kitchen cupboards, with a disk of mirror to fit the top. The piece can be rotated and also develops interesting reflections from the mirror. Cost of the stand was about $4.

to be carved easily and that will make the largest element cover 5 to 10% of the space at most. If, for example, the selected category is birds, I might decide to show the bald eagle—the American national bird—quite large, as well as the wild swan and Canada goose, both large birds anyhow. The eagle makes a good center element in a horizontal group, or a center top element in a vertical one. The swan and goose, being similar in shape, should probably face in opposite directions and be opposed in position—that is, one at each lower corner, for example. With these located, I can begin to build up my pattern, drawing other birds so they make a pleasing pattern around the three major ones. Birds in flight can be drawn so their outstretched wings are covered by parts of other birds, legs of long-legged birds like flamingos or storks can be drawn so portions of their legs are behind other birds, and so on, the object being to attain an overall pattern of bodies with wings and legs intertwined to some extent, and the open background spaces not too large. Ideally, poses can be varied and birds mingled without reference to their habitats or relative size. Thus a bird may be selected by the silhouette its picture makes, to fit in an existing space.

I do not introduce branches, nests, leaves, or other confusing background material. The important thing is to select subjects that can be carved and that have distinctive silhouettes insofar as possible. A subject like insects is difficult, because each "bug" is likely to have six legs and a pair of antennae (the alternative is the centipede and some bugs that have branching antennae), so the legs must be interwined across the spaces between insects and in some instances, in which legs are quite long, they may pass under or over several other insects. Thus I found myself, in designing the "bug" tree, alternating between a hard-shelled beetle and a winged insect, a long-legged one and several short-legged ones, and so on, to make the design work out.

A few general rules may be helpful: Do not design elements or areas into which your smallest tool will not fit. In other words, "design by tool." Tend to drop detail if possible, because it will not be very evident anyway in the finished overall pattern. Do not attempt precise scale—make the wren oversize with relationship to the eagle or the eagle will be too big or the wren so little that you'll be fighting grain size when you carve his eye and beak. Don't worry about the pose of one element with relationship to another; one can be walking and full front, the one beside it a side view seated, with no harm to the composition—unless its ultimate home is to be a museum. Do not select a series of subjects that have the same silhouette; in the absence of distinguishing color, they'll look like repetition.

Keep balance constantly in mind. The moment you cross the halfway mark, you must remember to keep glancing back at the first half to be certain that the spaces between subjects are roughly equal and equally dispersed, that the surface is not full of detail on one half and simply flat planes on the other. If you have an outstretched wing, for example, with all feathers detailed on one side, you'd better have a balancing detailed sec-

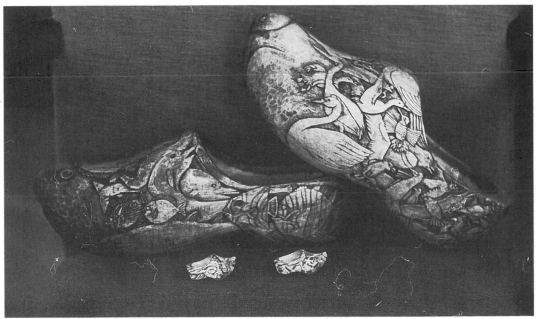

THESE DUTCH KLOMPEN came from a Curaçao hardware store; I bought them to wear. But the willow wood made penknife carving easy, so I covered one with birds and the other with tropical fish. String holes on the inner sides (to hold the pair together until sold) were incorporated into the design. Walnut-stained background and antiquing is a bit too dark for the whiteness of the willow. The miniature shoes, about 1½ in. long, carry the same designs, done under a magnifying glass. Finish is flat varnish and wax. Part of the design is sketched on page 21.

tion of about the same size on the other. If you show a great deal of detail on one element, place undetailed elements near it.

When my theme is animals, birds, or fish, I try to keep the heads free and clear. I'm perfectly willing to cross one body over another as long as this does not obscure a particular feature essential to identification. Thus the shoulder patches of a red-winged blackbird, or the crest of a cardinal, or the spots on a ladybug should be readily visible.

Keep constantly in mind that you are creating a third dimension, so make certain that the elements you want to appear nearer to the observer's eye are on top of objects farther away. Thus, when the legs of two animals cross, be sure that the near leg of the nearer animal is atop the far leg of the one farther back. In many cases like the side view of an animal, for example, you may want to place the crossing leg on an adjacent animal between the legs of the animal viewed from the side, as if they were really quite close to the same plane. I find myself changing leg overlaps in the middle of carving, getting mixed up where planes overlap.

Fragile elements that normally project, like a cat's whiskers, may be suggested by drilling tiny holes where the hair roots would be, or carving V-grooves along the muzzle.

WEARABLE WOODEN SHOES (my daughter's—also from Curaçao) were polyglot-carved with different subjects, the left a mass of flowers and the right a group of ancient musical instruments. Individual elements were based on handbook pictures, and were selected to fit spaces. String holes were worked into the design, one as the center of a flower, the other as the center hole in a mandolin. Background is under ⅛ in. deep, and toned with mahogany stain, which worked out better than the walnut on my pair. Finish is flat varnish and wax. A coat of varnish before staining reduces tendency of the stain to over-color end grain.

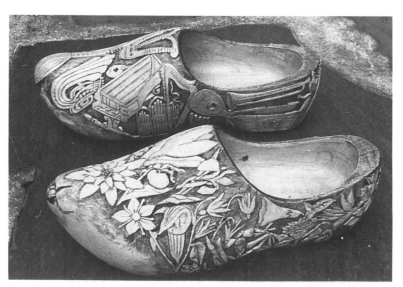

Eyeballs, which are really ovate convex surfaces, look "blind" if carved that way, even if eyelids are carved around them. So a tapered circular hole can be carved, or even a hole drilled, for the pupil. Scales can be suggested by crossed lines in areas which would be in shadow on the actual fish or dragon, leaving the rest of the surface smooth as if it were highlighted. (Cross-hatching or channeling also makes a surface appear darker than a smooth one because of reduced light reflection.) Buttons and frogs on clothing can be represented by depressions rather than elevations. Hair and shaggy fur may be represented by roughened areas or shaggy ends if grain permits. Attempting to show actual hair often results in an oily, stringy look. Major waves in curly hair, however, can be represented well.

Professional carvers often recommend roughing out the entire panel area before doing any finish carving, but I find that most of them do what I do—rough for a portion or area, then finish that area to see what I am getting—to balance subjects and ground, surface textures, light and shadow, and the like. It's also less boring and simplifies the design problem, permits the carver to suit his work to his steadiness or degree of skill at any given time, and makes it possible to test some particular finishing problem before that problem is created in other areas of the panel. Also, when an area is finished, the carver can "clean up" vagrant splinters and chips as he studies the whole carving, reducing the really boring finishing once the carving is done.

Putting in design elements as you go has its dangers, of course. You may not get everything in that you wish—the disaster made familiar by that plaque, "Plan Ahea[d]." There is no pattern for reference. (This forces you back to the original, which may be good!) Changes on wood are harder to erase, working over the surface tends to rub out the drawing (unless you go over the pattern with a "Magic Marker" or ink in one form or another). But the major problem is that, in your absorption with carving, you will work too close to the undesigned area, so elements you plan to insert may overlap into a space you've already grounded out.

Another danger is that the elements of convenient shape will be used up first, leaving a number of tricky or difficult ones for final insertion. Final elements can of course be made larger or smaller in scale to overcome some of these problems. I have also avoided relatively large and uninteresting areas in carvings by showing only the key parts of large elements, allowing the rest to "disappear" or "bleed" beyond the panel edges. Thus, a whale's head or the snake-haired head of Medusa can be shown, without the space-taking and nondifferent body.

It is not necessary to have exactly the same number of elements in each of a pair of panels or on the two ends of the same panel, as long as the major elements are in rough balance and background spaces are approximately equal. Thus, in the two mythology panels, the flying dragon at the top of one balances the sphinx in the other, the head of Medusa balances the head of Cyclops, the centaur balances the minotaur, etc. The panels are a pair although one has under 30 elements and the other almost 45.

As you decide on the design, it is advisable to go over it and strengthen the lines which define the areas to be grounded out. This will help avoid inadvertent removal of needed wood, help to make certain that you have transferred all parts of the design from the sketch or photo you used as a source, and indicate abnormally large background areas. On light woods, pencil lines will be readily visible, but on dark woods, you may want to strengthen the lines with a fiber-tip pen or the equivalent. (If you change the design, however, your lines must be scraped off.)

✳ The Ecology Door

A Case in Point

This door is a lineal descendant of the "bug tree"; its owner suggested a "bug door." The door was Sumatra mahogany, installed and operating; the problem was to appliqué around a large and unusual central knob. My solution was eight panels, all of different dimensions, each devoted to a different group of living things—both flora and fauna—but omitting man, the apes, arachnids, mosses, and basic life forms. Panels are arranged from top to bottom roughly by altitude of the subjects' environments. Top and bottom panels are basically linear in design; the remaining six "rotate" around the doorknob in dynamic symmetry.

There are 452 subjects: American birds,

51; insects & bugs, 47; trees, 26; mammals, 49; flowers, 57; shellfish and crustaceans, 71; amphibians and reptiles, 42; fish, 109 (salt-water fish on top, then brackish-water fish, then fresh-water types). Subjects are not to scale, nor are they all from the same point of view. But they are detailed for recognition. I tried to make each identifiable and to avoid other subjects with a similar silhouette or markings (which would require color for distinction). Supporting structure was omitted; there are no leaves with flowers, branches for birds, bugs, or animals, water for fish. Design is purely of the subjects themselves. All are properly grouped except for three mammals and two crustaceans among the fishes (we commonly call them "fish"), and some tree blossoms included in the flower panel.

Heavy carving was done with an assortment of tools and a light mallet; details were whittled with penknife. Ground was sunk about 3/16 in. Eyeholes in animals and fish were drilled with bits held in the fingertips—no power tools. Wood is Thai teak; all except the bottom panel came from one 1×12-in. plank 13 ft. long. So the bottom panel is a slightly lighter color which the owner insists upon leaving "as is." Finish is an oil-resin complex used by yachtsmen to preserve teak decks. It replaces surface finishes and adds a plastic seal, is a colorless fluid.

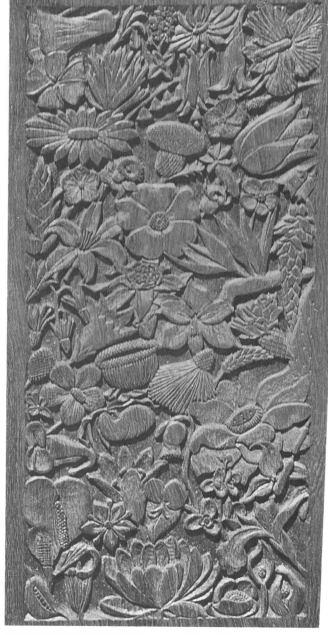

AMERICAN FLOWERS panel (ABOVE) is 10 × 20 in., contains 57 patterns. SHELLFISH AND CRUSTACEANS panel (FAR LEFT) is 10 × 21 in., contains 71 patterns. TREES panel 10 × 9¾ (wide) in., contains 26 patterns. Reproductions here are thus about one-third the size of the originals, large and clear enough for copying.

KEY—

AMERICAN

TREES

1. Swamp oak and acorn
2. Hickory and pignut
3. Crabapple and fruit
4. White spruce
5. White basswood
6. Dogwood flower
7. Cottonwood
8. Canoe birch and catkin
9. Hornbeam and seedpod
10. Hop
11. Red haw and seed
12. Swamp holly
13. Sugar maple and seed
14. Green ash
15. Pussy willow
16. Pin oak
17. Mulberry
18. Magnolia
19. Black cherry
20. Yellow oak
21. Sassafras
22. Yellow wood
23. Chestnut and bur
24. Holly and berries
25. White spruce and cones
26. Pecan

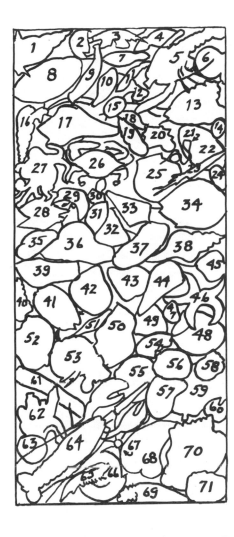

KEY—SHELLFISH AND CRUSTACEANS

1. Great pond snail
2. Scud
3. Water sow bug
4. Fingernail clam
5. Crayfish
6. Wheel snail
7. Flatworm
8. Pearl mussel
9. Horse leech
10. Turtle leech
11. See No. 53
12. Hairworm
13. Large round pond snail
14. Atlantic coffee bean
15. Limpet
16. Humble pond snail
17. Knobbed whelk
18. Tadpole snail
19. Rice snail
20. 3-keeled snail
21. Ribbon worm
22. Fat mucket clam
23. Squid
24. Eastern chiton
25. Scallop
26. Blue crab
27. 2-spotted octopus
28. Banded tulip
29. Beach flea or sand hopper
30. Rock barnacle
31. Slipper shell
32. Channeled top shell
33. Crown cone shell
34. Horseshoe crab
35. Striate bubble
36. Northern moon

37. Angel wing
38. Florida horse conch
39. Turkey wing
40. Wentletop
41. Measled cowrie
42. Giant Atlantic cockle
43. Astarte
44. Sawtooth pen shell
45. Fan worm
46. Ocre star
47. Marsh periwinkle
48. Northern quahog
49. Glass sponge
50. Apple murex
51. Lugworm
52. Tun or cask
53. Hermit crab in Atlantic nautica shell
54. Sandbug or mole crab
55. Sundial
56. Brain coral
57. Hooked mussel
58. Tegula
59. Sea fan
60. Jingle shell
61. Razor clam
62. Lime sponge group
63. Atlantic sand dollar
64. Lobster
65. Shrimp
66. Sand collar (worm case)
67. Green brittle star
68. Eastern oyster
69. Sea cucumber
70. Queen conch
71. Helmet
NOTE: Except for Nos. 11, 14, 17, 19, and 20, the first 20 or so are fresh-water residents.

KEY—AMERICAN FLOWERS

1. Wild morning glory or hedge bindweed
2. Arethusa or Indian pink
3. Forget-me-not
4. Black-eyed Susan
5. Angel trumpet (tree)
6. Hibiscus
7. Frangipani
8. Indian paintbrush or scarlet painted cup
9. Bluet or innocence
10. Wild Columbine, 4 o'clock
11. Oxeye daisy
12. Lily of the valley
13. Bull thistle
14. Phlox
15. English plantain
16. Darwin tulip
17. Heliconia
18. Mountain laurel
19. Daffodil, narcissus
20. Day lily
21. Swamp rose
22. Wild ginger
23. Indian pink or pinkroot
24. Common buttercup
25. Wintergreen or checkerberry
26. Bird of Paradise
27. Shell ginger
28. Shooting star
29. Solitary gentian
30. Bromiliad (air plant)

31. Amaryllis
32. Prickly pear (cactus)
33. Stone clover
34. Rose mallow
35. White violet
36. Queen Anne's lace
37. Yellow lady's slipper
38. Purple cone flower
39. Knotgrass
40. American lotus (water)
41. Jewel weed or spotted touch-me-not
42. Star of Bethlehem
43. Indian pipe
44. Day flower
45. Arrowhead
46. Purple trillium
47. Cattail
48. Anthurium
49. Wild geranium
50. Golden club
51. Arrow arum
52. Jack-in-the-pulpit or Indian turnip
53. White water lily
54. Cowslip or pond lily
55. Larger blue flag, iris, fleur-de-lis
56. Water arum
57. Skunk cabbage
NOTE: Nos. 5, 6, 7, 17, 26, 27, 30, 31, and 48 are tropical only. One blossom of a cluster is shown in Nos. 14, 18, 41.

IF YOU PLAN TO COPY

Both a large photo and a chart are given for each panel, so you can identify each design and use any or all for a pattern. Photos are about one-third size of the actual panel, so a ⅛-in. grid over the photo and a ⅜- or ½-in. grid on your wood would approximate the original size. But any can be made larger or smaller, to suit your need. Charts are not suitable for copying because they were traced over the finished panels for identification.

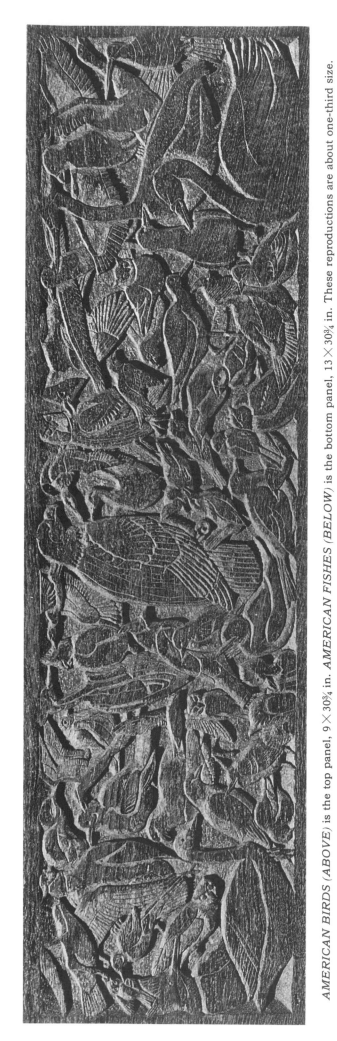

AMERICAN BIRDS (ABOVE) is the top panel, 9 × 30¾ in. *AMERICAN FISHES (BELOW)* is the bottom panel, 13 × 30¾ in. These reproductions are about one-third size.

SOME OBSERVATIONS ABOUT THESE PANELS

Note that views vary; not all are side silhouettes. Variation in aspect and pose helps maintain interest. Carving is essentially flat; details are limited to those vital for identification or textural effects. Excessive detail becomes confusing and increases fragility and wear. In the fish panel below, Nos. 1–55 are sea fish, Nos. 56–64 brackish-water, and Nos. 65–109 fresh-water fish. Nos. 45 and 55 are actually crustaceans, and Nos. 1, 52, and 54 are mammals, but are commonly thought of as fish because of their environment. Sizes of subjects are not to general scale, but are selected to suit the design. Portions of bodies of the whale at left and dolphin at right in the fish panel are "bled" into the frame because their bodies would create large flat areas in the design. "Frame" of ⅝ in. all around provides protection and untouched wood for screw holes. There are 51 different birds and 109 fish patterns.

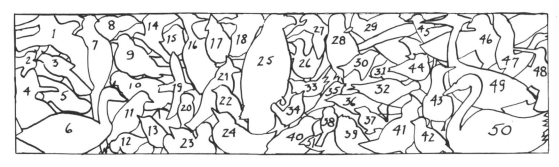

KEY—AMERICAN BIRDS

1. Duck hawk
2. Golden-crowned kinglet
3. Catbird
4. Kingfisher
5. Pigeon hawk
6. Canada goose
7. Ring-necked pheasant
8. Brown thrasher
9. Hermit thrush
10. Black gyrfalcon
11. Dove
12. Goldfinch
13. Green heron
14. Arctic tern
15. Quail or bobwhite
16. Ivory-billed woodpecker
17. Cardinal
18. Yellow-crowned night heron
19. Chimney swift
20. Burrowing owl
21. Cedar waxwing
22. Bluebird
23. Hooded merganser
24. Gannet
25. Bald eagle
26. Greater snow goose
27. Canvasback duck
28. Duck hawk
29. Blue jay
30. Redstart
31. Crossbill
32. Solitary sandpiper
33. Tufted titmouse
34. Marsh wren
35. Painted bunting
36. Yellow-billed cuckoo
37. Puffin
38. Chickadee
39. Screech owl
40. Robin
41. Ruffed grouse
42. Kingbird
43. Booby
44. Horned lark
45. Frigate bird
46. Osprey
47. Mallard duck
48. Hummingbird
49. Great white heron
50. Swan
51. Swainson's warbler (next to No. 40)

KEY—FISHES

1. Sperm whale or cachalot
2. Batfish
3. Lookdown
4. Reef fish
5. Sharpnose flying fish
6. Porkfish
7. Hogfish
8. Tiger shark
9. Blue tang
10. Guitarfish or fiddlefish
11. Cowfish or trunkfish
12. Beau Gregory
13. French angelfish
14. Moray eel
15. Spanish hogfish
16. Four-eyed butterfly fish
17. Red snapper
18. Yellowtail jack
19. Threadfish
20. Sailfish
21. Red grouper or sea bass
22. Sea robin
23. Scorpion fish
24. Balloon shark
25. Sheepshead
26. Blenny
27. Parrotfish
28. Common sturgeon
29. Rock beauty
30. Barracuda
31. Smooth flounder
32. Headfish
33. Dolphin or dorado
34. Coelacanth
35. Leopard ray
36. Lion-fish
37. Sprat
38. Gulper (long-tailed)
39. Northern stargazer
40. Flying gurnard or flying sea robin
41. Jackknife fish
42. Trumpet fish
43. Filefish
44. Butterfly fish
45. Pipefish
46. Bonito (mackerel)
47. Mudbelly (parrot fish)
48. Queen triggerfish
49. Southern puffer
50. Needlefish
51. Manta ray
52. Pilot whale
53. White marlin
54. Porpoise (dolphin)
55. Spotted seahorse
56. Chinook (salmon)
57. Spoonbill (paddlefish)
58. Shad
59. Halibut
60. Weakfish
61. Smelt
62. Alewife
63. Atlantic salmon
64. Common eel
65. Yellow perch
66. Pumpkinfish or sunfish
67. Lake lamprey on a . . .
68. Lake trout
69. Small-mouth black bass
70. Channel catfish
71. Killifish
72. Carp
73. Crappie
74. Brook lamprey
75. Comet goldfish
76. Pike
77. Blindfish (caves)
78. Eastern pickerel
79. Calico bass
80. Rainbow trout
81. Sculpin
82. Golden shiner
83. Large-mouth black bass
84. Red-horse sucker
85. Brook silversides
86. Bluegill
87. Bullhead or horned pout
88. Black-nosed dace
89. Stone roller
90. Fallfish
91. Common goldfish
92. Brook trout
93. Mud minnow or rockfish
94. Lungfish
95. Common white sucker
96. Cutlips minnow
97. Johnny darter
98. 3-spined stickleback
99. 10-spined stickleback
100. Stone cat or Mad Tom
101. Brown trout
102. Rio Grande perch
103. Grayling
104. Mountain sucker
105. Chilid or Grande Perch
106. Eelpout or yowler
107. Whitefish or chub
108. Quillback
109. Longnose gar

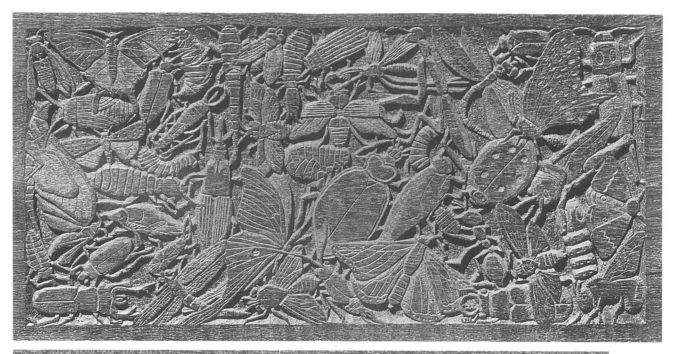

INSECTS AND BUGS panel *(ABOVE)* is 10 × 19 in., contains 47 patterns. *AMERICAN MAMMALS* panel *(LEFT)* is 11 × 18¾ in. and includes 49 patterns. *AMPHIBIANS, REPTILES, AND SAURIANS* panel *(BELOW LEFT)* is 12 × 18 ¾ in. and contains 42 patterns. Reproductions here are thus between a third and a fourth actual size and can be transferred as patterns with a small grid. Charts at right are not accurate as to outline, are merely for identification.

WHY TEAK?

The original door was Sumatra mahogany, stained quite dark, and the house itself was also dark brown. Natural-finish teak thus would stand out against the almost-black door, is hard and enduring, stable in sunlight and rain, does not rot, and resists insects and worms. Warping is slight and easily controlled, the color is a warm brown and even if neglected will weather to a pleasant gray. It also is a good carving wood, with no tendency to split and a dense structure which supports reasonable detail. Fortunately, it does not require varnishing for protection, but can be finished with a teak-deck preparation, which supplements its own oils and includes a plastic sealant.

KEY—INSECTS AND BUGS

1. Wasp
2. Western tiger swallowtail butterfly
3. German cockroach
4. Firefly
5. Potato beetle (larva)
6. Earwig
7. Bella moth
8. Mayfly
9. Psocid or bookworm
10. Hornworm (sphinx moth larva)
11. Boll weevil
12. Dytiscid beetle
13. Cicada killer
14. Glowworm
15. Goldsmith beetle
16. Stag beetle
17. Milkweed bug
18. Dragonfly
19. Luna moth
20. Stinkbug
21. Silverfish
22. Greenbottle fly
23. Termite (worker)
24. Potato beetle
25. Mosquito
26. Horn beetle
27. Human flea
28. Caterpillar hunter
29. House fly
30. Cricket
31. Monarch butterfly
32. Katydid
33. Aphid, milked by an . . .
34. Ant
35. Black beetle or pinchbug
36. Cicada
37. Spicebush swallowtail (larva)
38. Queen bee
39. Io moth
40. Grasshopper
41. Ladybug
42. Grubworm
43. Praying mantis
44. Damselfly
45. Japanese beetle
46. Black swallowtail butterfly
47. Click beetle

KEY—AMERICAN MAMMALS

1. Flying squirrel
2. Badger
3. Longtail weasel
4. Mountain vole
5. Mountain lion
6. Grizzly bear
7. Hoary marmot
8. Beaver
9. Pronghorn antelope
10. Mountain goat
11. Bighorn sheep
12. Jaguar
13. Wolverine
14. Chickaree (squirrel)
15. Hare
16. Sea otter
17. Collie dog
18. Red fox
19. Whitetail deer
20. Elk
21. Woodchuck
22. Pig
23. Striped skunk
24. Red squirrel
25. Mule deer fawn
26. Raccoon
27. American opossum and
28–31. Young opossums
32. Lynx
33. Horse
34. Cow
35. Wild burro
36. Peccary (wild boar)
37. Gray wolf
38. Muskrat
39. Townsend mole
40. Bison
41. Pika
42. Moose
43. Black bear
44. Harvest mouse
45. Porcupine
46. Marten
47. Least chipmunk
48. Little brown myotis bat
49. Shrew

KEY—AMPHIBIANS, REPTILES, SAURIANS

1. Eastern racer snake
2. Frilled lizard
3. Hawksbill turtle
4. Sand lizard
5. Chuckwalla (lizard)
6. Horned toad (lizard)
7. Ground Uta lizard
8. Red-spotted toad
9. Alligator eggs hatching
10. Garter snake
11. Collared lizard
12. Wood frog
13. Hognose snake
14. Softshell turtle
15. Worm lizard
16. Rattlesnake
17. Box turtle
18. Basilisk lizard
19. Leopard frog
20. Galapagos turtle
21. Tiger salamander
22. Iguana
23. Alligator
24. Indigo snake
25. Komodo lizard
26. Snapping turtle
27. Leatherback turtle
28. Fence lizard or swift
29. Tortoise
30. Cottonmouth or water moccasin
31. Green frog
32. Mud puppy
33. Spring peeper
34. Newt
35. American chameleon or Anole
36. American toad
37. Flying dragon lizard
38. Red eft
39. Gila monster
40. Canyon tree frog
41. Monitor lizard
42. Alligator snapper

HOW TO FASTEN THE PANELS

In applying the panels, adhesives were rejected because of possible differential expansion and the possibility that the owner might one day want to remove the panels. Panels are held to the 35 × 80-in. plywood door by No. 8 1½-in. flathead brass screws at 6- to 8-in. intervals in counter-sunk holes around the edges, with cross-grain teak plugs glued in and sanded down to hide the openings, as at A in the sketch. (Each panel has an uncarved edge ⅝ in. wide.) U.S. Forest Products Lab concurred in this idea, also suggested the alternate holding method at B, with roundhead screws and washers. In either case, holes are drilled oversize to provide clearance around screws, so differential expansion is provided for. Bearing and holding are done by the screw-head alone. After two years, there is no evidence of differential movement of the panels.

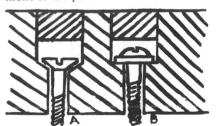

❋ A Montage of Monsters

Diptych in Polyglot Design

Supernatural beings have always played a part in man's life; it's a way of explaining the unexplainable. More-backward countries and rural areas of less-backward ones still have their chimerae, of course, but what of our Santa Claus, Cupid, witches, fairies, Loch Ness monster, gremlins, leprechauns, trolls, Man in the Moon, and so on, to say nothing of our science fiction? Depiction of weird beasts probably reached its peak in the medieval bestiaries, and these are the source of a number of the chimerae here shown, but modern mythologies, art histories, and the like also provide some.

These panels began as an idea for a summer screen for the fireplace. As teak was available up to almost 15 in. wide, I decided to produce twin vertical panels—a diptych. These are 1 in. thick, about $14\frac{5}{8} \times 22$ in. with a $\frac{5}{8}$-in. border on sides and top and a 1-in. border on the bottom. They are carved in low relief about $\frac{1}{8}$ in. deep, with the background

darkened and appropriate lines of the carving "antiqued" as described earlier. Most carving was done with tools and a mallet, but details often were done, or at least finished, with a penknife. The biggest tool was a $\frac{3}{8}$-in.-wide firmer, the smallest a veiner.

One panel was completed before the other was started. Design was started at the bottom in each. The left-hand panel includes only 29 figures, the right-hand one 43, yet they are a pair because principal elements balance. Note the similarity of design across the bottoms, the balancing of the Cyclops head with one of Medusa, the Minotaur balancing the centaur, and the "featuring" of a prominent center element at the top of

KEY—LEFT PANEL

1. Minotaur, human-headed bull from the Cretan maze.
2. Hydra, 9-headed dragon beaten by Hercules.
3. Man in the Moon, from modern sources.
4. Sphinx, with woman's torso, lion body, eagle wings, and dragon-headed tail. Best-known is the crop-haired sphinx at Gizeh, but this one is Greek.
5. Winged foot or shoe: Mercury and Perseus wore them.
6. Cecrops, first king of Attica, was born of a dragon.
7. Trolls abound in Northland fairy tales. This one is Norwegian, suggests the source of the legends as a bear at twilight.
8. Basilisk or Cockatrice; half chicken, half dragon, hatched by hen from a dragon's egg. Its very presence was poisonous.
9. Pegasus, Bellerophon's winged horse.
10. Satyrs, one of many woodland, meadow, and stream sprites, had a male upper body and head with horns, a goat's hindquarters. Pan was a satyr.
11. Mermaid, probably from sightings of manatees and dugongs, is half-woman, half-fish. Her male counterpart is the merman.
12. Dragon, in this case Chinese, after Arthur Rackham.
13. Harpy, a woman with wings and claws, or a bird (see other panel), who lured sailors to their deaths.
14. Phoenix reputedly lived for 540 years, then was reborn from its own corpse, or was consumed in flame which hatched an egg.
15. Flying dragon had many shapes; this one was partly determined by wood grain.
16. Cyclopes were one-eyed giants.
17. Cerberus, a 3-headed dog with dragon tail, guarded the gates of Hades, was brought back by Hercules.
18. Unicorn, a horse with a single frontal horn, reportedly easily tamed by a maid—whose boy friend then would steal the horn, reputed to have medicinal and other powers, hence immensely valuable. Probably narwhal horn.
19, 20. Goblins took both human and bird forms, were used to discipline children.
21. Flame-breathing bull was one of many fire-breathers.
22. Sea bishop, again probably from a miter-shaped head on manatee or dugong.
23. Sea dragon or sea serpent, ancestor of the Loch Ness monster.
24. Nightjar or goatsucker is the European equivalent of our nighthawk, said to suck milk from goats at night.
25. Toads and frogs were said to spit poison, and toads sometimes had jewels in their heads.
26. Sea elephant had head and forelegs of the pachyderm, tail of a fish.
27. Newt was a great help in witch spells and hellish brews, particularly its eyes.
28, 29. Whales were said to be able to spout and wash a ship under; were reported with horns or other appendages to attack ships.

each panel—the Sphinx in one, a flying dragon in the other. This is important in producing companion pieces, not the precise number of elements nor their relative size. Note also that while side views predominate there are front, top, and three-quarter views as well, all in the same panel.

Panels are reproduced roughly half-size here so elements may be used as patterns just as a drawing would be; the drawings are provided for identification only. There are no supernatural beings that *look* natural, like werewolves, vampires, warlocks, Indian tigers and American owls, goats, cows, the Valkyrie, Lorelei, roc—or even hairy and otherwise abnormal humans once thought to be lucky or unlucky.

My panels are backed by three strips of aluminum angle to prevent warpage and provide a mounting. Strips are at center, top and bottom, and each has the standout leg drilled at center to provide a hook hole or whatever. I mounted them originally on the feet of my andirons, so the firedog gave stability and the two brass legs a touch of color in front. But the brass proved to be a disturbing element, so the panels are now mounted on 4×4×12-in. mahogany blocks, chamfered and "relieved" at center front and stained to the darkness of the background. Flat varnish and wax kept the teak its natural color, while the background was darkened with walnut stain. In one or two instances, grain or fault in the teak surface led to a particular design—in No. 15, left-hand panel, the head and right-wing outline were in the wood.

KEY—RIGHT PANEL

 1. Cherub, familar at Christmas and as Dan Cupid.
 2. Bird-headed man with egg, an Easter Island fantasy.
 3. Flying dragon—an elaborate medieval form.
 4. Santa Claus is the classic elf, bigger than most.
 5. Centaur: half-human, half-horse. Best known: Nessus.
 6, 7. Totems have been tribal symbols or family symbols in many lands, like the African *mwikos*. Athabascan and Tlingit Indians, in British Columbia, had the American poles, combining several totems; here an eagle and a bear protect a man between the bear's knees.
 8. Make-make, sacred bird or totem on Easter Island.
 9. Grotesque-headed female, probably a seated dancer. From Jalisco, Mexico.
10. Mahiole, from Hawaii, is a plumed headdress worn by a dancer.
11. Gnome guarded mines and underground treasures.
12. Jackal-headed man from early Egypt, with lion-headed and bull-headed ones, guarded temples.
13. Siren, as imagined in early Greece attacking Odysseus.
14. Frigatebird figurehead from a Solomon Islands pirogue.
15. Genii, here Aladdin's, came in many forms from the Near East.
16. Manticore had human head, lion body, scorpion tail.
17. Eskimo evil sprite, from Greenland.
18. Triple-faced man is Celtic in origin.
19. Chimera once had three heads: goat, lion, and dragon.
20. Witch riding a broomstick—a modern version.
21. Chinese dragon, more animal than saurian.
22. Gremlin was a World War II sprite, making trouble.
23. Harpy, as a bird, an attacker of Odysseus.
24. Nataraja is a 4-armed Indian dancer, an impersonation of Shiva, one of many multilimbed or multiheaded monsters. Another . . .
25. Typhoena or Typhon had three male torsos, terminating in a dragon tail. Early Greek.
26. Leprechaun, Irish gnome, said to guard a crock of gold.
27. Mamassu was a genie in the form of a winged bull which guarded Assyrian sanctuaries.
28. Medusa was best known of the Gorgons and beaten by Perseus. Snakes were her hair.
29. Dwarf is a little man with powers to suit locale.
30. Chimera later had lion and goat heads, lion body and snake head on its tail tip.
31. Fairy, smallest of the little people, usually has dragonfly wings.
32. Bull-headed demon, as depicted in India.
33. Gorgon, in another version, had an armadillo body scaled all over, pig's legs, serpent tail, ox head. Eyes and breath were poisonous.
34. Vodyanoi was a dangerous Slavonic water sprite. Covered with grass and moss.
35. Nagini is a dangerous snake, ancestor to Indian royalty, still worshipped in south India. Male form is the Naga.
36. Griffin had head and neck of an eagle (but 100 times as big), lion's body (but 8 times as big), talons.
37. Pixie was almost as small as a fairy, winged and antennaed.
38. Whale sometimes had a human head.
39. Sea horse had a horse body, serpent tail.
40. Sea lion had a lion's head, serpent's tongue, fish body.
41. Salamander was a lizard that lived on fire.
42. Kraken was a Scandinavian island, 8-armed, that sank ships or made whirlpools by sinking itself. (From the octopus, probably.)
43. Taueret, also called Apet or Opet, was a hippopotamus deity in Egypt, which guarded nursing mothers.

✳ Carving Plastic Foam

Wave-edged Blades and Saws Do It

Styrofoam, the rigid plastic foam from Dow Chemical now commonly used as a base for floral displays, swimming floats, and for commercial settings, is a fast and easy material to carve, but requires special techniques. These do *not* include the hot wire suggested by some stage-set designers, because that releases toxic methyl chloride. The best tools I've found are ordinary bread knives and paring knives of the wavy or serrated-edge type. Cuts are made with a sawing action rather than by direct pressure. A knife or chisel tends to crush and tear.

Commercial Styrofoam tends to be large-celled, so is not suited to detail in its original

form. Also, the billet itself has a hard skin which must be removed before carving. Both of these difficulties are avoided if you start with pieces of the foam cut into blocks; they have no skin and their structure is more dense. Urethane foam from duPont is also now available in art stores ("Artfoam"), which is more dense and can be assembled into sections large enough for heroic sculptures, but it is much more expensive.

Several years ago, we needed a heroic-size angel in "Carrara marble" as part of one stage setting for the Thomas Wolfe play, *Look Homeward, Angel*. We got from the local distributor a section extruded for a float, 11×20 in. in cross-section and 9 ft. long, as well as several smaller pieces 2×12× 24 in. The float section, which required skin removal, provided the body of the angel, as well as a Grecian urn, a recumbent lamb, several pigeons, a cross, and similar appurtenances of a monument works. Two of the smaller pieces made removable wings, set into the angel's shoulder blades on 1½-in. dowels 5 in. long. Dowels are oversize to spread the load and hole interiors painted to reinforce them, because the plastic will crush from any concentrated pressure. Also, because the twin dowels on each wing were equally spaced, and the mating surfaces vertical planes, the wings could be inverted and interchanged, so the angel can have elevated or lowered wings, as desired.

FAR LEFT: Group of figures in Styrofoam for a stage set of a monument works in *Look Homeward, Angel.* The angel herself is about 7½ ft. tall with wings up. Off-white paint makes her look like Carrara marble under stage lights. *BELOW LEFT*—"Radiator" of Styrofoam slabs and spacers with broomstick piping, for a stage set of *Barefoot in the Park.* It was finished in water-based paint, then sprayed with aluminum. *LEFT*— Caricature in Artfoam about 12 in. high, showing a sore-backed "General Cornpone." All by the author.

To make something as large as the angel, it is advisable to make a full-size pattern and from it paper or cardboard templates to guide in carving. I drew the figure on the billet with Magic Marker, then sawed off slabs of extra material with a crosscut saw. The billet section, about 6½ ft. high, was then set into a wooden base platform about 4 in. deep and 2 ft. square, and hard original skin being left on the billet base to help resist crushing in a hole in the platform saber-sawed to fit. It was necessary to add material for the hands and lily, and this proved to be complicated. Plastic cements simply dissolve the foam, leaving runnels; water-based casein adhesives will not dry because no air can get to them between the plastic surfaces and the material will not absorb water. However, a thin coating of rubber cement applied to both 15×15-in. surfaces and allowed to dry to a quite-tacky consistency, did the trick. Most of the volatile escaped before assembly and so rapidly that the plastic was not dissolved.

Details are difficult to carve in the commercial material. When I got to details of the face and hands of the angel, she looked as if she had smallpox; cell structure was just too large. A couple of coats of casein paint (beware oil-based or resin finishes!) provided a more stable surface which could be detailed by carving with an ordinary knife, but the work is slow and painstaking because any deep cutting exposes the plastic structure and permits crushing. The answer is to repaint an area whenever the plastic is exposed.

Finishing is done with a couple of coats of off-white water-base paint, making certain the cell structure is filled. An oil-based finish may then be put on top if desired. But if it finds its way into the plastic—look out! A duck hunter told me several years ago that he had carved a dozen Styrofoam decoys, then started to put on a base coat of oil paint. As he was painting No. 8 or 9, he looked back to see that the painted ones were in process of shrinking to little hard knots.

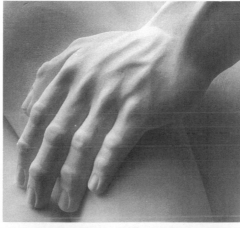

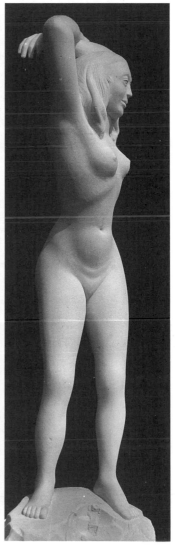

URETHANE-FOAM SCULPTURES by Domenico Martellotti. Boy and girl below, each over a foot tall, are made from single pieces, the life-size nude at right is assembled from blocks. The closeup of the hand of the nude at right shows veining and tendons, which illustrates how much detail can be gotten into Artfoam. All three figures look like marble as finished and can be detected only by close examination. The plastic is of course vastly lighter in weight, but does not have the translucence and warmth of marble, nor its delicate patterns of veining.

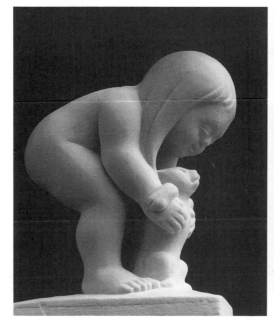

✳ Eskimo Carving

Soapstone, Ivory, Bone—and Sometimes Wood

Legend has it that whittling was a winter occupation in northern climes when the settler was largely pinned to his cabin. If this is true, it helps to explain why the Eskimo has been so prodigious a producer of objects carved in walrus and whale ivory, caribou bone, soapstone, and occasionally wood, sinew, and horn. But it does not explain why the Eskimo has produced so much more than the Lapp, for example, or why his work has so much artistic quality. Until a few years ago, Eskimo art was a prized possession of a limited number of travelers to the Far North, but nowadays the Canadian government sponsors both classes and marketing in urban centers, so quantities available have increased but quality has suffered a corresponding decline.

Early Eskimo art, untutored and evolved from the objects the Eskimo saw around him, has a strength and simplicity that is hard to describe. Only rarely does it depict religious subjects and only rarely is it larger than hand-size. If it is concerned with a man, it is often meticulously detailed, showing all of the tools he needs for the subject shown—like a kayak complete with oars, spears, and floats (next page). Even the decoration on his parka or anorak will be reproduced, as it is in Eskimo scrimshaw. It must be remembered also that all of this work was done with extremely simple tools.

LEFT—Caribou herd are all the same pose, mounted in random positions on wood base 4 × 7 in., with tiny chips glued on top to simulate moss. Antlers are whittled sinew. Probably missionary-influenced. *LEFT BELOW*—Unusually elaborate are these sledge assemblies, basically wood, complete with sinew harness, fur parkas, whittled loads lashed in place. *BOTTOM LEFT*—Walrus, duck, and mink are polished modern pieces in gray soapstone, probably produced with Government advice, but showing traditional flow and simplicity of Eskimo design. *BELOW*—2-in. polar bear in white soapstone, by the author, left rough to simulate heavy fur. *BOTTOM*—Eskimo fishing at seal's breathing hole, 4 in. long, whittled in wood from life by John Tangerman.

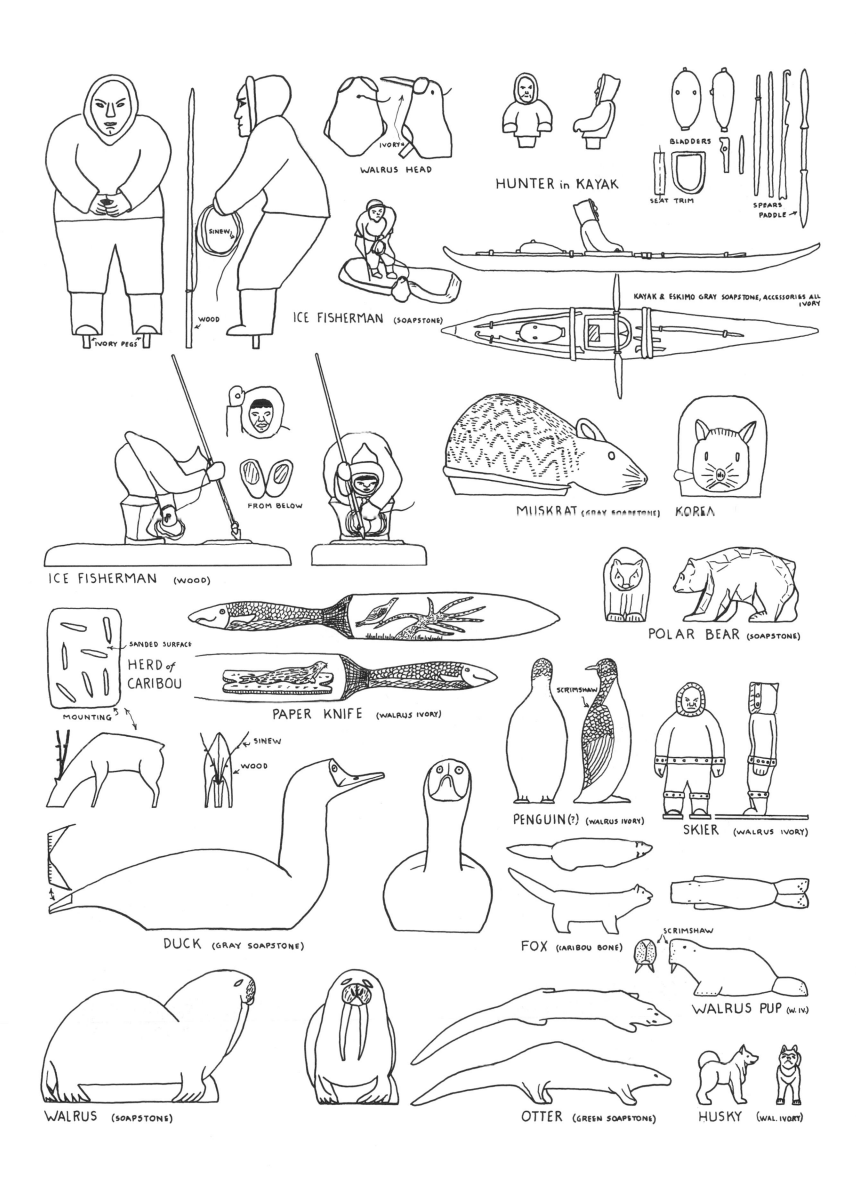

WALRUS HEAD

IVORY

HUNTER in KAYAK

BLADDERS

SEAT TRIM

SPEARS
PADDLE

SINEW

WOOD

IVORY PEGS

ICE FISHERMAN (SOAPSTONE)

KAYAK & ESKIMO GRAY SOAPSTONE, ACCESSORIES ALL IVORY

FROM BELOW

MUSKRAT (GRAY SOAPSTONE)   KOREA

ICE FISHERMAN (WOOD)

POLAR BEAR (SOAPSTONE)

SANDED SURFACE

HERD of CARIBOU

MOUNTING

PAPER KNIFE (WALRUS IVORY)

SINEW

WOOD

SCRIMSHAW

PENGUIN (?) (WALRUS IVORY)

SKIER (WALRUS IVORY)

DUCK (GRAY SOAPSTONE)

FOX (CARIBOU BONE)

SCRIMSHAW

WALRUS PUP (W. IV.)

WALRUS (SOAPSTONE)

OTTER (GREEN SOAPSTONE)

HUSKY (WAL. IVORY)

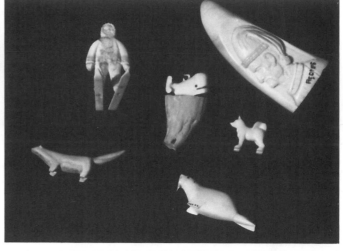

Soapstone is the familiar Eskimo carving material. The 5-in. ice hunter *(TOP LEFT)* is three pieces, man, floe, and walrus head, joined by ivory pegs, with ivory spear and tusks, sinew line. *BELOW* it is an Eskimo in 8-in. kayak, complete with ivory double paddle, spears, bladder floats, and cockpit coaming, with sinew lashings. The Eskimo torso is mortised into a square hole in the kayak. These are older carvings in gray soapstone with flat face and blocky figure. The paper knife of walrus ivory

(ABOVE RIGHT) is typical Eskimo scrimshaw work, showing a seal on an ice floe and a well-modeled fish. *ABOVE* it is a group which includes a skier, a husky and a baby walrus in ivory, and a fox or wolf in caribou bone, all Eskimo work. The 2½-in. whale pendant I made from a sperm-whale tooth, and the fisherman's head at upper right was carved by an Azores engineer in sperm-whale tusk also. The muskrat at *TOP LEFT,* also soapstone and scrimshawed, is primitive Korean.

✳ Elaborate Carving Can Be Done in a Prosaic Soupbone

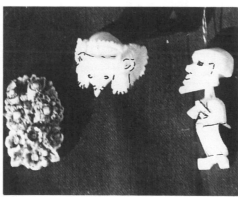

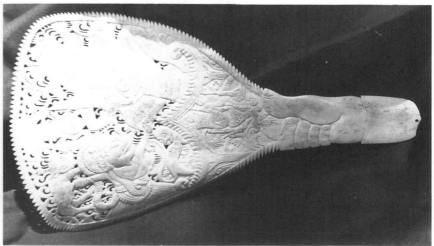

Balinese fan *(BELOW)* is a cow clavicle, pillar at *LEFT* a leg bone, as are Mexican pieces. Bali pieces are pierce-carved with intricate religious scenes, like Chinese or Indian ivory work. Mexican pieces include folk-hero statuette *(LEFT),* rose ring setting and skeleton pendant, the latter two made by prisoners for tourists, hence inexpensive. See next page.

✳Bones, Stones and Shells

You Can Carve Them All

If you want to carve other materials than wood and ivory, there *are* some readily available. One is animal bone (facing page). Indonesians in Bali, Indians in Mexico, Eskimos in Labrador, Africans, carve it now, and man in general has carved bone back before history. He has carved shell almost as long, and probably stone as well, particularly the softer varieties.

You can get bones at your butcher's, soapstone and alabaster at art stores, shell at the beach or the fish store. The latter, however, is not likely to be very rewarding for your efforts; American shells tend to be brittle and quite hard to carve, then aren't very good-looking or colorful either except for abalone, conch, and a couple of others.

A great deal of carving of cow bones is still done in Bali, most of it in leg bones, but some in clavicles (see left). The carvers are concentrated around one village, and are Hindus, so designs tend to be religious, scenes from the *Ramayana* and the like. The leg-bone carvings are pierced work and very, very delicate, with networks and filaments I had seen previously only in Chinese ivory. The carvers use knives, chisels, and burins, plus files and rasps, produce pillars, statuettes, rings, pins, necklaces, and fans—the fans from the clavicle. In Mexico, also, some cow-bone carving is done. I have one that is a miniature statuette of El Pipila, a national hero among the Indians, another that is a very complex full-relief rose pattern about ½×1 in. for a ring, and a third that is a miniature skull on a fully dressed body, with an ax made from a sliver of bone thrust under the arm. More utilitarian are crochet

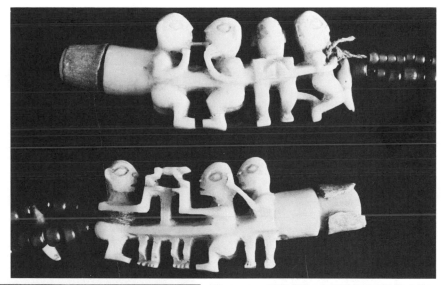

RIGHT—Ear ornaments carved of human bone, found in the Marquesas Islands in the 1880s by Hjalmar Stolpe. Courtesy National Museum of Ethnography of Sweden, Stockholm. Photo by Bo Gabrielsson. *BELOW*—Several pins and a Tiki pendant from Fiji, and an ashtray from Tahiti. All are carved shell except for the lion at *LOWER RIGHT,* which is coconut shell with a jeweled eye, and comes from Thailand. *BELOW RIGHT*—Bear and rhinoceros miniatures from India, apparently bone and tinted in natural color. The figure over the penny is a Mexican assembly carved from peach pits, of a man riding a bird.

hooks with various decorative tops. These were once common in the U.S. before plastics, still are in the Azores also.

Shell carving is still quite common in Tahiti and Fiji. In one small church on Moorea, the altar is decorated with flowers made of mother-of-pearl all around its perimeter. Pins in fish, bird, and animal shapes are common, as are trays, dishes, and small carved scenes. Some of these are obviously done on a production basis with grinders, but the better ones are hand-sawn to shape and hand-carved. Some of the scenes are very delicate and utilize the subtle shading of the shell; these have become expensive collector's items.

Coconut shell is also carved, in some of the Pacific Islands, into pins, pendants, and other small objects. This is a brittle material something like briar root in its reaction to the knife, but it can be carved much more easily than marine shell. Tortoiseshell, and some calabashes, are carved in Latin America.

Japan and China have of course carved very hard woods and soft stones for centuries. Chinese jade and jadeite carved into intricate shapes is collected and treasured, whether or not the work is antique, as is the *netsuke,* made in Japan. The latter is a tab

or knob once threaded onto the cords of the moneybag a gentleman wore on his sash or obi over his kimono. The *netsuke* could be ivory, wood, or stone, usually depicted an animal, bird, or similar rounded form. Similar gadgets have been made by woodsmen to thread on a cord on the end of a burl cup or bowl, so the cord can be thrust under a belt and held by the knob.

Somewhat akin as a mark of identity is the Chinese *chop,* a small stone statuette with the owner's ideograph carved on the bottom and used with ink to stamp documents. One I bought in Taipei cost only $6.25 in a red and white stone with a toad atop it, plus one dollar and three hours time to reproduce my *chop.* The Eskimos in Labrador have also carved soapstone and bone for many years, making simple but powerful figures of local scenes and characters— boats, dogs, walrus, deer. These have tripled or quadrupled in price recently.

Soapstone and alabaster and a few other stones can be carved with the knife or carving tools without too much damage to either. Many natives in various countries also carve much harder semiprecious stones. But in this case the tools are burins, riffler files, and grinding, thus beyond our present scope.

LEFT—Toad *chop* from Taiwan, a statuette with a seal in its base. The seal produces the stamp above it, showing my carving symbol and name in phonetic Chinese. Below the *chop* are two Japanese *netsuke* over 150 years old, the left one a badger in ivory and the right one a frog in wood with jeweled eyes. Each has drilled holes for the thongs of a purse which were looped over the belt of a gentleman of the time. *BELOW*—Latin-American Indian carvings, the *OUTER* two in soft shale and the *CENTER* one in an ivorylike Ecuadorean fruit pit 2 in. high. The shale carvings are miniatures of old Maya reliefs at Monte Alban *(LEFT)* and Palenque *(RIGHT)*, done by guards at these archaeological sites, probably lineal descendants of the original carvers.

✳ Carved Ivories

Many Materials, One Problem

Mention ivory carving and you conjure up a picture of an Oriental craftsman working on an elephant tusk. Yet there have been ivory carvers in Europe, India, Africa, and the Americas who have worked on many different kinds of ivory. Some of their work has been as artistic as any by the Chinese but possibly not as intricate. I own carved ivories from Germany, Russia, the Azores, Africa, and Labrador done within the past 15 years. The late Ernest Warther, whittler of Dover, Ohio, made a number of locomotive models, some solid ivory, some combining ivory with walnut, ebony, and mother-of-pearl. Carson Ritchie, an English ivory carver, has recently written a book showing a number of ivory carvings by other English craftsmen. And scrimshaw is coming back in the United States.

"Ivory" is a term applied to many materials, mostly tooth dentine. Sculptors have had, at one time or another, such divergent ivories as whalebone (jawbone of the sperm whale), walrus teeth, rhinoceros horn, hornbill (beak of the helmet hornbill, native to Indonesia), tortoise shell (usually from the hawksbill turtle), whale teeth, hippopotamus teeth, boar and warthog tusks, even mammoth tusks (mostly Russia and Germany). In Viking times, human teeth were carved into tiny idols in Scandinavia; I found crocodile teeth and boar tusks in Mexico.

Crocodile teeth are very hard and difficult to carve with anything except power tools. The enamel part of sperm-whale teeth and the outside of the narwhal tusk (now a collector's item when available and once the fabled unicorn's horn) are also very hard. Hippopotamus tooth is next in hardness, followed by boar and warthog tusks, rhino horn and the darker African ivory (which comes from forest elephants). Indian and African veldt elephant, mammoth, and walrus tusks are all relatively soft, but still harder than ebony. There are some variations in color too, but the usual idea of ivory is that it is white, so some carvers try to

RIGHT—The late Ernest Warther and his all-ivory model of the famed locomotive, "General." *BELOW*—Ricksha assembly of carved ivory tinted in soft browns, about 5 in. long. Carved in Japan. *BELOW CENTER*—Scene with two deer, from India, about 12 in. high with base and backing. *BELOW RIGHT*—Nested spheres (17, one inside the other) and a clamshell with village scene inside, typical of Hong Kong "ivory factory" work.

bleach any color away. In these days of plastics, however, the stains, spots, erosion, and growth rings of ivory help distinguish it.

Oriental carvers use the simplest of tools: thin saws (to save costly material), bow drills, small chisels, burins, knives, and rasps. Tools I've seen may combine a chisel tip and rasp teeth. For intricate work, they make special tools like L-shaped knives to separate the spheres. In Ehrbach, Germany, most carving is now done with a dental burr.

Tools are not pushed through ivory as they can be through wood, even though it has a definite grain and older pieces may have partially separated into concentric rings. The tooth enamel is removed, either by chipping or grinding (it is the ridged-looking portion usually nearest the gum line), then the design is drawn on (where there is one) in India ink, and the cutting done either with small chisels and a light mallet, or by forcing the tools along much as a silversmith does engraving, with a rocking motion that leaves

a line more like a worm track than a cut groove. It is a slow, meticulous operation. A tusk, or a large block of ivory, is very fragile and will split and crack when dropped or even with a sudden change of temperature. Smaller pieces are very durable and do not split, warp, or splinter during carving. Some carvers like the ivory to be wet, but boiling water can permanently damage the material, and sudden drying is bad for it also.

Polishing is a real secret of ivory carving. It must be very carefully done. Major nicks and scratches are removed by scraping with a knife edge or the equivalent. Then the surface is sanded with fine sandpaper or emery cloth and carved areas with bits of fine sandpaper glued to the ends of shaped sticks. Some parts can only be reached with riffler files. This must be done very carefully to avoid sanding away the sharp edges of cuts and the finer lines, because chamfered edges tend to make the whole carving a milky blur. Spots and hairline cracks are left as they are; they prove it's ivory. Power tools at this stage are quite dangerous; they tend to "run" and blur the lines.

Top carvers use as many as six powder or paste abrasives in final polishing, starting with a fairly coarse one and working up to something as fine as jeweler's rouge. They are brushed on successively with tiny stiff brushes—like a typewriter-cleaning brush or a denture brush—which are moved back and forth in the cut areas. The brush is kept damp and is dipped into a little mound of the

BELOW—A group of ivory miniatures, including a dragon from China, Brementown Musicians (one piece) and stag from Germany, fox and ermine from the U.S.S.R.
BOTTOM—Scrimshawed whale tooth, with designs of a flying fish, girl's head, and full-rigged ship, an antique by an American seaman; sailing junk from China, and openwork paper knife, also from China. *RIGHT*—Rearing horse from Germany, fruit knife (ivory handle and case) of unknown origin, elephant-chain letter opener from India, and ivory chopsticks with ivory-handled knife in a sharkskin case with Peking-horse caricature ivory inlays.
BOTTOM RIGHT—Chicken bridge, utilizing the curve of the tusk, from Hong Kong or China. About 9 in. long. All the above except the whale tooth are sketched on the next page.

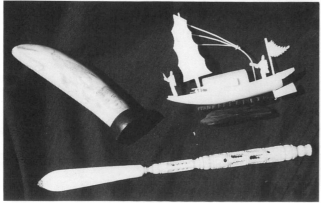

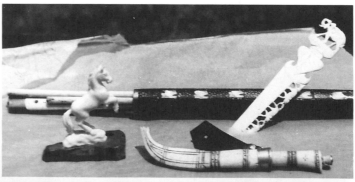

DRAGON - CHINA

THE BREMENTOWN MUSICIANS GERMANY

PONY - INDIA

CHICKEN BRIDGE - HONGKONG

CAMEL - INDIA

SUPPORT FIGURE - CHINA

PRANCING HORSE - GERMANY

WALRUS PUP - ESKIMO

SPERM WHALE - U.S.

ANTLERS PAIRED - OFF

REINDEER - GERMANY

LOW-RELIEF PANEL of DEER - INDIA

ARCTIC FOX - U.S.S.R.

OWL - CHINA

BENGAL TIGER - INDIA

OWL - JAPAN

STEM

WASP (TOP VIEW)

WORMY APPLE - CHINA

WILD BOAR - GERMANY

PUFFIN - ESKIMO

SCRIMSHAW

TOP

LION COUCHANT - INDIA

WALKING LION - INDIA

ESKIMO SLEDGE & TEAM

ERMINE - U.S.S.R.

ELEPHANT-CHAIN LETTER OPENER - INDIA

PORTUGUESE FISHERMAN in WHALE TOOTH - AZORES

SILVER FERRULE

FRUIT KNIFE UNKNOWN

LION & ELEPHANT CHARMS - INDIA

SPERM WHALE in TOOTH - E.J.T.

IVORY-NUT NEGROID HEAD ECUADOR (Stained Dark Brown)

SCRIMSHAWED PEKING-HORSE CARICATURES on a CHOPSTICK CASE - CHINA (2X)

GOOSE - CHINA (Tinted)

CHIPMUNK - CHINA (Tinted)

JUNK MODEL in IVORY - CHINA

IVORY-NUT PROFILE - ECUADOR

4 SCRIMSHAW DESIGNS - U.S.

165

abrasive. After a few minutes of the first, the piece is washed carefully and the next-finer abrasive applied, and so on. Each abrasive is used about twice as long as its predecessor, so the final one may involve several hours of work on a relatively small carving. Western carvers, however, tend to use only two abrasives, the first pumice powder and the second jeweler's rouge, then follow with a lengthy rubbing with soft cloths put over pieces of cardboard or a brush tip, with no abrasive at all.

Orientals have tinted ivory carvings for centuries. To color lines other than black, it is possible to use colored inks. Or indigo will give a deep blue, jeweler's rouge a deep red, Tripoli compound a brown. The agreeable light brown on some Chinese ivories is obtained by fumigating the piece with burning tobacco, tanbark, incense—or just soaking it in tea or dye. The Chinese also use lime chloride as a bleach, and have developed many soft colors from minerals and bark or wood: mercury chloride (cinnabar) for vermilion, red lead for an orange, red ocher (umber) for brownish red, azurite for

deep blue, malachite for green. But modern dyes and pigments thinned down will work.

Scrimshaw—the scratching of designs into the surface of ivory, particularly whale teeth and walrus tusks—was done with a variety of tools: the tip of a knife blade, a large needle, or whatever was available on shipboard with a sharp hard point. Some modern scrimshaw carvers use old diamond- or sapphire-pointed phonograph needles in a holder or even the old straight needles themselves. However, the Eskimos make the simplest tool. It is simply a block of soft wood, about $\frac{1}{2} \times \frac{1}{2} \times 3$ in.,with an onion-bulb shape whittled at one end. Into this they drive a headless brad or finishing nail, then file the end to a point of the desired width. Several tools give a variety of scratch widths. The tool is held in the fingertips around the base of the bulb, and will readily scratch the ivory. Patterns are drawn in India ink, and, after scratching, the whole tooth is sanded to remove any residual ink lines, etc., and polish the tooth, then the carving is polished as well with pumice or emery dust and a tiny stiff brush. India ink is carefully drawn into the scratches with a pen or a tiny brush and any excess sanded off. India ink does not stain ivory and any spillage can be sanded off easily, so some carvers simply wipe it on, then sand the surface after it dries.

BELOW—Fisherman (sketch on page 99) from China, and wormy apple complete with wasp, a Chinese tinted piece about 2 in. high. *TOP RIGHT*—Eskimo sledge and huskies of whale ivory, on a board, about 4 in. long. *RIGHT BOTTOM*—Miniatures include two lions, a chipmunk, a tiger, a goose, and an intricate stylized owl. Most are tinted and are from India, except the Eskimo scrimshawed penguin (?!) at left and baby seal at right. *RIGHT CENTER*—More miniatures, including Indian camel, elephant, and lion, German boar and horse, American sperm whale, Eskimo puffin, Chinese owl.

✳ Observations

Remarks You Wish Your "Friends" Wouldn't Make

It was nice of you to give me that carved pin. Everybody in our bridge club likes it so well that they want them too. Would it be asking too much for you to make me seven more?

Our church is having an auction. You're not a member, but I told them I just knew you'd be glad to donate a carving to be sold.

It really doesn't matter much what you make; we'll be leaving this apartment soon anyhow. I just want something a foot square to cover that hole in the wall.

I think this figure is perfectly lovely. You won't mind, will you, if I make one suggestion? Shouldn't that left foot be a little larger?

I know I ordered the carving of a bird, but right now I'm feeling a little broke.

We're having an art show, but none of the artists can make it. Would you mind sitting in and carving something—just so there's some action?

If you're such a good carver, how come you won't sharpen my ax?

I used to whittle when I was a kid, but I grew up.

I made one of your designs in clay, but I improved it.

You know, I could do that—I just don't have the time, that's all. Or . . . I just don't have the patience.

My husband collects figures of horses. If I buy you the wood, will you carve me one as a birthday present for him?

That's a pretty high price, don't you think, for a piece of wood that small? And it is all full of cracks to boot.

I think a fair price would be the number of hours it took you multiplied by the minimum wage.

We're fixing up a window for the Girl Scouts. We have some lovely birdhouses, quilts—oh, all sorts of things. Can we borrow this totem pole to go in it?

Why don't you stop carving figures and things and make ashtrays or something useful?

You do some things that show promise; where did you take lessons?

We won't need your carving after all; the artist we invited first finally agreed to put his in our show.

I picked up this Chinese mandarin cheap at an auction because I figured that you could replace the missing pieces. When you aren't busy, will you fix it up?

But this is just whittling, of course; it's not as if it were real art.

I've got to have a present for tomorrow and I can't think of a thing. Would you mind making something for me tonight after you get home from work—just a simple little figure about a foot tall?

I don't want to sound critical, but this arm seems a little out of proportion to me.

This year, don't spend any money on my Christmas present; just make a carved eagle to go over my fireplace.

I bought this genuine Sheraton chair—have the documents to prove it. What do you think of it?

I understand you wrote a book about wood. What kind of wood is this that I picked up on the beach?

If you're such a good carver, how come you're wearing a bandage?

I've heard all about your whittling. Some time you must show me your shop.

I don't want to spend that much for a carving; would you lend me the drawing to copy?

Who did the carvings on your door and mailbox? They look better than your normal work.

My wife asked me to carve a thing like this, but I just don't have the time.

Will you carve me a pair of deer for my lawn—lifesize? There's some wood piled up back of the garage.

Tangents—Some Thoughts and Comments about Carving and Carvers

Knowing all about baseball is about as valuable as knowing all about whittling.—ABE MARTIN

If a cut can go wrong, it will. COROLLARY: If you worry about cutting yourself, you will.

The last cut before supper will be a disaster.

The concept is more important than the details; the originality more important than the time.

If one of twenty tools drops or is nicked, that's the one you'll need immediately. COROLLARY: After you stop to pick it up or resharpen it, you'll wonder where you needed it.

The knot or check is always in the wrong place.

The detail that is hardest or takes most time is the one nobody will notice.

After you've finished a piece, you'll see a place that needs "just one cut." *Don't touch it!*

The more tools you acquire, the fewer you will need and use on most work.

When you show "how to do it," expect to look awkward, make a mistake, or cut yourself.

The tricky tools will fail you in a pinch; the simple ones won't.

The whittler makes one-piece carvings—often with the help of glue.

Many a good carving is ruined by poor finishing.

The major virtue of some woods—and some carvings—is that they will burn.

Many a carver holds his latest masterpiece in a bandaged hand.

Tool steel is harder than nail steel—except when a tool hits a nail.

Whittling is like chicken gravy; it's better with a little heart and giblets in it.

Barber and butcher both start a job by sharpening tools; a carver can profit by their example, even if he cuts flesh only by mistake.

The poet, author, and painter can boast of their ineptness with tools; a carver must first be a good mechanic.

A frequent fault in whittled pieces is too much detail; the artist suggests detail but doesn't emphasize it.

If you're a "primitive" carver, you can charge three times what you would if you just admitted you were crude.

A basic difference between a craftsman and an artist is that the craftsman can copy anything while the artist can convert his dreams to canvas or wood.

✳Checking and Cracking

What to Do—If Anything

Checking—the radial splitting, particularly at the ends, of green wood as it dries—and cracking—a result of sudden drying of humid wood—are in some respects the same problem, but differ in others. If checking occurs while you are carving, or if you plan to carve a checked piece, you can often modify the design to incorporate or allow for the check or to make it inconspicuous. But if the piece checks after completion, if you buy or make a carving of green wood, or if you bring to our steam-heated dryness a carving from the humid South Seas, you can expect conspicuous cracks that will require repair.

Carvers of large figures, who work from logs, expect checking as the wood seasons; many simply allow it to occur. Some even claim that it enhances the piece—"proves that it's wood." If the piece is to be sold, however, the check or checks may have to be repaired or treated, but it is most unlikely that checks will grow and damage or split the work, unless the wood is still quite green. After all, some carvers actually wet the wood upon which they are working. I read of a Japanese carver of woodblocks who actually works with the block under water; he claims the work is easier and surer—and the chips float away. In the Southern Highlands of North Carolina, carvers boil fruitwood and nutwood blocks in water for a half hour before they begin carving small animals and the like. They insist it makes carving easier and reduces the danger of splitting off legs and other possible cross-grain projections. There is no permanent damage to the piece; any discoloration when the piece dries is covered in the finishing anyhow. Carving green fruitwood is a lot easier than carving the seasoned wood, but checks will occur—and may make trouble later on.

So I asked Joe Clark, pathologist at the Forest Products Laboratory, Madison, Wisconsin. His reply: "Steaming does not physically damage wood, but may cause an appreciable loss of surface extractives, which lowers the natural resistance of the wood to stain and decay fungus infections." In other words, don't steam wood that is going to be exposed to weather or moisture

without protection. He also reminded me that wood can be *too* wet to carve well. This was one reason, presumably, why Indians of the far Northwest removed all sapwood before they carved totem poles of cedar.

Basically, checking seems to be greatest with fruitwoods and with woods that have seasoned naturally. Kiln-dried wood offers fewer problems—but also fewer prospects and greater cost. If you have good wood available and no way to kiln-dry it, *and the time to wait,* you can season it yourself. The need is to achieve uniform drying throughout the wood, to slow down moisture evaporation particularly at the ends. The log should be debarked, then coated at the ends with varnish, paint, or wax. Several carvers I know swear that the best treatment is to melt beeswax onto the end, then heat it with a blowtorch to drive it in. This will certainly get deeper penetration and will reduce the likelihood of spalling and flaking of the coating. Then the log can be placed under cover (but not inside) for weathering. Farmers used to do this with ash and hickory pieces for tool handles—putting them up in the rafters of a shed or barn. The time for weathering will vary with the piece and the wood. An old country maxim is "a year per inch of diameter," which seems excessive if one starts to consider a 1-ft. or 2-ft log.

Cracks and checks can be masked with reasonable success. Furniture refinishers use sealing wax colored to the same tone as the wood, which they "butter" into the crack with a heated tool, just as they fill scratches and holes. The only problem with this approach is that later working of the wood may cause some of the wax to be squeezed up into an unsightly ridge.

Somewhat safer is the use of plastic wood or glue mixed with sawdust of the wood being filled. The adhesive, however, has a different reaction to stains and finishes than the original wood, so some retouching is necessary, unless the whole piece is to be painted. The best method I've found is to make wedges of slivers of chips of the original wood, matching them with the wood surrounding the crack for color, grain, and pattern, and gluing them in, carefully removing any glue excess at once, then cutting and/or sanding when the repair dries.

PREVENTING CHECKING WITH PEG

Polyethylene glycol 1000 (PEG) is a preventive for checking of green wood, warping, and dimensional change if applied in sufficient quantity. To obtain high dimensional stability, penetration of the chemical throughout the wood is required and a uniform uptake of 25 to 30% of the chemical solution based on the weight of the dry wood is a necessity, according to the Forest Products Laboratory in its many tests.

This means that it is difficult to treat large logs. A better procedure is to rough-carve the green wood, treat with PEG, dry, then finish-carve the piece. Further, the PEG is hygroscopic, so a fairly thick finish such as polyurethane varnish is required; otherwise the treated wood will be sticky to the touch and bleeding of the PEG will occur during humid weather.

Tests with PEG over the past six years show that checking of small pieces in particular can be reduced by penetration of the outer surface. Surface treatment will *not*, however, prevent decay. Also, water will leach out the PEG rather readily, and leaves a waxlike tacky surface that must be polyurethane varnished if the carving is to be exposed to atmosphere and moisture. Ordinary varnishes will either not adhere or will dry very slowly.

A number of carvings from Liberia and Southeast Asia were protected at the Lab with PEG. They had checked as a result of our dry winter atmosphere—in as short a time as two weeks after receipt. The carvings were soaked in water for two weeks (which also removed the cheap varnish), then were soaked in a 50% solution of PEG for three to seven days at 140° F, or for three weeks in a 30% solution of PEG at 70° F.

Walnut, maple, and cherry are all likely to check seriously when they dry, particularly if they are dried quickly. In experiments with untreated walnut carvings at the Lab, 70% were rejects after drying at 80° F and 30% relative humidity, only 25% after drying at 65°. However, walnut carvings soaked in 30% PEG for two to three weeks at room temperature, or for four to 14 days at 130–140° showed no surface checks, splits, or warps. Even short soaks of 12 to 24 hours at 140–180° will do a job on a small walnut

carving, particularly if it is dried slowly thereafter at 65°.

Cherry soaks up less PEG than walnut, but the treatment works just as well. Maple carvings, on the other hand, soak up more PEG, but develop serious splits anyway. Maple must have a much heavier treatment, so it will retain 25–30% PEG. American elm, southern pine, red oak, and yellow poplar have all been treated successfully when quite green, but warp if the treatment is delayed until the wood is partly seasoned. Such wood must be soaked in water for several weeks before rough carving and PEG treatment. Burls and crotches can be stabilized with PEG too, but require 50% solution and as much as 60 days' treatment because of their dense structure.

In general, soaking time varies with wood density. White pine, spruce, redwood, soft maple, cottonwood, willow and the like require only half as much time as walnut. Hard maple, yellow birch, beech, the oaks, and apple require double or triple the time for walnut. Very dense woods like manzanita, mesquite, desert ironwood, myrtle, and burls of most species require long high-temperature treatment in most cases.

Wood in contact with the ground will rot out sooner or later and is also subject to attacks by termites, boring ants, worms, fungus, and others. The best retardant is to lift them from the ground and any contact with a frequently damp concrete or other base.

Dip treatment for as long as an hour in 5% pentachlorphenol or copper naphthenate in a heavy oil carrier (No. 2 fuel oil, for example) is the best treatment thus far offered by the Lab. Tests were made on southern pine in Mississippi, some pieces painted and some not, exposed to wetting and shade but not on the ground. Dip treatment will double or triple wood life and is much more effective than painting. In some cases, adding a water repellent seemed to help.

Preservative applications will help prevent rotting of a tree trunk in contact with the ground, but must be done frequently. Checking will expose untreated wood; the surface treatment tends to be shallow in penetration and is washed off by rain and weathering. Soil fumigants can be applied about the roots of a dead tree, but are temporary in effect. Root wood can be bored and treated with preservatives but is not very practical.

✳Repairing Broken Carvings

Solving Some of the Problems

While you're still carving a piece, a minor slip or split can often be repaired by slight redesign. But there'll be times when you have to repair your own piece—remember that Michelangelo (or someone else) repaired the fingers on the Pietà, according to recent X-rays. Also, there will be times when you see a carving in a shop, or an antique carving, low-priced because it is damaged. I've bought some for half price and repaired them, just as I have had to repair some that I bought abroad and found broken on arrival. And I've even had an instance or two of pieces that I found had been "repaired" by someone earlier, so clumsily that it was a major job to break the piece again so it could be repaired properly. One was an antelope, whose four spindly legs had been reinforced with a club-shaped brace at the navel!

There are only a few general rules for repair, because so much depends upon the piece and how it was broken. If it is a gluing job, I use a casein glue like Elmer's (why not—that's my name) for anything that will not be exposed to excessive moisture or go outside, the two-component plastic cements for what goes in the weather.

The old hot glues take too much time and involve too much waste for my kind of hobby operation, and I've been surprised to find that professional cabinetmakers are also abandoning them for the two types mentioned above, for reasons of economy, neatness, and convenience. After all, the modern glues dry transparent and are easily masked. Further, if there is a slight pit, it is easy to rub in some sawdust of the wood in

Girl at *CENTER* has replacement hands and tortilla. White pine, 6 in. long, shown before repainting.

question, thus approximating correct color.

When parts are to be replaced, it's a different story. You must start by hunting out wood that will match that of the original, unless the repair is to be painted. For example, I bought "The Storm," carved by "A Brande '32," in a small shop in northern New York State about 1950. It was broken and battered, so a bargain, and the "'32" was apparently 1832 rather than 1932. The high-relief plaque, 10 x 14 in., is carved in a piece of oak beam from a barn. While I was in the neighborhood, I found small scraps of old oak.

I shaped the broken ends of the carved sections flat for good joints and simply glued in he pieces. They've held for 20 years, because the plaque is not handled or subjected to pressure. In this case, a little delicate shaping could be done after reassembly, and the area of the joint could be sanded. Then the new wood and the sanded area were carefully toned with stain to as nearly the color of the original as possible. Time did the rest.

In another case, a friend knocked over his Balinese rearing horse pictured, then lost the broken bits. The base was far too small and light to make it stable. Our local amateur theater group decided to use it as a prop—if I'd repair it. The wood is similar in color to basswood with a creamy finish, but harder and more brittle, thus basswood could be used for the replacement parts.

There was a short sliver of the tail on the base, indicating the three-point support of the original, so I designed a new flowing tail. Then I made a new leg in the same proportions as the remaining one, and an ear the same way. The leg joint was reinforced with a brad through a drilled hole because the joint is inherently weak, being across grain. Both hoof tips had similar cut-off brads added to act as dowel pins.

With two sound legs, the horse could be positioned on the base and the tail fitted precisely. The broken spot on the rump was flattened so the tail had a firm gluing base and the joint was reinforced with two small brads. Then the joint between tail and tail-sliver in the base was made.

After a little shaping and sanding, the

new parts were tinted with pigment to hide the joints, slight grain, etc., and the whole horse given a coat or two of dull varnish, then waxed. Now it is good for another 15 years, and more stable because I hollowed out the base and put in lead sinkers.

Delicate parts must usually be fashioned almost completely before application, but it is sometimes easier to glue on a rough-shaped replacement and finish-carve afterward. For example, in the group pictured, a Mexican Indian and her daughter making tortillas, it was possible to take the girl off the base when her hands were discovered missing. I rough-carved replacement forearms and tortilla, then glued them in place and recarved the hands to an exact match with the original. This whole carving is white pine and painted, so grain and color are no problem. The somewhat dusty original, which I made about 20 years ago, has a music box concealed in the oven.

There are times, incidentally, when discretion is the better part of valor in carving as in everything else. I made an end table several years ago which featured Aztec and Maya designs, including two rain gods, which have projecting hooked noses. It was obvious that these would be broken off sooner or later. To delay the evil day, I reinforced them with cut-off brads in holes.

I also heard, years ago, of a carver who reinforced the staff or wand of a chess king he was making by drilling down through it and inserting a finishing nail. He knew that sooner or later some player in the grip of emotion would snap that small-diameter rod. So think about protective reinforcing.

When small pieces must be made, it is often easier to carve the piece on the end of the stock from which it comes, then cut it loose finally. Holding a small piece of wood in the fingertips can become frustrating. Also, there are times when a reinforcing pin must be put in as the joint is assembled.

One way to match the two holes is to drill one of the holes, then set loosely in it a brad with just the tip of the point projecting. The other section is then located properly and pressed down; the brad point will mark where the matching hole must be. In this case, be very careful to match the direction of the holes from the mating faces as well as the hole position. A hole at right angles to the joint face is the safest solution, if possible.

Another way to locate holes is to cut a template of paper the shape of the joint and locate the holes on it, then apply the proper face to each side of the joint in turn, marking the hole or holes.

RIGHT—Bali horse has new left leg, tail, and ear, plus lead counterweights in base to avoid further trouble. Overall height 22 in. Repairs of basswood on a creamy white original without apparent grain lines. *BELOW*—Knee of leader, umbrella edge, and handle (withe), scroll and pegs of third figure's violin are all replacements in this oak high-relief panel, "The Storm."

✳ Carving Tools and Accessories

From Knife to Riffler File

What tools does the beginner need? It depends upon the beginner—his age, his previous knowledge of tools (if any), and the projects he plans. Youngsters ordinarily start with a pocketknife (Sketch A), because this is a minimum investment and pocketknives are easy to find, although many are ill-suited for whittling anything except newspapers and fingernails. Oldsters have been known to acquire all the possible carving equipment at once—then wonder what to make.

My suggestion is to hold tools—and hence investment—to a minimum initially, until you find out just what you want to do. If you plan hand-size figures in relatively soft woods, and you hope to have the setup portable, get a pocketknife. But get a good one, with carbon-steel blades rather than stainless; they hold an edge longer and can be sharpened to a keener edge. The knife should not be too heavy or clumsy. Two blades are enough, the smaller a pen shape, the larger a clip or spear point (Sketches B), which makes hole-drilling and deep-recessing easier. Blades should not be too thick. My long-term favorite for small work is a penknife, but I find that long hours of using it tend to cramp my hand nowadays. A slightly larger handle is better, but it should

Well-equipped carver keeps his tools aligned on the bench with edges toward him, proper for a Western-world carver.

be free of blister-making projections like those of an auxiliary bottle-opener or other gadget. One danger with a pocketknife or most clasp knives is that you may catch the point in the wood and close the blade on a finger. The Swedish barrel knife or sloyd knife avoids this, but usually has a thick blade with center ridge—only one.

If portability is not the basic criterion, a carver's knife is very useful (C). This has a stubby, pointed blade and a large handle, so can take quite heavy cuts. It is also possible to use one or a kit of interchangeable-bladed knives, particularly for very small work, model-making, and scraping cuts. I know several whittlers who use nothing else, and discard the blades when they are dull to avoid the nuisance of resharpening. I have found, however, that for steady whittling, the blades tend to be too thin and to rotate in the chuck under stress, with bloody results. There are several forms of leatherworking and skinner's knives that have plastic handles molded to an adult hand and take interchangeable blades. If you are willing to start by grinding the blades down to suit your purposes, they work quite well. Some carvers make knives from kitchen paring knives, straight razors or the like. All things considered, a couple of knives, one large, one small, is probably the best bet for versatility. These can be supplemented by tiny knives made by breaking off the edge of a razor blade with a pair of pliers and binding it into a piece of ¼-in. dowel for such jobs as putting a ship into a bottle or making a figure an inch high, or whittling a chain from a matchstick. For chip carving, a knife like a skew chisel is handy (D). If figures are your "thing," add a tiny gouge, called a "veiner," for making grooves, plus a ¼-in. scroll gouge for fluting. And of course a small oilstone and hone.

The dedicated whittler starts with a rectangular block and his knife and makes a one-piece object with only one tool. But for the rest of us, who haven't time to quibble or to dig ditches with teaspoons, I'd suggest a scroll or compass saw (or access to a bandsaw) to cut out blanks. This will get rid of excess wood faster, provide a silhouette for the carving, and may salvage valuable wood in some instances. You can also try dental drills or hand grinders for roughing or cutting away the background of a panel and for surface textures, but I find that they chew the wood and have a tendency to "run" and cause trouble. I use them only on very hard materials like ebony, ivory, or bone.

If your inclinations, budget, and projects are larger, you'll probably want to add carving tools and a mallet (H). Of course, if it's totem poles or trees you're carving, you'll also want a shingling ax or equivalent, relatively light in weight and with a thin blade that will take and hold a razor edge. But this is a different sort of thing. Tool sizes and shapes should be suited to the kind of work you do, but a basic group of about a dozen tools will handle the normal series of jobs. These can be supplemented with other, more specialized tools as you gain skill or tackle more ambitious projects, but if you tend to try something new each time, as I do, you'll probably stick with a limited number of more-or-less standard types, changing size to accommodate the project. Thus I have firmers (E—like carpenter's flat chisels, but sharpened from both sides) of many widths from $\frac{1}{16}$ to 2 in., and flat gouges in the same general range. The big tools will remove chips faster, but the small ones are needed for details. A few rounder gouges and special shapes are helpful, but may require more space than you have readily available, take time to find, and are harder to sharpen.

But, before we get into tool selection, it should be pointed out that the basic difference between the knife and corresponding chisels is that the latter usually require two hands to control properly. They take off chips faster, and in some cases more accurately, but because the basic cut is a push rather than a hand contraction, one hand must do the pushing while the other guides and restrains the tool. (Usually, the right hand pushes and the left restrains, but it is important to be able to learn to use tools with either hand in a pinch. Ambidextrous carving saves time and changes of position, as well as reducing problems with grain, light, and holding of the work.) It seems paradoxical to have one hand push and the other hold back, but unless this is done, the extra pressure required to start the cut may cause the tool to run or overcut immediately thereafter. This is likewise true, but to a lesser extent, when the mallet provides the propelling

force. It permits more exact control of the blow, and is almost essential in cutting hard woods like walnut, ebony, and teak, but again ties up both hands.

All this means that if the piece is small, it must be held in some way other than in the hand, unless just veiner lining or some similar small operation is being done. (Besides, it's much safer not to hold the piece in one hand while trying to make a chisel cut with the other; I have the scars to prove it!)

Thus, if you decide to use chisels (F and G), you'll also have to consider having a series of them and space to lay them out, as well as a good, solid support for the workpiece and necessary holding devices. Large panels and big in-the-round blocks will be stable of themselves, particularly if you stick to relatively small tools and slow chip removal. That last is what carvers in Bali, India, China, and Japan do, but their work tends to be small and very intricate, and they sit on the floor tailor-fashion, so can hold the work in their laps and put tools on the floor. They take time to nibble away at the hard woods they usually cut; but you may want to work softer woods and may want to get the job done over the weekend. You may also want to use power tools or rasps and files, and these again frequently require both hands and a conventional shop setup rather than a chair next to the fireplace in the living room.

Carving tools are sized by width of cutting edge or "sweep," stepping from $\frac{1}{16}$ to $\frac{3}{8}$ in. in sixteenths, in eighths to 1 in. and on up in larger steps. Some may be in millimeter widths: 1, 2, 3, 5, 6, 7, 8, 10, 12, 16, 20, 25, 30, 35, etc. (1 mm = 0.037 in.) The first set of carving tools I had were English in origin

Eastern carvers have few tools and fewer accessories. Here a carver at Mas, Bali, squats on a mat with his tools —none with handles and all small—at his left knee. The carving is a figure in ebony, his leg is his vise.

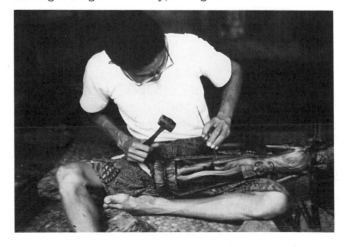

and came in a canvas roll. Included were nine tools: ½-in. firmer and skew firmer, ½-in. scroll and hollow gouges, ½-in. short-bent scroll gouge, ¾-in. extra-flat gouge, ½- and ⅜-in. hollow gouges, and ½-in. parting or V-tool, with sharpening slips in end pockets. This would have been better with a veiner replacing the corner or skew firmer. My first supplements were a veiner, larger gouges and firmers, then smaller ones, some bent to handle grounding (cutting away the background in a panel). I soon learned that the V-tool cut a sharp-bottomed channel and the veiner and gouges cut grooves of varying shape and depth, all faster and better than I could have done them with a knife, but they do add complications to a job I dislike anyhow — sharpening. Veiner and V-tool also require razor edges to work as they should, plus added technique, because in a diagonal cut across grain, one edge is going with the grain but the other against it, so burring, splitting and running off a line into the grain are easy.

Practically any of these tools can be obtained with a bent rather than a straight shank (F). These add cutting convenience but increase sharpening difficulty. The spade or fishtail tool, on the other hand, makes it easier to get into corners and undercuts, is lighter and easier to sharpen, and does not conceal so much of the work, particularly in sizes of ½ in. and wider. The edge cross-section is the same as on a straight tool, but it rapidly narrows.

The long-bent tool is called a "grounder" in England, because that's its major use. The short-bent and knuckle tools are used to form spherical or cylindrical cross-sections and are supplemented by the back-bent tools for undercutting. There is also the dogleg tool, sometimes also called a grounder in this country. The fluter or deep gouge will cut deep channels but can also be used to cut larger cross-sections by rotating it slightly to right or left. But a combination of scroll and flat gouges will do the latter job quite well also. Various special shapes and shanks were formerly available but are now hard to come by, except for the macaroni, a 3-sided tool for cutting flat-bottomed grooves and the like. Other tools had a bend to one side or the other, but really do not normally justify their ownership. There are also burins (J) or gravers (solid chisels) developed for wood-block engraving, which work well in end grain.

All things considered, the most useful tools are the flat gouge for roughing, shaping, and cleaning up, the firmer for flat surface and finishing, the veiner for outlining and emphasizing a line, and the V-tool for square corners and angle-bottomed grooves. On large work, I find standard carpenter's chisels and gouges better for roughing because they are heavy tools and will take a beating in hard woods where a carving tool will break. I have them ½, ¾, 1, 1½, and 2 in. wide.

The easy way to work is standing up at a bench heavy enough so it won't shift. For heads and similar figures in blocks, a small stand weighted at the bottom with a rock or anchored to the floor is excellent, provided there is room on it or on a nearby shelf for the tools in use. In low-relief carving, I find I can work on the end of a card table or on an outdoor trestle table, and sit down part of the time, because the panel itself absorbs the shock of mallet blows. The problem in any instance is to have all the tools you need conveniently at hand, preferably laid out in a loose row with their ends toward you, so you can select a desired tool rapidly.

Common commercial handles are round or octagon, tapered toward the cutting edge. The round ones are maple, beech, ash, or boxwood, the octagonal may even be dogwood, which they use in Oberammergau. The octagonal handles have less tendency to roll on the bench or turn in the hand. If you're cutting hard woods, you'll want handles with brass ferrules to keep them from splitting at the tang.

Other tools are familiar woodworking tools like the scraper and hand router, rasps, and riffler files (I). The latter come in various shapes and sizes, some straight, some bent, and have a different surface at each end. They are useful for finishing in tight areas or over knots and faults.

Holding can be done with wood or other clamps, in a vise with soft jaws, or by clamp blocks screwed to the work surface. If a hole in the base is not objectionable, there is a specialized tool called a carver's screw, which comes up through a hole in the table and screws into the workpiece, then is locked by a wingnut beneath the table. This has the advantage that the block can be rotated around the screw, but it cannot be tipped or lifted easily. In some instances, the workpiece can be set up on blocks to permit easier access to the base, but blocks may shift too, if you become aggressive.

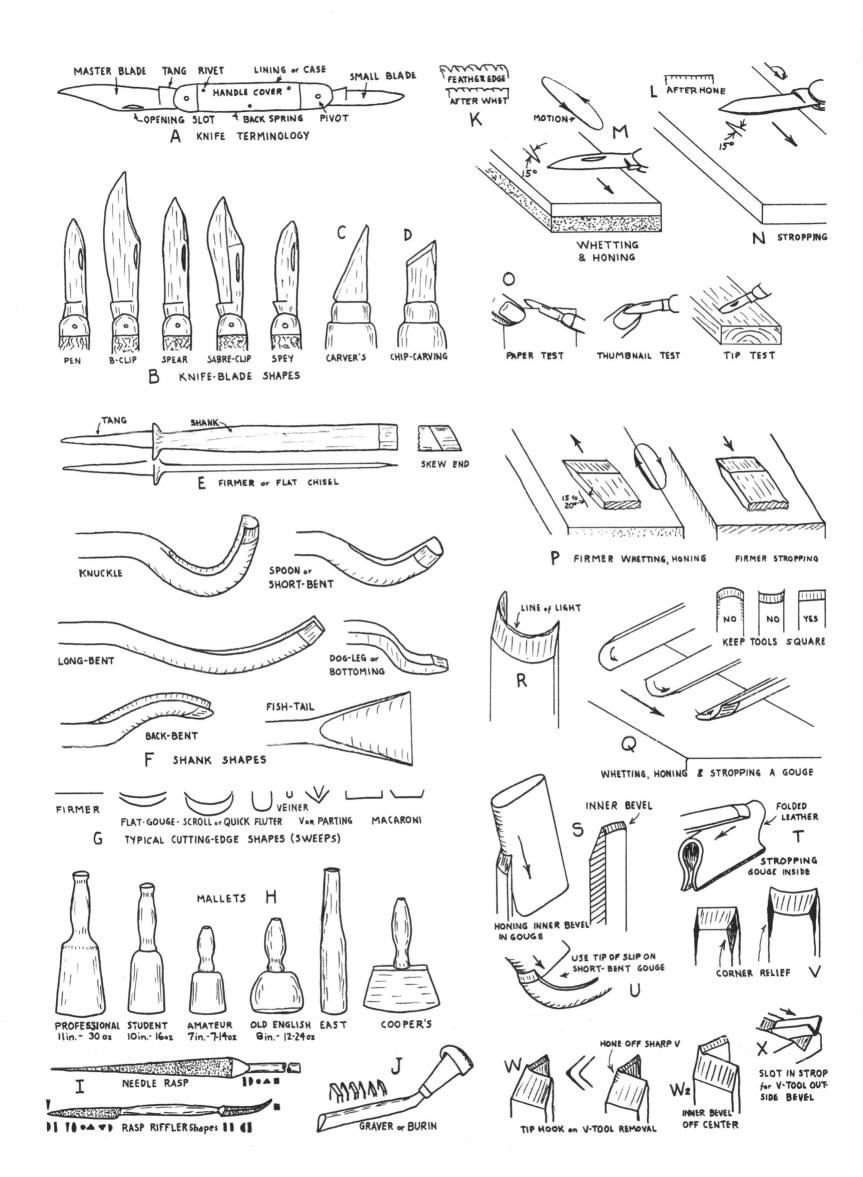

A KNIFE TERMINOLOGY

MASTER BLADE · TANG · RIVET · LINING or CASE · SMALL BLADE · HANDLE COVER · OPENING SLOT · BACK SPRING · PIVOT

B KNIFE-BLADE SHAPES

PEN · B-CLIP · SPEAR · SABRE-CLIP · SPEY · CARVER'S **C** · CHIP-CARVING **D**

FEATHER EDGE · AFTER WHET **K**

MOTION **M** · 15° · WHETTING & HONING

L AFTER HONE · 15° · **N** STROPPING

O PAPER TEST · THUMBNAIL TEST · TIP TEST

TANG · SHANK · SKEW END · **E** FIRMER or FLAT CHISEL

KNUCKLE · SPOON or SHORT-BENT · LONG-BENT · DOG-LEG or BOTTOMING · BACK-BENT · FISH-TAIL · **F** SHANK SHAPES

P 15 to 20° · FIRMER WHETTING, HONING · FIRMER STROPPING

LINE of LIGHT · **R** · NO · NO · YES · KEEP TOOLS SQUARE · **Q** · WHETTING, HONING & STROPPING A GOUGE

FIRMER · FLAT-GOUGE · SCROLL or QUICK · FLUTER · VEINER · V or PARTING · MACARONI
G TYPICAL CUTTING-EDGE SHAPES (SWEEPS)

MALLETS **H**

PROFESSIONAL 11in.-30oz · STUDENT 10in.-16oz · AMATEUR 7in.-7-14oz · OLD ENGLISH 8in.-12-24oz · EAST · COOPER'S

INNER BEVEL **S** · FOLDED LEATHER **T** · STROPPING GOUGE INSIDE · HONING INNER BEVEL IN GOUGE · USE TIP OF SLIP ON SHORT-BENT GOUGE **U** · CORNER RELIEF **V**

I NEEDLE RASP · RASP RIFFLER Shapes

J GRAVER or BURIN

W TIP HOOK on V-TOOL REMOVAL · HONE OFF SHARP V · **W₂** INNER BEVEL OFF CENTER · **X** SLOT IN STROP for V-TOOL OUT SIDE BEVEL

✳How to Sharpen Tools

Essential for Good Carving

Most carvers hate resharpening tools; it takes time to do properly. The time is recouped through faster, safer, and more-accurate cutting, but it doesn't seem that way. It's a necessary evil to most of us.

There are actually four operations involved: grinding, whetting, honing, and stropping. Most tools are ground when you get them, so any grinding you may do will be because you decide to modify the edge shape, you nick the edge, or from wear.

A ground edge is like a very fine saw — microscopic teeth projecting to the sides, with feathers trailing from them — the so-called wire edge (see Sketch K, preceding page). Whetting and honing are really progressively finer grinding operations, so they reduce the size of the teeth and remove some of the wire edge, but it takes stropping to align the teeth and get rid of the feather (L). (That's why a barber strops a razor.) Once this edge is aligned and cleaned, it will stay that way as long as it is honed and stropped frequently — until it finally wears too blunt.

Grinding was once done on grindstones, but nowadays is done on small-diameter, high-speed and fast-cutting wheels, so there is constant danger of overheating and burning the thin cutting edge — or the tip of a knife. Steel is tempered by heating, quenching, then drawing a temper very exactly. That temper, which is what gives a blade its hardness, can be removed by overheating. Once the temper is drawn, you may as well grind that part away; it won't hold an edge anyway. (You can see a burned spot as an aura of straw, blue, and purple on the surface of the metal.) The only way to avoid it is to cool the tool in water frequently — about twice as often as you consider necessary.

Grinding is a special skill; unless you do a lot of it and have a good power grinder, you'd be advised to let a professional regrind your broken, chipped, and dropped-on-the-concrete tools — I did just that for years. The wheel must be fine-grained, clean, steady (no portable grinders!) and equipped with a tool rest. If the wheel has been used to sand or sharpen pencils or is grooved, you'll have trouble. A nicked or broken tool should first be fed in perpendicular to the wheel axis until the fault is ground out, then resharpened. The tool is held so the wheel turns *toward* the cutting edge, and the ground face is 15 to 20 degrees with the axis of the tool — a bit more than the angle of a pocketknife blade. The edge is fed across the wheel. Both sides of a firmer are ground, but just the outer side of a gouge, but the included angle of the edge will be about 30 degrees because of the way tools are ground. (If you're an accomplished grinder and carver, you may want to make the edge angle smaller for cutting thin woods and greater for hard, the range being 15 to 25 degrees on a side.)

If a flat tool is held and moved properly across the wheel, and a gouge is rocked slightly as it is sharpened, the result will be slight hollow grinding as a result of the curvature of the wheel perimeter. This is good; it makes the tool easier to whet and hone, reduces drag behind the cutting edge, even may make the tool retain sharpness longer. But be sure the ground edge is straight and square; a gouge should not be rounded at the corners or dip in the center, and a firmer's cutting edge should be in the center of blade thickness.

I have tried to sketch how to whet, hone, and strop, the operations you'll be doing more often. Whetting and honing are exactly similar in technique; both are done on hand stones, whetting on the coarse side and honing on the fine if you have a 2-faced stone. If you're using natural stones, whetting is done on Washita, a yellowish or grayish natural whetstone. Honing is done on Arkansas, a white, very hard and uniform fine-grit stone. The latter is the common material for "slips," the small shaped stones for honing the inside of gouges, veiners, and V-tools.

To prevent the stone from "loading" or filling with the fine particles of steel cut from the tool, it should be lubricated with a thin machine oil or even a 50-50 mixture of machine oil and kerosene. When the lubricant turns gray with steel particles, it should be wiped off and replaced. Periodically, also, a natural stone should be washed thoroughly with benzine or gasoline, or boiled in water containing a little soda. This lifts out the soaked-up oil and grit. A manufactured stone usually can be cleaned just by heating it in an oven and wiping it while still hot, because the heating causes the oil to exude.

Stropping is done on a piece of leather like a razor strop, except that it is usually mounted on a block or otherwise held so both your hands may be free. Professionals have two strops, the coarser impregnated with crocus powder in oil, the second with oil alone. (Obviously, the blade being sharpened should be wiped free of grit between steps of the sharpening operation, because bigger grit will be transferred and ruin the effectiveness of the finer cutting material otherwise.) Stropping, by the way, is not done by moving the blade edge-first, but with the edge *trailing*.

Sharpen your knife on hand stones only, unless you nick it badly or break off the tip and must reshape the blade. The original wedge shape of the blade gives proper clearance and support for the cutting edge, so all you need do normally is renew the edge wedge and realign the tiny saw teeth. If the blade is very dull, take a few strokes on the coarse stone (or Washita), holding the blade at a slight angle above the stone and drawing it down the length. With a little practice, you can develop a sort of oval motion (M), in which you press on the draw stroke and lift on the return, without ever really taking the blade off the stone.

When the edge shows no line of reflected light or tiny nicks, move to the fine-grit side (or Arkansas) and repeat the process, taking the last stroke or two at very light pressure to help remove the wire edge. Then strop—in this case moving the knife heel-first, trailing the edge (N). Again, you can develop the barber's trick of fast stropping, rolling the blade *over its heel or back* at the end of a stroke so a return stroke can be made. After a dozen or so strokes on each side (half on each leather if you have two), give the blade a strop or two on the palm of your hand. Then test it.

There are three common tests for sharpness (O): The first is to hold a piece of thin paper between your fingertips and to draw the blade over the top edge. It should cut the paper, not fold or bend it and not drag. The second is to draw the edge across the end of your thumbnail; it should tend to stick—in other words, *cut*—rather than simply sliding across. Third, make an oblique or slashing cut with the tip in a piece of soft wood; it

should cut in without drag. This tip test is important, because it is easy to get a razor edge on the blade and still have a dull tip.

Sloyd-bladed knives, because they have a thicker wedge shape (edge to center rather than edge to back), are laid flat on the stone.

Firmers and chisels are sharpened like knife blades, except that the blade is pushed over the stone. Also, because the blade is narrow, you may have a tendency to rock it or tilt it slightly, thus grinding away the corners and getting a rounded cutting edge. A firmer with rounded corners is good for only one thing that I know of: smoothing a background without catching and grooving at the corners. For carving you need a flat edge with sharp corners, because the corners replace the tip on a knife blade. Hold the firmer up at a slight angle, 15 to 20 degrees, above the stone, and sharpen with an oval motion similar to that described for the knife (P). Carpenter chisels are sharpened just as the firmer is, except from one side only, with just a final stroke or two on the other side, with the chisel lying flat, to wipe off the wire edge.

Tests for sharpness are the same as for a knife, but one can be added: chamfering

José Ramón Trujillo, self-taught carver of Jocotepec, Mexico, has only a few tools, but has demonstrated his skill at the Casa de Las Artesanias in Guadalajara on several occasions. Here he works on my Madonna.

off the corner of a piece of soft wood with a single push. The blade should cut smoothly and evenly across the grain.

Sharpening a gouge is somewhat trickier; the method is diagrammed (Q). A new gouge will normally have a 15-degree angle on the bevel, so this is laid flat on the hone with the handle out to the side, then the tool is moved down the hone and rolled slightly against the stroke direction as it moves, so the entire bevel is honed equally. You must learn just how much to twist so you do not overroll and round the corners. This wiping process is continued until the edge shows no line of light (R). Then the inner bevel is honed on with a slip (a wedge-shaped hand stone with rounded edges to fit the contour of the gouge. The slip is simply moved down in a wiping motion, each stroke being a little farther around the curve. The slip should form a short inner bevel of about 15 degrees as well, so the included angle of the gouge is 30 degrees. This gives better clearance and slipperage for the chip, makes it possible to turn the gouge over for convex cuts without sticking the handle against the work, and gives a sturdier edge. Done well, this inner bevel will be about a quarter of the length of the outer one, and it is often possible to keep the gouge quite sharp simply by dressing this inner bevel. When the two bevels approximate each other in length, it's time to whet the outside.

A gouge is also stropped as it is honed,

Cremations in Bali involve the burning of two or more images of bulls. Here a carver works on a head in soft wood with only a few tools.

with a wiping sidewise motion (Q). This removes the wire edge or burr. A piece of soft leather impregnated with crocus powder in oil can be folded and used to give a few strokes on the inner bevel (T). The object is partly to get the bevel surfaces polished; this makes cutting easier and leaves the wood surface smoother, almost polished.

A minor point or two: The short-bent gouge is difficult to hone internally, because only the tip of the slip can be used (U). However, it is used only rarely, so doesn't dull too fast either. Some professionals relieve the heel behind the cutting edge of both firmers and flat gouges (V) so they can get into' tighter places with them. Both sides must be ground this way on a gouge, and both sides of one face of a firmer.

The V or parting tool is a difficult one to sharpen because of the thickness of metal at the point of the V. With continuous sharpening, a tit tends to form at the end of the V (W) because the slip wears into a curved edge, hence doesn't hone a sharp angle. The remedy is to hone away just a little of the outside of the tip so the cutting edge is in effect two chisel edges joined by a tiny arc. On a small V-tool, it is also easy to overhone one side (W2), so a slight depression occurs there, matched by a slight hook on the other side. The remedy is of course to equalize the honing, but it may be necessary to whet the end square by holding the tool perpendicular to the stone, then re-create the bevels by watching the line of light along the edge. Cut a V-groove in your strop for easier honing of the outer bevel (X).

The best habit to develop, in connection with keeping tools sharp, is to strop or hone (if necessary) while you plan the next cut. If you do this regularly, the most-used tools will be kept sharp almost unconsciously. Some professionals simplify the whole operation by having some form of shaped hone and strop—like a larger-diameter wood roll with grooves cut in it corresponding to the inner faces of the common tools. This dips in a bath of crocus powder and oil as it rotates, so all the carver has to do is hold the tool against it to renew the inner bevel. Other carvers use emery-cloth pads and similar devices, but these tend to round the edge rather than maintain the angle. It also goes without saying that tools must be arranged, stored when not in use, and kept oiled so that their cutting edges are protected.

✳Woods—Kinds and Characteristics

How to Select Them

While quality and sizes available may have declined in recent years, the varieties of woods available to the carver has increased, partly because of our own efforts, but also because of the activities of amateur woodworkers and cabinetmakers and of groups like the International Wood Collectors Society and the National Wood Carvers Association. Members of these latter groups exchange usable pieces and sources.

For the whittler, however, it is most important to have good sources for white or sugar pine and basswood. A high percentage of his projects will be made in these soft and readily workable woods, particularly if he is addicted to small figures. But if it is a decorative panel, or the design is quite small or complicated, denser, harder woods are required. Most of us do not have lime, English oak, box, olive, or other standbys of the European carvers available, so we make do with fruitwoods, holly, mahogany, walnut, and teak.

Mahogany, for example, is a name for a variety of woods, ranging from the solid structures of the Latin American and African varieties to the open structure and softness of Philippine mahogany. (Even the latter may be a misnomer; I have six samples of differing Philippine woods, all loosely called mahogany but ranging from soft to quite hard and dense!) Ironwood is also a common name for very hard woods, which sometimes turn out to be lignum vitae, cocobola, or some other wood—like Osage orange in the United States. "Pine" can mean yellow pine, which is very hard and difficult to work; "maple" can mean silver, red, or big-leaf maples, which are softer and poorer cutting woods than sugar, white, or hard maples. "Hardwood" and "softwood" are also confusing because they are commercial and botanical terms, a hardwood being from a broad-leaved tree. Thus basswood, poplar, cottonwood, and aspen are called hardwoods, although they are quite soft; yellow pine, because it is a coniferous or needle-leaved tree, is called a softwood although it is quite hard.

White pine (called "yellow pine" in England) has tints of pink and yellow, although northern or sugar pine is usually quite white and better to carve. It is the commonest wood for carving, now and in early America. *Basswood* (called "bee tree" in some areas and somewhat like the lime and linden of Europe) has less resin and is a bit softer, is quite durable too, and may have a light tan or yellow tinge.

Cypress and *butternut* are soft and easy to carve, but don't wear too well. *Red cedar* has attractive color and odor, but pieces available tend to be narrow and knotty. The purplish color of new-cut cedar fades in sunlight. *Redwood* (sequoia) is dull red and very soft but quite durable. *Sweet gum* (American satinwood), brownish, is more uniform and durable than cedar. *Holly* is our whitest wood, medium hard, but tends to check. *Beech* and *sycamore* are of similar hardness, good for shallow carving.

Red oak is darker, softer, and has a greater tendency to splinter than *white oak*. The latter, seasoned, is very hard and difficult to carve, but very durable for outside furni-

Balinese mother and child *(LEFT,* 1½ ft.) is in a wood without figure, so the carver put texture in the headcloth and a pattern in the skirt. Paul Parrass, however, carving a stylized nude in cocobola *(RIGHT,* 4 ft. high) capitalized on the figure in the wood.

ture and exterior decoration. *English oak* falls between our two types in hardness, is close-grained and ages to a dull yellow. *Austrian oak* is somewhat coarser in texture.

Walnut is dark brown with light-yellow sapwood and a visible grain. It is a highly satisfactory carving wood, although it does check and split if mishandled. It is harder and more close-grained than mahogany. *English walnut* usually has too much "figure" for carving; *Italian* can be close-grained and good. *Mahogany* can be red or brown, is easy to work and close-grained, suitable for indoor things, hence a furniture favorite. The best comes from Central America, particularly *Honduras,* but is now becoming scarce. *Cuban* is harder and has better color. *Spanish mahogany* may also come from Santo Domingo; it is close-grained. *Mexican mahogany* is usually fairly poor, as is *Philippine,* with coarse grain and poor color. (My best source for mahogany was old aircraft patterns and furniture.)

Chestnut is fairly soft, light brown, and coarse-grained, with an interesting figure. However, it splits between the summer (hard) and spring layers and tends to warp. *Maple,* whitish-pink, is hard, quite long-wearing, and a favorite for furniture. *Birdseye* and *curly* figures make attractive surfaces but are difficult to carve. *Buckeye* is quite similar. *Pecan* is harder and coarser in grain, as well as darker.

Among fruitwoods, *cherry* is the favorite. It is pinkish to red, takes sharp cuts, wears well, but is often available only in limited size. It can be stained to look like mahogany, was used extensively in the Midwest for furniture. *Apple* and *pear* are lighter in color (as is *box*) and great favorites with German and Swiss carvers. Fruitwoods are subject to insect attack, rot easily, and check and split if not carefully handled and dried.

Among imported woods, *teak* is expen-

Osage orange, hardest United States wood, has sharply contrasting growth rings of brilliant yellow and orange, thus made my tropical-fish group interesting. It is, however, an exercise in frustration, brittle and hard.

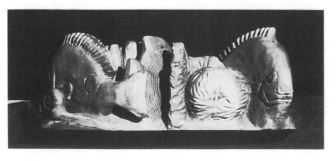

sive but an excellent wood. It cuts well, will support detail, is durable, and does not warp noticeably. It is brown, sometimes with darker streaks, weathers untreated to a soft dark gray. *Ebony,* which comes from Africa, India, Ceylon, and the Dutch East Indies, is a favorite of African, Japanese, and Balinese carvers. The *Gabon* variety from Africa is dead black; *Macassar* (Dutch East Indies) and *Calamander* (Ceylon) are brown with a black stripe. Sapwood is lighter-colored, as in walnut. It is very hard, as are *lignum vitae* (another African favorite) and *cocobola. Lancewood, box, pear, briar,* and *sandalwood* are also very hard but will take fine detail.

Rosewood ranges in color from light red to deep purple with streaks of yellow and black. It is very hard and close-grained and has much figure. The *Brazilian* is darker and more uniform in color than the *East Indian. Satinwood* is a close-grained golden yellow wood, usually cut in striped or mottled graining. The East Indian has more pronounced figure than the Brazilian.

Lacewood, from Australia, is pinkish or reddish brown, with satiny spots, so is called "silky oak." *Avodire* is a close-grained light yellow wood from Africa that looks like moire silk when quarter-sawed. *Zebrawood,* close-textured with prominent brown stripes on yellow or gold, also comes from Africa. *Harewood,* also called *English sycamore,* is really white, but when properly cut and dyed silver-gray it has an elaborate fiddle-back pattern. *Tamo,* or *Japanese ash,* has an open grain, is cream or straw-colored, with elaborate curly figure. Among others, *purple heart* is purple, *greenheart* green-yellow, *thuya burl* rich red brown (but almost impossible to carve because of its hardness and brittleness), *madrone burl* deep pinkish with a figure like an overlapping knot, *myrtle burl* pale gold and with a curly figure, *English ash burls* dark greenish yellow with brown figure.

Warping: Most woods that have been kiln-dried and properly cared for are relatively stable, but any wood is affected by the alternate moistening in summer and drying in winter of American central heating. Also, any wood that is carved green or dried in the open air can cause trouble when brought inside, although the problem is more likely to be checking and splitting than warpage unless the piece is very thin. If wood cut

Table No. 1 WORKING PROPERTIES OF COMMON WOODS

Name of Wood	Weight Per Cubic Foot (1)	Hardness	Strength (2)	Stability (3)	Gluing	Nailing (4)	Steam Bending	Planing and Jointing (5)	Turning (6)	Sanding (7)	Shaping	Mortising (8)	Remarks
	General Characteristics							Machining					
Ash	35	Med.	Med.	Best	Fair	Good	Good	Good 10-25	Fair	Best 2/0	Best	Fair	Tough—Hard to work with hand tools
Basswood	24	Soft	Weak	Good	Best	Best	Poor	Good 20-30	Poor	Poor 4/0	Poor	Fair	Excellent for toys, drafting boards, corestock
Beech	39	Hard	Med.	Poor	Poor	Poor	Good	Fair 10-20	Fair	Good 4/0	Fair	Best	Not durable outside. Hard on tools because of mineral deposits in cells
Birch	40	Hard	Strong	Good	Fair	Poor	Good	Good 15-20	Good	Fair 4/0	Best	Best	Excellent for furniture, turning, dowels, handles
Butternut	25	Soft	Weak	Best	Good	Fair	Poor	Good 10-25	Good	Fair 4/0	Fair	Fair	Furniture—Perfect for walnut imitation
Cherry	36	Med.	Med.	Good	Best	Fair	Poor	Best 10-25	Best	Best 4/0	Best	Best	Furniture, boat trim, novelties
Chestnut	27	Soft	Weak	Best	Best	Good	Fair	Good 15-20	Best	Best 3/0	Good	Good	Stains badly in contact with wet iron. Very dusty in all machining operations
Cottonwood	27	Soft	Weak	Fair	Best	Best	Poor	Poor 5-20	Poor	Poor 4/0	Poor	Fair	Excellent for boxes and other nailing jobs. Wears very well for a soft wood
Cypress	29	Soft	Med.	Good	Fair	Fair	Poor	Good 15-25	Poor	Fair 2/0	Poor	Poor	Tends to splinter. Most durable of American woods for outdoor and soil exposure
Elm (Southern)	34	Med.	Med.	Poor	Fair	Best	Good	Poor 15-20	Poor	Good 2/0	Poor	Good	Very durable under paint. A good furniture wood despite difficulties in machining
Gum (Red)	33	Med.	Med.	Poor	Best	Good	Fair	Fair 10-20	Best	Fair 4/0	Fair	Fair	One of the most used furniture woods for imitations of walnut and mahogany
Hickory	42	Hard	Strong	Good	Good	Poor	Good	Good 10-25	Good	Best 2/0	Fair	Best	Excellent for furniture and long a favorite for steam bending, tool handles, wheels
Magnolia	30	Soft	Weak	Fair	Best	Best	Best	Good 5-15	Fair	Good 4/0	Good	Poor	Excellent for steam bending, although little used as such. Often marketed as poplar
Mahogany	35	Med.	Med.	Best	Best	Good	Poor	Good 5-25	Best	Good 4/0	Best	Best	One of the best furniture woods
Mahogany (Phil.)	33	Med.	Med.	Best	Best	Good	Poor	Good 5-25	Good	Poor 3/0	Fair	Fair	Generally coarser and softer than true mahogany. Furniture, boat planking, trim
(9) Maple (Hard)	41	Hard	Strong	Good	Fair	Poor	Fair	Fair 15-20	Good	Good 4/0	Best	Best	Fine furniture, flooring, turnings, bowling pins. One of the best hardwoods
Maple (Soft)	31	Med.	Med.	Fair	Good	Fair	Fair	Poor 10-15	Fair	Good 4/0	Fair	Poor	Same uses as hard maple but an inferior wood. Difficult to machine smooth
Oak (Red)	39	Hard	Strong	Best	Good	Good	Best	Best 10-25	Good	Best 2/0	Fair	Best	Substitute for white oak in cheaper work
Oak (White)	40	Hard	Strong	Best	Good	Good	Best	Best 10-20	Good	Best 2/0	Good	Best	Interior trim, floors, furniture. One of the most used American woods
Pine (White)	25	Soft	Weak	Good	Best	Best	Poor	Good 10-25	Good	Fair 2/0	Good	Fair	Best all around soft wood. Excellent for paint
Pine (Yellow)	38	Hard	Strong	Fair	Fair	Poor	Poor	Good 10-25	Poor	Fair 2/0	Good	Good	Main uses—House construction, trim, floors
Poplar	29	Soft	Weak	Good	Best	Best	Fair	Good 5-20	Good	Poor 4/0	Poor	Fair	Excellent for carvings, toys, corestock
Redwood	29	Soft	Med.	Best	Best	Good	Poor	Good 10-25	Fair	Poor 2/0	Good	Poor	Excellent for outdoor furniture, window sills, etc.
Sycamore	35	Med.	Med.	Poor	Good	Best	Poor	Poor 5-15	Good	Poor 3/0	Poor	Best	Interior trim, furniture. Difficult to machine, but excellent appearance
Walnut	36	Med.	Strong	Best	Best	Fair	Good	Good 15-20	Best	Best 4/0	Good	Best	Has every good feature for furniture and cabinet work

NOTES

Data in this chart is largely from extensive tests made by U. S. Forest Products Laboratory, with some additions.

1. Pounds per cubic foot, dry. All woods vary in weight, even in the same tree from trunk to top. A variation of 10% over or under average should be allowed.
2. Composite strength value. Woods rated weak are strong enough for all average work.
3. Rated on unrestrained warp. Most woods are quite stable if properly seasoned and cared for.
4. Rated on ability to take nails near end without splitting.
5. All flat grain stock, shallow cut. Rating is average from runs at 15, 20 and 25-degree cutting angles. Bottom figure is best knife angle for smooth cutting.
6. Rated on smooth cutting and ability to hold detail. Not much difference between best and good.
7. Rated on freedom from fuzz. Bottom figure is coarsest abrasive grit which can be used without scratching.
8. Rated on smoothness of cut. Work speed decreases with hardness of wood and this factor might be of more importance than smoothness in production work.
9. Sugar, white or hard maple. Should be distinguished from silver, red, big-leaf or soft maple, which is an inferior machining wood although often marketed simply as "maple."

Table No. 2 WOODS-FINISHING DATA

Note: NGR = Non-Grain-Raising (Applies to stain)

	Natural Color	Usual Grain Figure	Stain: Type (1)	Stain: Color	Filler: Wt. (2)	Filler: Color	Bleach	Paint	Natural Finish	Remarks
Alder (Red)	Pink to Brown	Plain or Figured	Wiping or Water	Red or Brown	None		Yes	Yes	Yes	Principal hardwood of Pacific coast. Like red gum
Amaranth (Purpleheart)	Purple	Mild Stripe or Mottle	None		None or 6	Match Wood	No	No	Yes. Pref.	Usually finished natural to retain purple color
Ash (U.S.A.)	White to Brown	Plain or Fiddleback	Any	Any	15	White or Brown	Yes	Yes. Fill First	Yes	White filler used for frosted finish (3)
Basswood	Cream	Very Mild	NGR	Red or Brown	None		Not Nec.	Yes	No	Fuzzy grain. Usually muddy under oil stain
Birch	Cream	Mild	Any	Walnut or Mahogany	8	Natural or Brown	Yes	Yes. Interior	Yes	Used extensively for walnut and mahogany
Butternut	Heart: Amber Sap: Cream	Like Walnut	Water	Walnut or Oak	14	Medium Brown	Yes	No	Yes	Good for amber walnut without bleaching
Cedar (Aromatic Red)	Heart: Red Sap: Cream	Knotty	None		None		No	No	Yes. Pref.	Red wiping stain can be used to blend sap wood
Cherry	Red to Brown	Good	Water	Red or Brown	6-8	Red to Black	No	No	Yes	Takes excellent finish. Good for brown mahogany
Chestnut	Gray-Brown	Heavy Grain	Oil or Wiping	Red or Brown	15	Red or Brown	No	Yes	Yes	Large pores. Good for novelty finishes (3)
Cypress	Heart: Brown Sap: Cream	Plain or Figured	Water, Oil or Wiping	Red or Brown	None		No	Yes (6)	Yes	Good for sand blast (4) If water stained, see (5)
Ebony	Dark Brown to Black	Plain or Stripe	NGR	Dark Red or Brown	None or 3	Brown or Black	No	No	Yes	Oily. Gaboon ebony is blackest
Elm (Southern)	Brown to Cream	Heavy Grain	Water	Red or Brown	12	Dark Brown	No	Yes	Yes	Cross-grained. Sometimes hard to get even color
Fir (Douglas)	Cream to Red	Plain or Wild	Wiping or Oil	Brown	None		No	Yes (7)	No	Good for sand blast (4) Not pleasing stained
Gum (Red)	Heart: Br. Red Sap: Cream	Plain or Figured	Any	Red or Brown	None or 3	Match Wood	Yes	Yes	Yes	Most used wood for walnut and mahogany imitations
Hickory	White to Cream	Usually Straight	Water	Red or Brown	15	Brown	Yes	No	Yes	Good walnut or mahogany—blond finishes
Holly	Silver White	Mild	Water	Amber	None		Not Nec.	Yes	Yes	One of the whitest woods. Usually finished natural
Magnolia or Poplar	White to Yellow	Mild	Oil or Water	Red or Brown	None		No	Yes	No	Usually painted. Makes fair satinwood imitation.
Lacewood (Silky Oak)	Medium Brown	Flake	Water	Oak or Lt. Walnut	12	Dark Brown	Fairly Well	No	Yes	Excellent cabinet wood. Very decorative
Mahogany	Brown to Red-Brown	Stripe	Water	Red or Brown	12	Red to Black	Yes	No	Yes	Best known cabinet wood. Excellent for finish
Mahogany (Philippine)	Brown to Red-Brown	Stripe	Water or Wiping	Red or Brown	18	Red to Black	Yes	No	Yes	NGR stain preferable to minimize grain-raising
Maple	Cream	Varied	Water and Wiping	Maple	None		Yes	No	Yes	Use NGR stain and tone with wiping stain after sealer
Oak (English Brown)	Deep Brown	Plain, Flake or Swirl	NGR	Brown	15	Brown to Black	Yes	No	Yes	One of the best cabinet woods. Also "Pollard Oak"
Oak (Red)	Red-Brown	Plain or Flake	NGR	Green Toner (8)	15	Brown	Yes	Yes	No	Bad grain-raising with water stain, hence NGR stain preferable. Good for novelty finishes (3)
Oak (White)	White to Light Brown	Plain or Flake	NGR	Brown	15	Brown	Yes	Yes	Yes	
Orientalwood	Light Brown	Stripe Crossfire	Water	Amber or Brown	12	Brown	No	No	Yes	Good walnut effects
Pine (White)	White to Cream	Mild	Water (5) or Oil	Brown Only	None		No	Yes	No	Best for painting
Prima Vera	Yellow-White	Stripe Crossfire	Water	Amber	12	Natural or Dark	Yes	No	Yes	Also "White Mahogany". Excellent "blond" color
Redwood	Red	Mild St. Grain	Red only for toning		None		No	Yes	Yes	Excellent exterior wood. Best painted
Rosewood (Brazil)	Red-Brown	Varied	NGR	Red	15	Dark Red or Black	No	No	Yes	Oily. Wash off with lacquer thinner before staining or finishing
Rosewood (East Indies)	Red-Purple	Stripe	NGR	Dark Red	12	Dark Red	No	No	Yes	
Sapeli	Medium Brown	Stripe	Water	Red or Brown	10	Dark Brown	No	No	Yes	Very similar to striped mahogany
Sycamore	White to Pink	Flake	Water	Amber or Brown	None		Seldom	Yes	Yes	Good for natural finish
Walnut	Heart: Brown Sap: Cream	Varied	Water	Walnut	14	Brown to Black	Yes	No	Yes	Obtainable in all figures
Zebrawood	Tan with Brown Stripe	Heavy Stripe	Water	Light Oak	12	Natural	No	No	Yes	Very pronounced grain. Good for modern effects

NOTES

1. Where water stain is indicated, NGR (non-grain-raising) stain can also be used. "Oil" means penetrating oil stain; "wiping" means wiping oil stain.
2. Pounds of filler paste per gallon of thinner.
3. All coarse-grain woods are good for novelty finishes, using contrasting filler, usually white.
4. Woods with alternate hard and soft streaks can be sand-blasted or burned with torch to cut out soft wood.
5. Water stains take better on resinous woods if wood is first sponged with 4 oz. sal soda and 1 oz. washing soda to gallon of water.
6. Add 1 pt. benzol per gal. of paint for better penetration (primer only).
7. Special sealers available to kill grain.
8. For brown tones, first spray weak green stain to kill red color of wood.

green is end-coated with varnish, wax, or shellac and allowed to season slowly under cover, much of this can be avoided. Warpage is one of four kinds: crook (a side bend, bow); a bend in the flat side of a board; twist; cup (curling of a board), the most-common warp in flat wood. All are caused by shrinkage in drying and are functions both of the kind of wood and the way in which it was cut. Quarter-sawed or comb-grained hardwood, in which the grain lines through the thickness are at 45 to 90 degrees with the width (edge-grained or rift-sawed softwoods) is much more stable than flat-cut (also called plain-sawed), the common form, which has grain lines running across the face or radiating from the center. Flat-cut boards always curl away from the heart, so any carving should be done on the heart side and the panel mounted that way. Then if it curls more, it will bulge rather than hollow. See the "Stability" column in Table I for relative warpage of various woods.

Moisture Content: Any wood air-dried and stored outside will have a moisture content around 20%, as compared with 8% for kiln-dried lumber stored inside. Thus, wood stored outside should be kept inside for a month or more before being used in critical applications. If it is a log that is air-drying, be careful of checking and cracking.

Carving: "Machining" information in Table I will be helpful in determining how easily a wood may be carved. Walnut, for example, can be cut clean in a jointer, while soft maple is very rough. Rake angle of most jointer blades is about 30 degrees—that is 30 degrees off the perpendicular. If a bevel is cut on the face of the blade to reduce this angle to 15 degrees, the jointer will cut better on woods like poplar, soft maple, Philippine mahogany, cottonwood, and sycamore. This suggests that if you must carve these woods, the tool can have a blunter edge than normal.

Another exercise in frustration—a peasant cart carved of cork slabs and assembled with glue in Portugal. It uses a local product, but is as fragile as an Eiffel Tower model glued up of match sticks.

Style: Greeks and Romans carved cedar; Gothic carving was mostly in oak; Renaissance in walnut; Chippendale, Hepplewhite, Sheraton, and Duncan Phyfe in mahogany; Gibbons used lime or pear. If you're striving for authenticity or period you'll have to match them.

Finishing: In cabinet work and panel carving, the finish a wood will take may be a prime factor in selection. Table II will help you select a wood for finish and also suggests how it should be finished. Obviously, the grain and figure have much to do with the natural beauty of the wood and may strongly affect whatever carving you do. This is a whole study in itself; you can find information in books for cabinetmakers and familiarize yourself with it even more by getting a set of wood samples and studying them. For example, wood may have a narrow lengthwise stripe—called "pencil"—or a wide one—called "ribbon." Or it may have "mottle," "quilted," or "flake" surface. Burl and crotch wood have elaborate figure which will not only make your carving more difficult but will also affect final appearance.

The whittler, as I said earlier, commonly selects soft pine or basswood for figure-carving. Or he may choose a locally available wood, like apple, pecan, cherry, pear, or butternut, if he wants something harder and capable of taking a better finish. The sculptor very often goes as far as possible in the other direction—to ebony, lignum vitae, cocobola. My own preference is somewhere between, among the so-called furniture woods like walnut, mahogany, and teak.

My favorite for whittling is basswood because of its almost total absence of grain peculiarities, ease of cutting, and reaction to pigment wiped on. For panels, I like teak best because it is very stable, between mahogany and walnut in hardness, takes a good color, and has its own oil content which makes carving fun. Walnut and mahogany are more readily available in blocks for figure carving and result in a good job. Maple is better than other woods where surface abrasion is involved—as in a breadboard—or where a near-white color is wanted. Holly is whiter and can be finished to an ivory look, but is hard to find. Fruitwoods are good carving, particularly cherry because of its finish color, but they do have a tendency to split, check, and splinter. They also are prone to insect attack if exposed.

✳Finishing and Finishes

Sanding, Filling, Varnishing, Staining, Polishing

To finish or not to finish—that's the question. Some Oriental carvers lacquered teak black; medieval European carvers polychromed and gilded their best work. The wood was merely the base material. Many modern carvers follow the same theory, finishing with paint that hides the wood or shellac that makes it shine.

Sculptors, on the other hand, have gone increasingly toward exotic woods, with abstract designs that emphasize the grain or figure, or the color variations of the wood. Some carefully sand away every evidence of a tool mark; others add tool marks to give a surface texture after the carving is done. Some carefully delineate hair and feathers; others merely suggest them. Some add studs, nails, gold or silver wire, shell or plastic inserts, and other devices to attain highlights and contrasts in texture. Some antique a carving by rubbing dark stain into recesses and background, or suggest non-wood colors by rubbing on a little pigment, then rubbing most of it away so the wood grain shows. Others bleach the wood so it shows little or no color. Some leave parts of the surface rough, others sandblast or blowtorch the edges to remove any "fuzz."

There are, of course, reasons for all these things. Sandblast eats away soft spring wood to leave a ridged surface and make the piece look older. A blowtorch adds brown color here and there, just as a pyrotechnic pencil does. A group of pieces—like a Noah's Ark—all of almost-white basswood, seems to need a little color to distinguish its parts. Statues of saints made out of basswood, while pine, or cedar may look flat to the parishioner's eye—and to professional carvers, at least, the taste of the buyer can be important.

If the wood and work are good, I prefer no sanding—unless I'm trying to suggest a very silky surface. But if you must sand, use the fine grades: ½, 0, 3/0, 5/0, and 8/0, preferably in the modern papers with synthetic abrasives. Garnet paper will outlast flint or sand paper about three to one. For sanding of surfaces with some finish, use only 3/0, 5/0, and 8/0, discarding them as soon as they load up with particles of finish—otherwise they'll scratch.

Sanding can cause trouble by getting dust on the work, by scratching the surface, by eroding sharp edges and erasing fine lines. Therefore, it is best to do even rough sanding with No. 0 paper. When the work is smooth, dampen it with an almost-dry cloth or sponge, allow it to dry, then sand off the raised "fuzz" with 3/0 paper. It is advisable to sand off outer edges of a table or similar surfaces slightly; if they are too sharp, they "wear white" in use. Sanding a flat surface is done better with a small block backing the paper, but carving detail can be worked over with a finger or stick behind the paper, or with pieces of sandpaper glued to shaped sticks or fine riffler files.

Sometimes, a surface will have a discolored spot or the piece may be too dark for its application. Laundry bleaching solutions will take out some surface spots and are easy to apply. The traditional bleach is oxalic acid, made by dissolving ½ lb. of oxalic-acid crystals in 2 qts. of warm water, brushed on freely and allowed to dry. This is rinsed off with several applications of water (don't soak it or you may warp the piece), then a wash containing a little white vinegar. Then sand to remove fuzz.

STAINING

Staining comes next. Water stains are more permanent and easier to use than oil stains; brush on with a soft brush in a series of thin, even coats and wipe wherever it tends to pool or collect. It's safest to test a stain on a scrap piece first; some stains darken when varnish or lacquer is applied. Walnut, in particular, has this tendency.

NOTE: For other information on staining, filling and finishing, see Table II, page 181.

FILLERS AND FILLING

Cabinetmakers fill open-pored woods like oak, walnut, and mahogany to build a level surface for finish coats, to emphasize grain, or to get a coloration. The normal filler is a little darker than the wood, so merely emphasizes the pores, but it can be very dark (almost black), white, or a bright color for novelty effects. I almost never use them, but if you are making a piece of furniture of a suitable wood, or planning a high, smooth finish, they may prove very helpful.

Filler is applied after staining and a coat of very thin (6 thinner to 1) lacquer or shellac to seal the surface. This is sanded lightly with 5/0 paper and cleaned thoroughly to remove dust before the filler is applied. The filler is a heavy paste, mainly of powdered rock quartz (silex) with a little linseed and japan drier or equivalent synthetics. It comes in cans, by weight or volume. This mix is thinned with naphtha or gum turpentine; a pint of mix covers about 35 sq. ft., and no more should be mixed than will be used. The mix depends upon pore size of the wood. Woods like basswood, cedar, cypress, fir, hemlock, magnolia, pine, poplar, spruce, and willow need no filler. Thin filler (½ lb. of paste to ½ pint of thinner makes 12 oz.) is required for alder, beech, birch, boxwood, cherry, gum, ironwood, maple, sycamore, and tupelo. Medium filler (½ lb. paste to 5 ¼ oz. of thinner makes 9 oz. of mix) is required for amaranth, avodire, benin, butternut, mahogany, orientalwood, primavera, purple heart, rosewood, walnut, and zebrawood. Heavy filler (½ lb. of paste and 4 oz. of thinner makes ½ pint) is needed for ash, bubing, chestnut, kelobra, locust, Philippine mahogany, oak, padauk, teak, tamo.

Add the thinner a little at a time, particularly at the beginning; it's easier. Naphtha sets up the filler quickly; turpentine holds it open longer. For a very fast setup, add a little japan drier; for a very slow setup (35 or 40 minutes) add a little boiled linseed oil. Color can also be added, although many stores carry it in a variety of colors. Ready-mixed colors are easier to use in mahogany, walnut, and oak. They can be darkened or lightened by adding a little pigment color ground in oil or japan and mixed with a little turpentine before adding. Special colors can be produced by starting with white or natural. A very small amount of color will do the job, particularly if it's black.

The filler is brushed on liberally, with the grain. When the surface begins to turn dull, the coat is "padded in" with a felt block (felt glued to a wood block) or a smooth cloth pad. This is a circular motion, mostly across grain, to force or pack filler into the pores. (On carved pieces, your fingertips or the heel of your hand may work better than the pad.) Next the filler is "towed off" with tow, moss, burlap, excelsior, or some other cheap wiping material. This is across grain to remove excess filler and should be done thoroughly, a small area at a time. If the filler has set up too hard, the pad can be moistened with a little naphtha.

Lastly, do final wiping with the grain. A soft, lintless cloth, moistened with benzine, does this best. Also clean out inside corners and hard-to-reach areas with a "picking stick"—a ⅜-in. dowel 7 in. long, with a chisel point at one end and a round point at the other. Intricate carving can be cleaned with a bristle brush, but only if the area cannot be wiped clean.

Fast-drying fillers are ready for finishing in 6 hours, slow-drying ones in 24 to 36. Then they are sealed with a light coat of shellac or lacquer sealer, sanded again and varnished or lacquered. This will fill the tiny pores, ready for final sanding and finishing.

It is possible to get special effects, like lighter-colored bands and two-tone surfaces, by masking an area before applying filler. If the surface shows pinholes, the filler was probably too thick and bridged the pores. Remedies are a thinner filler, less japan drier, and/or more thorough dusting before finishing. If the grain is raised, the filler wasn't given enough drying time. (It's a good rule to make the drying time half again what the maker recommends.) Or the surface fuzz wasn't thoroughly sanded off before and after staining. Gray pores are the result of moisture in the wood, insufficient drying

Ebony is sanded, then finished with Kiwi black shoe polish in Bali. Apprentices and women do finishing in the Tilem compound, squatting on mats on a platform.

time, or a filler too light in color. The remedy is to make sure the wood is dry, and to be sure the filler is darker than the stain. A streaked, cloudy finish results when the filler is not cleaned off completely, or wood turpentine instead of gum turpentine is used in mixing. A wiping rag moistened with naphtha may correct this in final wiping.

As I said initially, I rarely do any filling; I prefer the natural look of the wood. Much of the preceding, therefore, is taken, with permission, from an article by Sam Brown in *Popular Mechanics* for January 1944.

FINISHING

Finishing of carvings is such a variable thing that I have tried to mention it with each project. As a general rule, I have gradually gotten around to flat varnish as the basic finish for any indoor piece, just to avoid dust and dirt impregnation. Any staining or coloring I do is on top of the varnish—that prevents running of color in end grain and makes it easier to correct mistakes. Then another coat of varnish or two holds the color or stain. Waxing helps the feel and adds a soft glow. For outside pieces, there are four options: 1. Leave the wood natural, merely soaking with a bug killer once a year or so. 2. Paint in colors and renew the paint as needed. 3. Varnish with a high-gloss marine varnish, if the weather is severe. 4. Finish with one of the colorless deck preparations, a mixture of oil and sealer in a volatile. My preference is for No. 4 on carvings in stable wood like teak or walnut, and No. 1 for other things.

The traditional finish for utilitarian carved objects was nothing, except possibly rubbing with the tool handle or a handful of shavings—and regular rubbing with the hands over spilled grease, candlewax, soot, oil, butter, milk, that gradually made the surface almost translucent and built patina.

Later on, linseed oil, in multiple thin coats, became an accepted finish, but it does tend to oxidize and darken. A head I carved in pine 40 years ago and finished with linseed now has a good gleam but is chocolate brown in color.

The medieval carver also finished pieces with several coats of wax: beeswax shredded into turpentine to make a butterlike mixture. This is warmed before it is used, rubbed in, and cleaned carefully from corners and pockets. "Benzine wax" is the same thing, except with benzine as the solvent. Wax is allowed to dry, then polished with a soft bristle brush and a clean cloth in turn.

FRENCH POLISH

An elaborate finish for surfaces is "French polish," put on over raw linseed oil. It is a mixture of ⅜ lb. of pale orange shellac per pint of alcohol. The surface should be unfilled, smooth, and wiped clean. Make a cloth wad and cover it with a piece of *old* lintless cloth, smooth out the wrinkles, and pour on a little polish. Add a droplet of linseed to the middle of the pad with your fingertip and immediately begin polishing, working in circles or loops in a small area and never stopping. If you stop, the pad will stick. Continue the process in overlapping small areas, being sure to get plenty of polish into any carved areas. Don't ever let the pad become dry and don't press too hard. Give the surface several hours of drying time, then sand lightly with 5/0 paper and do the whole thing over. Repeat until the grain is filled, then give a final rubbing with alcohol alone. This is obviously a trick, combining know-how and elbow grease.

To repolish such a surface, use a mixture of equal parts of alcohol, raw linseed, strong vinegar and turpentine. Start with the turpentine and vinegar, shake thoroughly, add the alcohol and shake again, add the vinegar and shake again. Shake during use.

VARNISHING

Furniture-style varnishing usually involves at least three coats. First is a good interior varnish, dried, then sanded with 5/0 or 8/0 paper to remove gloss and high-spots, then dusted. The second coat is a good clear rubbing varnish, which is rubbed with pumice after it dries. The pumice is finely powdered and worked with water. Sprinkle the dry pumice all over the surface, then dampen it and redampen from time to time. Rubbing with a cloth should be done all over the surface, not from spot to spot. Care is essential on edges, or the rubbing will cut through the finish.

Wash the pumice off with a sheep's-wool sponge and dry with chamois or cheese-cloth. Give it plenty of time to dry, out of the dust, then put on the third coat of rubbing varnish. When this is thoroughly dry, rub it with fine pumice in crude oil—less abrasive than pumice in water—and you should get a dull, silky finish. Shellac finishing is done the same way, except that the pumice is carried in paraffin oil or kerosene, thinned for very hard finishes with a little benzine. After the third coat, the rubbed surface is wiped dry and clean with soft cheesecloth.

If color is too light after preliminary coats, it can be darkened or changed with alcohol-soluble aniline dyes. Make a weak solution, strain it through cheesecloth, add a little white shellac as a binder (2 tablespoons per pint of color), and apply with a pad in a series of thin coats to the desired color. Thick coats will cause streaks, as will applying color across grain. White pine or basswood can be reddened with raw sienna, browned with burnt umber, yellowed with linseed or a mixture of linseed and crude oil. Too-red mahogany can be mellowed with a touch of gamboge or browned with a very little of a thin solution of malachite. Brighten dull mahogany with Bismarck brown containing a little orange. Grayish or very dark walnut can be cleared with orange. Too heavy or streaky color can be rubbed with fine steel wool.

REPAIRING SCRATCHES AND DENTS

To repair deep scratches or cuts, start with sticks of transparent shellac in proper colors and an alcohol lamp. (Candle or gas flames deposit carbon and blacken the spot. You can make an alcohol lamp by shortening the spout of an ordinary oilcan and inserting a wick.) Heat a scalpel or other old knife blade over the lamp until it will melt off a little of the stick shellac and putty this into the scratch or gouge mark until it is filled. Be sure the tool doesn't get too hot or it will damage surrounding finish, and keep it clean. Sand the filled area even with its surroundings and refinish. Dents can sometimes be swelled up flush with the surface again by applying hot water or steam from a steam iron. (Be careful not to burn the surface.) If this fails, fill with the shellac.

To refinish repaired spots, as well as fine scratches and worn spots and rubbed edges, rub over them with a piece of felt soaked in alcohol colored with stain to match the piece. Rub down surface scratches with a mixture of ⅔ crude oil and ⅓ benzine. Then rub over the whole surface with a rag soaked in crude oil and dipped in 0000 pumice powder, then with a dry rag. This should give you a surface ready to be repolished.

Index